WHILE THE GODS WERE SLEEPING

A JOURNEY THROUGH LOVE
AND REBELLION IN NEPAL

Elizabeth Enslin

SEAL PRESS

While the Gods Were Sleeping
A Journey Through Love and Rebellion in Nepal
Copyright © 2014 Elizabeth Enslin

SEAL PRESS
A Member of the Perseus Books Group
1700 Fourth Street
Berkeley, California 94710

Library of Congress Cataloging-in-Publication Data

Enslin, Elizabeth,
While the gods were sleeping : a journey through love and rebellion in Nepal / by Elizabeth Enslin.
pages cm
ISBN 978-1-58005-544-4 (paperback)
ISBN 978-1-58005-581-9 (Indian Ed.)
1. Enslin, Elizabeth, 1960- 2. Nepal--History--1951---Biography. 3. Nepal--Politics and government--1990- 4. Enslin, Elizabeth, 1960---Marriage. 5. Americans--Nepal--Biography. 6. Women anthropologists--United States--Biography. 7. Intercountry marriage--Case studies. 8. Brahmans--Nepal--Chitawan (District)--Biography. 9. Women--Nepal--Chitawan (District)--Biography. 10. Women--Nepal--Chitawan (District)--Social conditions--20th century. I. Title.
DS495.592.E56A3 2014
954.96--dc23
[B]
2014009242

10 9 8 7 6 5 4 3 2 1

Cover design and Interior design by Gopa & Ted2, Inc.
Map of Chitwan Valley by Stephanie Poulain
Printed and bound in India by Replika Press Pvt. Ltd.
Distributed by Publishers Group West

For Parvati Parajuli

Contents

❖

Author's Note

To write this story, I have relied heavily on memory but have also drawn from research notes, personal journals, and interviews (some recorded on tape in Nepali). All the events described here did take place, although some people may remember them differently. I have not, as far as I can remember, invented any events or exaggerated their details. For the sake of readability, I have, of course, omitted much, but I have not consciously compressed or moved events around in time. Nor have I created composite or fictional characters. For those who shared their lives and stories knowing they would be made public, I use real names. Where I have doubts about permission to publicize, I have changed names.

Notes on Terminology

For simplicity, I use the term *caste* rather than more accurate terms like *jati*—endogamous kin and occupational groups—and *varna*—a ritual taxonomy that arranges jati into hierarchies.

In the same spirit, I use *Hinduism* and *Hindu* as convenient catch-all terms for philosophies, groups, and people while recognizing that there is no singular Hindu religion with one founder, one text, one god, or one institution. It would be more accurate to speak of Brahmanism (or Vedantic Brahmanism), Vaishnavism, Shaivism, Bhakti, and so on.

Rather than the foreign word *Nepalese*, I use *Nepali* to refer to anything of or from Nepal: the language, the people, the food.

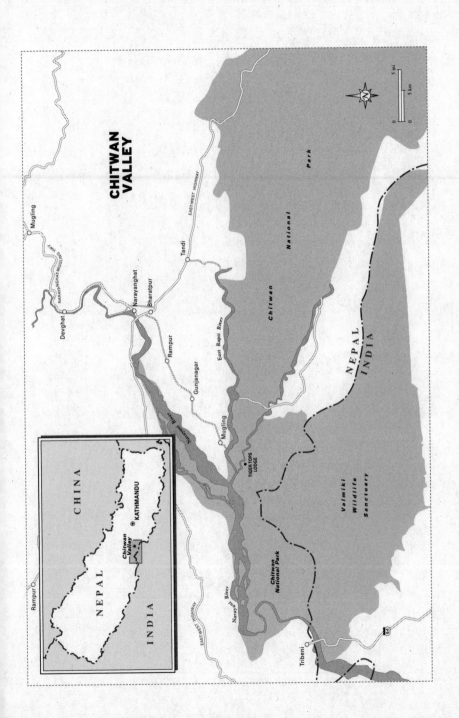

BASE CAMP

By the time light slivered Nepal's horizon on that November morning in 1987, I'd already spent forty hours in labor. The earliest contractions may have been false labor. But I can't pinpoint when the pain turned from false to true. Or where the feminist anthropologist in me ended and the Brahman wife began.

I don't remember much beyond pain. Yet from the loft I shared with my husband, Pramod, over the buffalo shed, we must have heard the usual dawn chorus in the family compound: the *ku-ka-RI-ka* of roosters, the monotone chants of my father-in-law reading the Vedas, creaks and splashes at the water pump, the whiz and ping of milk squirted from buffalo teat to tin pail, shouts to bring this or that and hurry up, some Hari-Shiva-Narayans for all that had to be done. No matter what, animals had to be tended, food prepared, gods and goddesses worshipped. And cursed.

Pramod sat beside me on our bed. For days, he had hovered nearby, only leaving to bathe, visit the outhouse, or fetch whatever I asked for. Yet, like many women in labor, I could not remember what had ever attracted me. The wide, full lips? The silly puns and optimism? The brown eyes and how they curved up at the outer corners?

Voices murmured in Nepali in the background: "Why is it taking so long?" "What's wrong?"

For once, Pramod stopped trying to console me with words. Through the rise and fall of each scream, he rubbed my back. Even my mother-in-law, Aama—who tried to please everyone—had given up trying to please me. She brought no more eggs floating in soup, eggs burned in ghee, or other culinary experiments I'd never before seen served in Nepal. She squatted nearby, her face paler than usual. Between contractions, I wondered why she didn't refasten oiled strands of white hair that had fallen loose from her tight bun.

Years later, I troll for memories and snag a sense of myself as driftwood: bleached and bloated, smashed onshore, pulled out beyond the breakers to rest a moment, then picked up by a cresting wave and slammed on sharp rocks again. At times, a finlike thought breached: make a decision by morning. Then, morning came. But I didn't want the bother of deciding whether to go to the hospital. I wanted sleep, and pain was the fee I paid every few minutes for another ride on the lullaby swells behind the surf.

Neither here nor there, I think now. I'd often heard Brahman women in our village sum up their lives like that. Belonging to the highest caste in Nepal, they enjoyed some privileges. But they also had to follow strict rules to uphold ritual status and keep ancestral lines pure. On marriage, they leave their *maiti*—maternal home—to spend the rest of their lives in their *ghar*—their husband's extended household. They never return to the place they feel most at home, except to visit. Nor can they be full members of the place where they'll live until death. Yet, by giving birth to children, especially sons, a woman crosses a threshold where, with skill and luck, she can claim some power in her ghar.

My maiti was Seattle. When homesick, I most longed for the driftwood-strewn beaches of Puget Sound where I'd grown up snorkeling, digging clams, and collecting shells.

My ghar was landlocked in Chitwan Valley, a wide basin in Nepal's *tarai*—a narrow strip of lowlands that belts the base of the Himalayan foothills before the Indian subcontinent drops south-ward and flattens out into the vast Gangetic plains. Flanked on the west by the Narayani River and on the south by the low Siwalik hills along Nepal's border with India, Chitwan used to be marshes, grasslands, and jungles. An influx of foreign aid after World War II transformed Chitwan to farmland. In a country outsiders have long associated with mountains, exoticism, and poverty, Chitwan began to draw Nepali newcomers with flatness, practicality, and opportunity. Residents often likened it to the United States, where—so they had heard—pioneering immigrants had driven out indigenous peoples and wildlife, felled trees, drained marshes, planted grain, and built great towns and cities.

Chitwan translates from Sanskrit as "Heart of the Jungle." In 1987, near the rivers and game reserves, one could still find jungle remnants. But Pramod and I lived with his middle-class family in the western part of Chitwan in the nondescript village of Gunjanagar. Far from Royal Chitwan National Park and about an hour by bullock cart from the Narayani River, our hamlet in Gunjanagar sprawled in flat, cultivated fields dotted by thatch or tin rooftops mostly sheltering families like ours—neither rich nor poor. It all looked so settled, a visitor might assume it had been that way for hundreds of years.

In the months before my due date, I deluded myself into thinking I could orchestrate a beautiful home birth in my jungle-hearted ghar. I'm still trying to make sense of my reasoning.

A twenty-seven-year-old doctoral candidate, I sought guidance in books friends sent me: *Our Bodies, Ourselves, The Womanly Art of Breastfeeding, Every Woman*. I pondered heartburn and hemorrhoids and believed myself cosmic for having them and naming them. I studied diagrams of cervical dilation. I memorized passages detailing the onset of labor and the first, second, and third stages. From photos, I learned the preferred settings for women in labor: pleasant rooms with soft beds, fluffy pillows, clean carpets.

Poorer women in our village gave birth in homes without toilets or outhouses, where water came from open wells, and food—often meager—was prepared and cooked on earthen floors. In comparison, my ghar didn't seem too bad. At least, that's what I told myself after I'd grown used to it. Like most families in rural Chitwan, we had sufficient land to grow our own rice and lentils plus some corn, wheat, and oilseeds. And Pramod's eldest brother earned enough income as a teacher to make up for any shortfalls, hire laborers now and then, and buy some luxuries: a radio, kerosene lanterns, packaged noodles. We also had an outhouse, a roomy kitchen, and a hand pump that delivered clean water.

Rather than claiming a room in the crowded cement house, Pramod and I opted for privacy in a makeshift loft over a storage shed next to the buffalo stalls. It was clean and spacious and provided a good view of fruit trees and fields through the open end. Yet each day, pioneers of jungle restoration invaded. Mice shredded our clothes to make their nests. Brown huntsman spiders as large as my hands lurked in dark corners of ceiling thatch by daylight and skittered across floorboards at night. Their molts floated down ghostlike onto sheets, clothes, and books. Bats fluttered through the open-air room every evening. Ants paraded in and out of my jars of muesli and Horlicks if I failed to tighten the lids. When I lifted the straw mat on our wooden bed, tiny scorpions curled their tails.

The presence of the two water buffaloes that lived beneath and off to the side of our loft cheered me with a vague sense of something more familiar. Not that I had ever lived with buffaloes or cows. But they, at least, were tame. Their plops and splashes on the wooden slats of their stalls and the smells that followed came with comforting regularity. And the way they gushed milk, tail-swatted flies, bellowed for food, and keened for male calves sold for slaughter enveloped me in a snug bovine sisterhood. There was so much else I didn't understand at the time, but buffaloes: they made some sense.

During the monsoon and rice harvest months, I grew accustomed to our loft. But I still longed for what I couldn't have. On the broodiest days, I let go of plush and beautiful and hoped for quick and painless, like those women you hear about who have babies without knowing they're pregnant. It had happened to a landless Tharu woman whose family worked for ours. She went out to defecate in the cornfields one evening and returned with a newborn.

A few weeks before labor began, I could have given in to doubts, taken the bus to Kathmandu, and made arrangements in any number of hospitals. But I wanted a home birth. We held family meetings and agreed on protocol. Pramod and I crawled on hands and knees along our loft floor, scrubbing every crack and crevice in the rough-hewn planks with water and antiseptic Dettol soap. Then we washed the bed platform, bookshelves, posts, and walls. Our room was as clean as it had ever been—cleaner, I told myself, than most local hospitals. The faint medicinal smell lingered and reassured me.

Yet when nature meets culture, I now understand, soap, family meetings, and dreams get you only so far.

During labor, I had vague moments of longing for the person I'd been a few years before in Seattle: a young woman smiling behind a customer service desk. I had supported myself through college with a part-time job at the original REI (Recreational Equipment, Inc.) store in an old warehouse on Capitol Hill. Biting my tongue through what managers reminded me was our sacred mantra—"the customer is always right"—I helped people exchange worn boots, skis, and parkas to make sure they had the right equipment for their adventures. We served backpackers, river rafters, and bikers, but the store's roots stood firmly among those who scaled high peaks. And with eight of the ten highest peaks in the world, Nepal was a prime adventure destination for REI employees and customers alike. I helped climbing teams bound for Nepal order their gear and often saw Jim Whittaker—the first REI manager and the first American to summit Everest—passing through. On my way to the break room, I scanned glossy, framed photos of Himalayan peaks I couldn't name. By coincidence, I even roomed for a few months with a geologist who'd been on the all-women team Arlene Blum led up Annapurna.

I went on to become a cultural anthropologist and met other globe-trotters who talked of reasons besides mountains for dwelling in Nepal: to work for aid agencies, study tantra or shamanism, flop in cheap lodging and smoke ganja or hashish. Yet despite all that and a childhood and adolescence spent daydreaming about travel to remote places, I never fantasized about Nepal.

When I finally decided to live in Nepal, I came to carry out a pregnancy and give birth—reasons that would have made little sense even to the most devoted Nepalophile. And in that country famed for high peaks, I landed in flat Chitwan. There, I—who had once badgered REI customers to buy Gore-Tex, bug spray, and sweat-wicking liner socks—still hoped to summit my own Mount Everest in the plains without bottled air, drugs, or any luxury gear.

I seemed to be failing that plan, too. Forty hours of frequent and painful contractions hadn't—according to our midwife—moved me beyond a cervical base camp of six centimeters.

"She should go to the hospital." That morning, everyone agreed: Pramod, Aama, my brother- and sister-in-law, my nieces and father-in-law, the midwife, all the neighbors.

"Take her. Quickly," Aama said.

Unlike Brahman women in Nepal, I could have returned to my maiti to give birth. In our family, my status as Euro-American usually trumped that of Brahman wife or pregnant woman—at least so far. But for reasons I'll get to, the time for playing that queen had passed. Stuck in my ghar between pregnancy and motherhood, I gave in to popular opinion. Pramod sent his brother, Siddhi, by bicycle to fetch a *tempu*—a three-wheeled motor rickshaw—from the main road.

That had always been our backup plan, but we hadn't reckoned on needing it. Pramod stuffed some clothes and toiletries into a duffel bag. Several of our nephews promised to come later by bus to fetch other essentials in the bazaar.

For all of Chitwan's supposed progress, the sound of a motor struck us as unusual in 1987. So when we heard the slow crescendo of an unmuffled hum, we knew the tempu was for us. Pramod led me down the wooden ladder from our loft.

Family and neighbors crowding our courtyard moved aside to let us through. They must have looked as they always did: fair-skinned Brahman and Chhetri women saried in every shade of red; Tamang, Magar, and Gurung women saronged in colorful dragon and flower prints; Tharu women muted in grays and greens, backs straight as sal trees. Men were there too, most wearing traditional, handwoven caps. Children swarmed among the adults, sniffling and wiping their noses: some uniformed in blue and white with book-heavy satchels, others warmed by tattered sweaters and shawls, shepherding cows and goats with long sticks. I remember a neighbor, Kansididi (literally, youngest sister) Tamang, best. A field separated our homes. In the previous months, I'd often walked up the lane to visit her and her talkative ex-army husband and their numerous children. Pointing to my baby bump, I refused the millet beer they and others in Tibeto-Burman groups frequently offered. But I welcomed their earthy humor, so different from the prudish conversations of Brahmans.

I waddled through the crowd leaning on Pramod's arm. In a raspy smoker's voice, Kansididi walked beside us and said what Pramod didn't dare say anymore: "Don't worry. You'll be all right." Another wave of pain bent me over. With so many eyes on me, I muffled the scream into whimpers.

Kansididi barely waited for me to finish. "The same thing happened to me with my first. Labor went on for days and days. I thought I was going to die. I was afraid to go to the hospital. But the baby did come out."

I studied her face: tired, slightly pockmarked, framed by a green acrylic shawl wound over her ears to keep out the morning chill. Like other Tamang neighbors, she was usually playful and upbeat. Now a seriousness belied her words. And why did she look at me like that, as though trying to memorize every detail?

"You'll be all right too," she said. "Don't worry."

Pramod helped me into the tempu, placed a duffel bag at my feet, and then squeezed in beside me. The engine revved and spewed black fumes. More neighbors crowded in. I read both worry and relief in their faces and didn't understand. I was grateful for their concern, but why the relief?

I trembled as the answer hit me. Months before, I had felt queasy while visiting the world's most famous memorial to a woman who had died in childbirth. Like other tourists that morning, Pramod and I had gaped at the minarets and mottled marble of the Taj Mahal, astounded to find them as gorgeous as advertised. After several hours, increasing nausea drove me back to our windowless hotel room in Agra. I hoped it was heat or the stench from garbage and sewage along the Ganges River. But the discomfort persisted all afternoon, and then swelled into a dinnerless evening. I probably pondered Mumtaz Mahal's death, but whatever empathy I felt for a seventeenth-century woman didn't translate into seeing myself as the kind of woman who might, like her, die in childbirth.

I had become pregnant while traveling in India—a country outranking most for percentages of women dying in childbirth every year—and then decided to wait for my due date in Nepal, ranked even higher. There in our village, I studied the lives of landless, agricultural laborers among whom maternal mortality rates surged higher still. Throughout pregnancy, I had felt fear—fear of my changing body, fear of not knowing how to be a mother, fear of giving birth far from my maiti. But I didn't think much about dying until I waved goodbye from the tempu.

"How sad it will be if we don't see her again," I imagined neighbors saying to themselves. "Yet many mothers die this way. Better to have an Amrikan die in the hospital than bring blame and trouble to the village."

I'd traveled enough to know how to get out of trouble: pack up the soggy tent and sleeping bag and hike out, buy a bus or plane ticket to somewhere else, hurry to my hotel room and lock the door, line up at the local embassy to replace a stolen passport. I didn't have the strongest legs or the most robust bank account, but I could always trust my brain or feet to move me forward. Now, I had to put faith in internal organs I did not understand.

The tempu set off across the common pasture in front of our house. I had to put trust in that vehicle without shock absorbers too. It beetled us away from my ghar along a dry irrigation canal while I convulsed inside. I had to believe it would successfully dodge buses and trucks on the potholed road to the small town of Bharatpur, forty-five minutes away. There, I would turn myself over to doctors and nurses in the district headquarters hospital. Of all the available options for giving birth, that had been my last choice. Now I felt as if it might be my last hope.

Before the sun set that day, I gave birth to an underweight but otherwise healthy boy. Despite my worst fears and failings, he thrived. By becoming a mother in Nepal, I learned to see myself and local culture through a new lens. Yet scenes from before and after delivery sank like silt along a stream bottom and disappeared into my pebbled subconscious. For six years, my fluid memory slid fast over that stretch so as not to raise the murk.

PART I
1985–1987

NOT INDIA

Pramod Parajuli and I fell in love at Stanford University in 1985, a situation I soon found myself explaining to acquaintances. The conversations usually went something like this:

"What country did you say he's from?"

"Nepal."

"Where?"

"You know, where Mount Everest is, between India and China."

"He's from India? Cool!"

"Well, Nepal is not in India, just next door. He's Ne—"

"Of course. I've always wanted to go to India, see the Taj Mahal. Do you like Indian food?"

"I do, but Nepal is its own country, not India."

I didn't know it then, but Not-India would turn out to be a fair way of generalizing the complexities of Nepal, at least for beginners.

If I had time in those conversations, I might try to share the basic picture Pramod had painted for me. Never conquered by the British, never a colony, and never, ever a part of India, Nepal had become an independent Hindu monarchy with scores of different languages and dialects in a geographic area a bit larger than Greece. Most citizens identified as Hindu, but there were also Buddhists and animists with tantra threading through all spiritual practices. Of course, I couldn't have explained then what tantra was. Pramod sometimes applied the word to what we did in bed, but I knew there was more to it than that.

And the language? Like Hindi in grammar and vocabulary,

Pramod had told me. But as different from Hindi as French is from Italian.

"Easy to learn, if you want to try."

With his passion for teaching, Pramod snuck some basic Nepali into our earliest conversations, like *namaste*—a hello that translates to something like "the spirit in me greets the spirit in you." Over meals, Pramod sometimes drilled me on words and phrases I could use if I ever went to Nepal: *Mitho cha* (tasty). *Pugyo* (enough).

Harder to explain than Nepal in casual conversation was what first drew me to Pramod.

I'm sure I crossed paths with him at Stanford many times before I noticed him. I was a graduate student in anthropology and he was in international development education, but we probably attended the same films, speaker events, and rallies. We also haunted the same aisles on Third World development and radical politics in the library.

I first met Pramod when we—and eight or so others—joined a weekly reading group on political theory. Pramod was funny and smart, but I didn't pay much attention to his charms until the day we talked about *Selections from the Prison Notebooks* by Antonio Gramsci. Looking for key points on consciousness and hegemony, we all flipped through pages from the English translation of the notes Gramsci made from Italian prison from 1929 to 1935. I barely understood what *hegemony* meant then, but like my peers, wanted to learn how to use it to talk about the insidious ways one country or social class can rule another without direct force. Pramod let us fumble for a few minutes. Then, without looking at his voluminous notes or opening his dog-eared copy, he said, "Look at page 333." We did. Then he paraphrased for us what was making Gramsci so popular in cultural studies in the 1980s, what Gramsci had to say about the "man-in-the-mass":

One might almost say that he has two theoretical con-
sciousnesses (or one contradictory consciousness): one

which is implicit in his activity and which in reality
unites him with all his fellow-workers in the practical
transformation of the real world; and one, superficially
explicit or verbal, which he has inherited from the past
and uncritically absorbed.

I understood that to mean we humans often can't see through the
cultural baggage that inspires us to work against our best interests.
Without thinking through the consequences, we undermine ourselves by handing our power over to others.

I wanted to get to know Pramod better. In the days that followed,
I scanned campus crowds for glimpses of his thick salt-and-pepper
hair, how it V-ed down the nape of his neck underneath a tweed
fisherman's cap. When he caught me staring, he smiled. At campus
lectures and receptions, we sought each other out for playful banter.
One evening, we fell back to the edge of the crowd. Pramod was
about two inches shorter than my six feet, but I'd learned by then
that height made little difference in sexual and intellectual compat-
ibility. He whispered something about a film or speaker in my ear
and brushed his lips against my pale cheek.

"What?" I said, hoping he'd do it again.

Between Pramod sightings, I debated the wisdom of getting
involved. For several years, I'd been in a series of casual relationships. Some had ended in shouts and tears. Others had yawned
into boredom. In all cases, they'd taken too much energy. For several
months, I'd sworn off men to focus on pending decisions about my
professional path. Except for his interest in radical politics, Pramod
didn't fit into my plan to be an anthropologist of eastern or southern
Africa.

On further encounters, Pramod's lips lingered and traveled more
—from cheek to nose's edge to earlobe. And I dared to pull him
closer as I leaned in to listen. At some event, we left the crowd,
found a quiet hallway, and kissed.

Soon, we couldn't imagine being apart.

Long before I traveled to Nepal, I met Pramod's family. Not in person, of course, but in that feverish soul-baring of early romance. Pramod could not explain himself without bringing in all his relations.

Unlike many foreign students at Stanford, Pramod had not come from a wealthy, urbane family. His father was a Brahman, the highest Hindu caste, and served as a *pandit* (priest)—the ideal path for a Brahman. But he came from a relatively poor lineage and could not live on payments he received for officiating at weddings, initiations, and funerals. Like most rural Brahmans in Nepal, he and his ancestors had always been farmers.

Pramod had never lived in Chitwan, his parents' current home. He had grown up in Kahung, a small village in the foothills of central Nepal where his father's predecessors had lived for generations. In a worn photograph Pramod showed me, I saw his tall father dressed in tunic and pants and his shorter mother in a red sari. They stood before a multistory earthen house surrounded by greenery.

Pramod's father, Pandit Kedarnath Parajuli, was already in his twenties when he married Pramod's mother, a ten-year-old. Such matches were customary in that generation. Girls had to be locked into marriage before sexual desires led them astray. Yes, Pramod admitted before I interrupted, what he and I were doing would be considered scandalous among Brahmans in rural Nepal. But men got away with it. And in some other ethnic groups, sex before marriage was the norm. He'd had some non-Brahman girlfriends in Kathmandu and in distant villages where he'd taught literacy. Men used to be able to have multiple wives too, he said. Some still did, although changing customs and laws made it harder.

Pramod said his mother had never learned to read and write; most women of her generation didn't, even if they were the wives of learned priests. Still, she took a keen interest in politics. "You two would get along well," he often told me.

Some afternoons, Pramod and I hiked through oak groves and pastures in the Stanford foothills. Cattle grazed spring grass there, so we often had to dodge fresh cow pies. That spurred Pramod into one of his favorite childhood stories.

"I had to pick up dung like that with my bare hands. Can you imagine?"

I had learned at an early age to gut fish but couldn't imagine handling dung with my bare hands. I would later learn its value: composting, of course, but also purifying altars and mixing with clay to make earthen plasters for floors and walls. But that spring, I saw only feces.

"And no matter how often I washed my hands, the smell of poo stayed there for days."

That I could imagine. Unconsciously, I lifted a hand to my nose.

"I can't do it, Father," Pramod said, imitating a child's voice. "It smells so bad. Please don't make me."

Pramod's older brothers and one younger brother picked up dung and also planted rice and weeded corn without complaint. Still, Pandit Kedarnath often released Pramod early from daily farm chores so he could return to his books. But it wasn't all studies and farmwork in the hills. Pramod also painted vivid pictures of happy hours spent with cousins climbing mango and guava trees.

When Pramod was twelve, his father opened a school in a Magar village several hours away. Magars were Tibeto-Burman speakers with their own language and culture and often asked the more learned Brahmans to run schools for their children. Busy with his own duties in Kahung and eager to turn over some responsibility, Pandit Kedarnath sent Pramod to the Magar village to be headmaster. I wondered at a father sending a small boy off for such a big job, but Pramod said it was not uncommon. Children had to grow up quickly in Nepal, at least in those days.

"I walked downhill through that jungle every morning. Then every evening, I walked back up. Such a big jungle, and I was so small. Can you imagine? I was sure a tiger would jump out and snatch me up. Mom used to tell me about ghosts there too. I was so scared. But that's where I learned to love teaching and working with the poor."

Pramod told that story wherever we went: at potlucks, over beer with friends. On every telling, I marveled at the courage of that boy and the wisdom of the father who prodded a son toward his passion.

Pramod's eldest sibling was his sister, Madhumaya. With traditions of arranged child marriage still common in her generation, she had left home to live with her older husband when she was twelve. Since Pramod was second to the youngest among six siblings, he grew up knowing her as a married woman who lived elsewhere.

Pramod and his five brothers came of age when social democratic and communist parties were organizing to defeat entrenched systems of caste privilege, authoritarian government, and corruption in Nepal. The eldest brother, Purushottam, staged dramas to entertain villagers, question inequality, and portray how families suffer when men drink too much or gamble. Pramod idolized his eldest brother and hoped to emulate him—the beginnings of his interest in popular education and social justice.

When Purushottam was in his early twenties, he married a teenager his parents had found for him. Soon after, he left to study in India. Within months, the family received word that Purushottam's body had been found by a train track in North India. They never knew whether it was suicide, murder, or an accident. In a decision considered progressive at the time, Pramod's parents released Purushottam's young widow to marry elsewhere.

Pramod often spoke of Purushottam's death when I prodded him about his lack of sentimentality. He did not seem visibly saddened by films or stories that made me dab my eyes. It was not because he was a man, he said. It was because his brother's death had been so painful for him that he had since found it hard to cry over anything else.

Three of the four remaining brothers continued Purushottam's strong commitment to social change and education. Siddhi took on the role of eldest. He had been working toward an advanced degree in agriculture but had to forgo further study, bring a wife into the family, and look after his parents. That freed the next youngest brothers, Tirtha and Pramod, to study at boarding schools, and later college, in Kathmandu. Tirtha went on to become a professor of education at Tribhuvan University's satellite campus in the tourist town of Pokhara, west of Kathmandu. The success of the brothers helped raise living standards in the extended family.

After graduating with a degree in education, Pramod taught literacy to remote and underserved communities throughout Nepal. But he wanted more challenges, so he applied for graduate programs in the United States and landed a full scholarship to Stanford University.

Pramod's youngest brother, Udaya, had fallen ill with polio as a child. His parents had already lost several other children in infancy and prepared to grieve Udaya's passing too. But after months of illness, Udaya recovered. Pramod showed me a photo. He was shorter and leaner than Pramod with a bent jaw. And because polio stopped one leg from growing, he tilted to his left. Despite his physical ailments, Udaya had a fun-loving, compassionate spirit that made him beloved in the family.

Like Madhumaya, Pramod's two eldest brothers had already married and had children. In photos, I saw them lined up in school uniforms in front of their parents. Pramod recited their names as if he expected me to meet them someday. But that was more than I could digest at such an early stage of romance. We had not yet agreed on where we were headed.

What was I looking for in a Nepali intellectual from a poor farming family who could quote an Italian rebel-philosopher? I didn't want another casual relationship, yet where would a serious one take us?

I knew Pramod wanted to research popular education among grassroots movements in India. "Why not your own country?" a member of our reading group had asked him when we first introduced ourselves and our interests. "Why do you American anthropologists go to Nepal or Zimbabwe?" Pramod replied. "Why not work in your own country?" Touché. Besides, in India, he told us, he could see a longer process of globalization and how people organized alternatives to it. He could then share those insights in Nepal.

Pramod knew what he wanted. Did I? I probably looked like someone set on a clear professional course then, but I had been wrestling with doubts for a while. My most recent notion was to study women's participation in rebel groups in eastern or southern Africa. My faculty advisors were urging me to settle on specifics soon. Ethiopia? Tanzania? Mozambique? I couldn't decide.

What had led me—once a quiet conformist—to an interest in women and armed struggle? And before that, how had I found a path into anthropology? It wasn't so long ago I had hoped to study animals. In my twenty-five years, I'd devoted myself with great passion to many things and then changed course. I felt myself to be odd scraps of this and that, never adding up to what I wanted to be. Trailing remnants from childhood and adolescence, I sensed I was looking to Pramod to start me over at another beginning, help me seize a new shape.

Since childhood, I had fantasized about a career that would take me to the East African savanna. I had initially seen myself as a zoologist there, tracking lions or giraffes. I memorized zoological taxonomies, aced all the science and math classes my schools offered, began a life list of every bird I identified. In my senior year of high school, I also volunteered at the Nocturnal House at the Woodland Park Zoo, where I swept up the feces of civet cats and giant sloths.

No one in my family had ever finished college. I fully intended to, but I lacked the confidence to take aptitude tests and fill out applications, and my family lacked money for an out-of-state or private college. I knew I would need a scholarship but didn't know how to get one.

By default, I settled for Shoreline Community College in the north end of Seattle. I had no patience for the math and chemistry required before I could enroll in a life sciences class. I wanted to leap ahead to elephants and chimpanzees. After one miserable quarter of molecular compounds and quadratic equations in 1978, I gave up science and meandered through the humanities.

I loved literature and philosophy but couldn't settle on a direction. When I took a class on sociocultural anthropology, I saw a new possibility. I could ponder humanistic concerns—even poetry— without abandoning science. When the anthropology professor told our class about a study tour she'd be leading to Kenya, I knew I had to join. I'd get to go on a safari and see elephants and zebras in the wild. I'd also have a chance to explore new interests in early hominid history and cultural diversity.

I convinced my mother and stepfather I'd already saved them thousands by attending community college. Compared to what a private liberal arts college might have cost, I said, a donation to my Africa trip fund was a bargain. Then I guilt-tripped my father. He had disappeared for a while after my birth and dodged child support payments to my mother over the years. For those lapses, he had agreed to pay for college and had mostly followed through. But so far college hadn't cost him much.

Family contributions bought me a deposit. A part-time job at REI gave me the rest. From Sea-Tac Airport, my mother and stepfather waved me onto the British Airways flight as though they might never see me again. Aside from my father's and stepfather's military service during the Korean War and a grandfather's occasional visits to explore his heritage in England and Wales, no one from my immediate family had ventured farther abroad than British Columbia.

No other arrival would ever make me gasp the way I did at the first sight of acacia trees and round huts as the plane descended toward the Nairobi airport. No curiosity would burrow in and take root like those first discoveries in Africa of the rich histories and cultures of people other than Europeans: Swahili cosmopolitans and seafarers, Kikuyu farmers, Turkana and Rendille camel herders. And no scents would intoxicate me like those of Kenya's highlands: wood smoke, iron-red dirt, and equatorial bloom and decay. More than thirty years later, the scent of a certain glycerin soap and how it mingled with those Kenya smells still overwhelms me with so much longing, I don't use it anymore.

Perhaps like a kiss, there's no foreign adventure like the first. I continued my undergraduate education at the University of Washington and followed what looked like the surest route back to East Africa: a major in cultural anthropology with a focus in African studies. I began to drape my eclectic interests on a broad question: Why do hunter-gatherers, pastoralists, and small-scale farmers all over the world cling to practices that globalization and development have deemed inefficient or destructive? And what might they have to teach the industrialized world about sustainability? Based on library research, I wrote my senior thesis on government efforts to settle nomadic pastoralists, such as the Maasai, and make them into agriculturalists and how the Maasai adapted those schemes to suit their own values.

Meanwhile, I steered through African studies toward an even grander sense of mission. I read Kwame Nkrumah, Frantz Fanon, Julius Nyerere. I told myself that anthropology could be an ally in the ongoing struggles they had inspired: struggles to dismantle what colonialism and racism had left behind, struggles to rebuild African countries from their own roots. Around that, I wrapped an even broader mission: to educate people in the United States about the richness of indigenous cultures. If people in the United States could see that places like Africa did have histories, cultures, and political philosophies as sophisticated as any in Europe, they would better appreciate cultural diversity. Africa was so amazing that people would slap their foreheads and say, "Now I get it." Racism would end. Inequality would fall away. Finally, world peace.

My decision to pursue my PhD in anthropology at Stanford

University was mostly financial. Other universities had accepted me and had stronger programs in African studies or pastoralism studies. But Stanford offered me the best deal: a full scholarship.

In my first quarter, I began discovering history I'd missed in my previous education. Yes, colonialism had mostly ended. But then came the Vietnam War and U.S. support for dictators in Central America, the Philippines, Iran. Surrounded by better informed and more eloquent peers from Tanzania, Jamaica, Bangladesh, India, and Nicaragua, I sloughed off layer after layer of naiveté and good intentions. Providing culturally correct information might change some minds, but there were deeper forces at work. Some people and institutions profited from the poverty and misery of others. They would not be swayed by anthropologists like me who urged them to appreciate cultural diversity.

With the zeal of a recent convert, I turned to action. I joined protests against the U.S. invasion of Grenada and CIA subversions of democracy in Nicaragua and El Salvador. But I wasn't sure how my new passion for politics would fit into my plans for fieldwork.

Through my first year and a half at Stanford, I proceeded with my studies, hoping that the act of trying to understand other cultures through anthropology would, if done right, be political enough. At the same time, I read books like *Reinventing Anthropology* and learned how my discipline had girded colonialism in Africa, Asia, and Latin America and provided intelligence for U.S. counterinsurgency efforts during the Vietnam War. Some well-known and respected anthropologists had willingly collaborated on projects to resettle or pacify "natives" to clear land for dams, industrial farming, or weapons testing.

Worried about being a handmaiden to neocolonialism, I lost touch with my initial idealism and enthusiasm for anthropology. Advisors encouraged me to contribute to emerging studies on the anthropology of women and gender. No matter how I approached that broad topic, they said, I would always be looking at politics.

I could study pastoralists but zero in on women's experiences. Or maybe I could study women and economic development more broadly.

But I wanted more politics. At the time, I believed I could best avoid anthropology's ethical pitfalls by hitching my work to an ongoing liberation struggle somewhere in Africa. I tried to picture myself collaborating with women involved in armed struggle. Could I embed myself among anti-apartheid guerrillas in Mozambique? Or should I give up anthropology and its tainted past and find another profession? I had boxed myself into a mindset in which those extremes seemed like my only choices. I couldn't decide.

Then, I fell in love.

My romance with Pramod in the spring of 1985 escalated in tandem with my activism in the campus divestment movement: Stanford Out of South Africa (SOSA). As part of similar efforts on other U.S. campuses, our main goal was to convince the Board of Trustees to withdraw investments from companies doing business with the apartheid government. Because of Stanford's large endowments, the work seemed particularly critical on our campus. Along with many others, I gave speeches, facilitated meetings, wrote letters to the editors of campus and community newspapers, and helped organize rallies and sit-ins. Pramod attended some SOSA events and cheered on my efforts, but chose to stay more focused on his own studies and his work-study job in the library.

One afternoon, I gave a speech at a SOSA rally. I can't remember now what specific actions we called for that day: Another sit-in before the dean's office? Letters to the trustees? In any case, we had a fine turnout. And every speech whipped up fervent chanting and applause.

Pramod was in the audience. After the rally, we sat on the edge of the fountain between the bookstore and Old Union for a quick lunch. He hugged me, congratulated me on a job well done, and then took my hand and stroked it. I wished we had a room nearby, or at least some tall grass or bushes. But we were surrounded by hundreds of other students basking in California sunshine. I also sensed that this wasn't just seduction. Pramod seemed more serious than usual.

"What's wrong?"

"I've had some news ... from Nepal."

"What? Your family? Are they okay?"

"No, no, not them. Everyone's fine. It's something else—" He hesitated. "Bombings. In Kathmandu. It's what we've been waiting for. The opposition is making a move."

Knowing my interest in politics, Pramod had shared many details about his involvement in the Nepali Congress Party and its twenty-year effort to restore multiparty democracy in Nepal. I didn't catch all the details in that moment. My head was full of the history and politics of South Africa. Until I grew curious about specifics on my own, Pramod had to explain his country's history many times in our first year together. What I loved was how important—like family—that history was to him. It made me increasingly certain that Pramod was the man for me.

Pramod's relatives traced their arrival in the Himalayan foothills to the eleventh century or so when Muslim Mughals were invading the Gangetic plains. Historians debate whether Hindus had reason to fear death or conversion. Modern politics that pit Muslims and Hindus against each other and fan the flames of fundamentalism offer competing versions. In any case, some Hindus—including Brahmans and other castes—fled into the hills. There, they settled among diverse ethnic groups, mostly Tibeto-Burman speakers like Magars, Tamangs, and Gurungs. Over time, the different groups forged interdependent communities.

By the 1700s, small kingdoms ruled throughout the Himalayas and competed for power. None dominated for long. In 1743, Prithvi Narayan Shah succeeded his father to the throne in Gorkha, eighty miles west of Kathmandu. For the next three decades, Shah conquered—or sometimes brokered alliances with—neighboring kingdoms to win control over a five-hundred-mile belt of foothills and plains and founded the Kingdom of Nepal.

Shah described his empire as a yam between two rocks: India and China. In previous centuries, Himalayan rulers had amassed wealth and power by controlling the trade between the two. By Shah's time, the Qing dynasty was expanding its empire southward into Tibet, and the British East India Company had begun the long process of colonizing India. Whether he intended it or not, Shah's conquest and unification—along with the region's hills and mountains—protected Nepal from invasion.

Shah and subsequent rulers planned to create an ideal Hindu kingdom, untainted by the corruptions of Mughal or British invaders to the south. Like most monarchs, they faced challenges from disgruntled and impatient relatives seeking their time on the throne. The result: feuds, massacres, and frequent turnovers of power. In 1846, a queen's love affair and intrigue to make her son king sparked a bloodbath. With ninety aristocrats dead and six thousand more exiled, members of the Rana family wrested power from the Shah kings and established themselves as hereditary prime ministers. For the next one hundred years, the Ranas ruled Nepal. The Shahs held figurehead status but little power. Throughout Rana rule, some Shah descendants resided in India rather than Nepal and plotted with others to return royal power to their homeland.

Opposition to the Ranas also grew among Nepal's educated, progressive elite. Many were inspired by the Quit India Movement, Mahatma Gandhi, and Jawaharlal Nehru—all espousing various theories on democracy, socialism, and strains of egalitarian thinking in Hindu philosophy. By 1947, the anti-Rana leaders, many of whom resided in India, formed the Nepali Congress Party. India finally won its independence from Britain later that same year.

With India forging the most populous democracy in the world, the Nepali Congress Party organized their takeover. They wanted to build democracy in Nepal but first had to remove the Ranas. And to do that, they needed allies. So they partnered with those who wanted to revive the monarchy. In 1951, a coalition of the Nepali Congress Party and royalists returned King Tribhuvan to Kathmandu, restored the power of the Shahs, and revoked the special powers given to Rana prime ministers.

The alliance between the Nepali Congress Party and the monarchy was never easy. King Tribhuvan did allow democratic elections for a prime minister and parliament. The Congress Party faced competition from communist parties but won a majority. They gave people a taste of a social democratic platform: free speech, free elections, greater respect for lower castes and women. However, the era of multiparty democracy was short-lived. After Tribhuvan died in 1955, his son Mahendra began chipping away at fragile reforms. By 1960, he had reestablished an absolute monarchy. He gave lip service to new enthusiasm for party politics and elections in the country, but made sure only one party was allowed to play: the Panchayat Party.

Panchayat. Pramod always spat out the word in angry syllables: Pan-CHA-yat. He hated it. And it used to be a good word, he said. It means "Rule by Five," describing how South Asian villages once governed themselves, and might have been a good basis for democracy. But in Nepal, Panchayat became a political party under the rule of Hindu monarchs. King Mahendra headed the Panchayat Party and the country and banned all other political parties. He also banned political meetings, outlawed free speech, and censored the press—all in the name of Hindu self-governance.

After Mahendra's death, his son, Birendra, became king. Along with his wife, Queen Aishwarya, and numerous councilors, Birendra continued to steer the country in the same direction as his father. The Panchayat Party arrested, tortured, and sometimes assassinated and executed those who defied them. Despite the risks, opposition groups—the Nepali Congress Party, student clubs, and various communist parties—organized underground to overthrow the Panchayat system. Pramod and his elder brothers were all active in those illegal groups. Siddhi became a communist, while Pramod and Tirtha supported the Nepali Congress Party.

The hanging of two Congress activists in 1979 led to widespread protests, especially among students who were also unhappy with changes stultifying the education system. To forestall greater violence, Birendra announced in 1979 that a referendum would be held the following year. People could vote on whether to retain the Panchayat system or replace it with a multiparty democracy. For six months, Nepal experienced something like free speech and free assembly. Opposition groups could publicly make their case in towns and villages throughout the country. I would later hear from Pramod's mother about her own efforts to sway opinion for "multiparty" by walking from village to village in the hills. Out of four million votes cast, the Panchayat won by a slim margin of four hundred thousand. There were accusations of rigging, and both sides attempted to buy votes by distributing food, alcohol, and even land rights in places like Chitwan.

After the referendum, the Panchayat reimposed its authoritarian rule. But people had experienced what it was like to air opinions in public without retribution. Many believed change was only a matter of time. Opposition groups now had some measure of how many people supported them. They continued organizing underground, building their constituencies and exposing the weaknesses of the Panchayat system.

Not long after Pramod told me about the bombings in Kathmandu, we began talking about a future together. Then Pramod dropped his grenade: "I'm not going to follow you to East Africa, you know. If we're going to be together, you'll have to come with me to India."

The explosion brought a relief that surprised me. I had latched on to African studies in a period of political naiveté. When I met Pramod, I had been trying to figure out how to move on to a new phase, collaborate with Third World activists, and tie my research into some grassroots struggle for social change. Pramod did fit that plan. Perhaps the place did not matter so much anymore. The next hurdle was convincing my dissertation committee.

"In India," I told them, "people are organizing for change—not just politicians, but farmers, low-caste women, and indigenous peoples." I reminded them that I had been planning for some time to focus on women, and then described India's strong national feminist movement and all the small grassroots women's groups working to save trees, prevent big dams from flooding sacred lands, fight for better wages, and protest rape and domestic violence.

"For studying women's activism," I said, "India is the place to be."

With reservations about my lack of preparedness, my committee allowed me to change research fields. Part of me questioned their wisdom as much as mine.

I had a little less than a year to prepare for my qualifying exams, in which students are grilled in both writing and oral presentation on a chosen area of expertise. I wanted to organize my exams around comparative systems of social inequality: gender, class, race. Adding caste in South Asia to that mix allowed me to delve into some history that would, I hoped, ease my way into India.

To describe the caste system, scholars often invoked a body metaphor from the oldest Hindu texts, the Vedas. Brahman priests and teachers orchestrate from the head, Kshatriya rulers and warriors govern with powerful arms, Vaishya merchants and financiers circulate goods and wealth from the belly and torso, and Sudra farmers, builders, and artisans undergird the body on firm legs. The metaphor illustrates the ideal hierarchy and the relation of each caste to ritual purity. As the head transcends bodily impurities, so Brahmans may rise above the unsavory aspects of ruling, trading, and banking. Yet the body analogy also captures how priests, rulers, and financiers cooperate to animate and control the system.

The caste system is an abstract ideal that gets messier in practice. It originated as a division of labor at a time when people could, in theory, fill roles based on merit and interest. Over the centuries, the roles became more rigid as kin groups claimed particular occupations and ritual status through hereditary membership and endogamy. Sub-castes within the broad categories proliferated and mixed with language, ethnic, and tribal distinctions. Castes often lived in interdependent but segregated communities. Each group observed detailed rules about diet, ritual purification, and interaction with members of other castes.

As groups became more rigid, the powerful began to relegate kin groups that did the most "impure" work to a status beyond the pale of the caste system. Those outcastes who swept streets, washed clothes, crafted clay pots, and worked metal and leather became known as "untouchables." By the twentieth century, more and more embraced a new collective identity as Dalits (literally, the Oppressed).

Longing for simplicity, I wanted to conflate caste and class. But even though they overlapped, they didn't line up. Although they lacked the spiritual purity of Brahmans, the Kshatriya and Vaishyas on the second and third tiers headed up the most powerful political and economic classes in South Asian history. They became the kings and queens, lords and ladies, rich merchants and industrialists. Like religious advisors in the courts of Europe, some Brahmans granted spiritual favors to Kshatriyas and Vaishyas in exchange for political influence and wealth. Other Brahmans renounced the material world and became humble farmers or even poorer forest-dwellers who lived off alms. They claimed ritual superiority, but many ate less than those they considered untouchable.

As South Asia became part of a global capitalist economy, many farmers, outcastes, and even some in higher castes became generic wage laborers on agricultural estates and in factories. The occupational specialties of the caste system began to break down. However, other traits of caste, such as endogamy, segregated living, and rules about intercaste relations, did not.

With my new focus on women, I wanted to explore how gender intersected with caste in India. I read scores of books and articles, most of which argued for more attention to regional specifics rather than gross generalizations. But to prepare for my exams, I had to paint some broad strokes.

In general, I learned, higher castes defined their ritual purity and superiority by how well they controlled women by marrying them off as virgin child brides, criminalizing their adultery, restricting their visibility and mobility in public, preventing divorce and widow remarriage, and punishing those who transgressed. Yet while higher-caste women endured domestic restrictions, they shared some benefits with their fathers, husbands, and sons. Those varied over time and place but included power over lower castes, access to wealth and learning, political influence, protection from public violence, and the ability to direct others to work for them.

Because lower castes had less ritual purity to lose, women in them generally experienced fewer constraints on sexuality and marriage. But they shared with their menfolk vulnerability to economic exploitation and physical abuse from higher castes. And, of course, women also faced sexualized violence at home, from higher-caste men, and from marauding armies and police.

With that broad understanding, I wondered how caste, class, and gender played out in a particular region of India undergoing capitalist development. Did women in different castes find enough in common around gender to organize for change as women? Or were they more likely to identify as a particular class, such as poor agricultural laborers, or with a caste or ethnic identity?

I added a Hindi class to my busy fall quarter. Pramod and I also hired a tutor to help us learn Marathi, a related language dominant in Maharashtra State. We pooled our meager savings and bought plane tickets to Mumbai. We planned to start there and meet with academics, journalists, and activists who might help us direct our research. From Mumbai, we would take a train to do the same in New Delhi. Pramod hoped to work with indigenous activists who were using drama, song, and dance in creative ways to mobilize actions against land grabs, big dams, and resource extraction. I hoped to focus my research on indigenous or Dalit women, or maybe women agricultural laborers. I wasn't sure yet. Although we had only three weeks, Pramod suggested we also take a side trip to meet his family, so we made arrangements to fly back to the States from Kathmandu.

True to my dissertation committee's predictions, I was poorly prepared for any of it.

A LONG NIGHT

O N MY FIRST trip to Nepal with Pramod in January 1986, a train rocked us overnight from New Delhi to Gorakhpur Junction. From there, a minibus dropped us at the border town of Sonauli nearly twenty-four hours after we'd left India's capital. With passport stamped and tucked back into a hip belt under my jeans, I dodged garbage and potholes, and crossed an invisible line from India into Bhairawa, Nepal. Like beads broken off a cheap necklace, the ramshackle buildings that lined the muddy highway running north through town seemed to belong more to a land of border towns than to any specific country.

Bent forward by overstuffed backpacks, Pramod and I trudged toward the bus station. We shoved our way into seats on the bus bound for Chitwan's urban center, Narayanghat. I tuned in to sing-song cadences and admired women with heavy gold ear- and nose rings and men in *daura suruwal*—tunics and pants more form-fitting than those in India—and *dhaka topi*—colorfully embroidered caps. As the bus trundled onto the highway, a boy bowed a four-stringed instrument and sang. The sounds and colors and something more I couldn't pinpoint gave me a palpable sense of being somewhere other than India. That, at least, was a relief.

What I'd liked best about India—*puri, saag paneer, mango lassi* —had been my downfall. A Delhi doctor had called my condi-tion gastroenteritis and prescribed bland foods. I'd recovered from fever, delirium, diarrhea, and vomiting but hadn't held down more than yogurt and boiled rice for five days. Now, my stomach hosted nothing but a war between nausea and hunger. Whiffs of masala, peanuts, urine, chai, vomit, and cigarettes from fellow bus passengers waging their own bodily battles intensified the discomfort.

I noted a few other foreigners on the bus: all budget travelers with dusty backpacks and clothes as colorful and mismatched as the bazaars they must have wandered through in India, Morocco, Thailand. Some flipped through their Lonely Planet guides. Part of me I thought I'd left behind wished I could first arrive in Nepal as they did, with grand plans for trekking and adventure. But as an aspiring anthropologist, I wanted to be so much more than a tourist. I reminded myself I'd fallen in love with a Nepali but didn't intend to succumb to Nepal the way tourists do.

I wonder now at that young woman arriving in Nepal with more dread than curiosity. Maybe stomach troubles tangled with other worries: strained finances, so many new people to meet, the discomforts of travel, all I had to learn about India to pass my PhD qualifying exams in several months. Pramod had already convinced me to give up plans to work in Africa and follow him to India. Two weeks of being sick there had depressed me about that decision. So any hint Pramod dropped that I should one day consider working in Nepal too made me mortar another brick in a growing wall of resistance. I had no plans to be an anthropologist of Nepal. Ever. I was a scholar of conflict and rebellion. Pramod was too, which is why he had planned research in India rather than in his country. Like Pramod, I saw Nepal as a theoretical backwater. Under stifling authoritarian rule for decades, the country seemed to attract anthropologists most interested in religion and ritual. And what did religion have to do with me? My mother and grandmother rarely talked about religion when I was growing up and never took me to church. My father was a devout atheist.

From my habit of staring at maps long before a trip, I knew we would skirt the base of the Himalayan foothills. At some point, we would pass near Lumbini—Buddha's alleged birthplace. Despite my stubborn resistance, I peered out the grimy bus windows hoping for a glimpse of the beauty I'd seen on postcards: hillsides dotted with red rhododendrons, rice paddies carved from steep slopes, peaks so high they appeared more rooted in clouds than in earth. But dense fog—and later, a moonless night—hid the landscape.

An hour or so past the border, the bus stopped. Two police boarded. They strutted down the aisle, jostled bags in the overhead racks, and poked bundles under the seats.

Pramod leaned into my ear and whispered, "All these police! It's because of the bomb that exploded in Kathmandu. Remember? I told you about it."

"Of course." I thought back to that spring day early in our romance when Pramod had described the news he'd heard from Nepal.

The police paused near our seats and scrutinized us. I smiled at them in the way I imagined a tourist with no political thoughts might smile at police in an authoritarian state. The police did not smile back. They looked away and continued down the aisle. They looked ready to rough someone up, more out of boredom than Panchayat loyalty.

A few minutes after boarding, the police stepped down and waved us through.

"Searching for arms smugglers," Pramod said. "It's a sign. The opposition is growing stronger."

He was trying so hard to spark my interest. I liked that.

"You think people would carry bombs on a bus like this?"

"Shhh," he said and looked around. "Keep your voice down."

I had studied autocracy and advocated uprisings against it, but I had no idea how to participate in the kinds of coded conversations rebels employed. Many of Pramod's friends had spent time in jail. Some had been tortured. Assassinations and executions happened more often in this alleged Shangri-la than most foreigners knew.

I looked around at the Lonely Planet travelers. I probably knew less about Nepal than they but felt smug knowing tidbits about its underside.

"Well?" I whispered.

"Maybe."

"You really think change is coming so soon?"

"I don't know when. But it will come. These police! They do surveillance like this, but they can't stop change."

I wondered if Nepal would be more interesting than I had imagined but hardly had the energy to ponder that for long.

Except for a flat tire and a few more checkpoints, the rest of the trip passed uneventfully. A little after midnight, the bus crossed a bridge over the Narayani River and pulled into a petrol station in Narayanghat. Fluorescent lights inside cast a wide beam across the muddy parking lot. Bundled in worn fiberfill jackets and scarves, several men huddled in the eerie glow and blew into their cupped hands. Streetlights illuminated rotting garbage piles and the cement buildings that paralleled the wide, empty road leading east.

The bus unloaded Pramod, me, and several other passengers. Taking on a few more people, it honked several times and, with shouts and slaps on the side, rolled into the otherwise silent night. Heading north on the highway through Narayanghat Bazaar, it would wind through steep foothills and follow the Prithvi Highway along the Trisuli River toward Kathmandu. The major road leading from the plains to Nepal's capital, it was a route I would come to know well over the years. If there were no breakdowns or accidents, the bus would reach the city in six or seven hours.

Standing in the lot of the petrol station, I wondered if we should sleep in a hotel. Pramod had suggested the option if we couldn't find transportation to his village. If we could find a room away from the street smells, I would have been willing to pay.

A tall young man staggered toward me.

"Which lodge you are staying in?" Puffs of whiskey breath floated out with his words.

"I'm not staying in a lodge. I'm with him." I pointed to Pramod, who was negotiating transportation with the drivers of assorted vehicles parked along the roadside. Trying to keep his balance, the man looked toward Pramod and waved him away.

"Him? Not good tourist guide. I give you good tour—elephant ride, canoe ride, tigers, rhinos, crocodiles."

Stabbed by nostalgia for safaris in Kenya, I remembered a coffee table book on the world's wild places I'd flipped through at Kepler's Bookstore in Palo Alto. It included a chapter on Royal Chitwan National Park, the oldest national park in Nepal and a designated UNESCO World Heritage Site. Covering about 360 square miles, the park preserves a remnant of the tarai as it used to be: hardwood forests, savannas, and marshlands that once stretched from India to Bhutan. A few weeks earlier, the naturalist buried inside me had noted some numbers on the back of an old receipt: 40 kinds of mammals, 40 different reptiles and amphibians, 113 species of fish, 489 resident and migratory bird species.

"I'm going to his village, Gunjanagar." I pointed to Pramod again and waved to get his attention.

The man laughed. "Gunjanagar? Not near park. I give better tour."

Pramod returned and gathered our backpacks. He wore blue jeans and a denim jacket, clothing that looked out of place in Nepal in 1986. And although a bit shorter than my six feet, he was tall for a Nepali. The drunken man addressed him in English.

"Where you want to go? I take you too."

Pramod responded in terse, angry-sounding Nepali. I didn't understand the words then. The tourist guide looked surprised, not expecting this foreign-dressed man to speak Nepali. Pramod gave me my pack and nudged me toward the road.

"You be sorry!" the man yelled after us and stumbled a few steps forward.

I looked at the two rickshaws waiting for us, stopped, and then glanced back at the drunk for a moment. Even then, some part of me sensed something amiss in the life changes I'd made over the last few years. Each one had prodded me farther from what I had once hoped for and then obscured the path back. That I glimpsed a faint hope of return in a drunken tourist guide loitering at night near a bus station in a bleak town should have been a sign to ponder my next steps more carefully.

"You don't want to stay here, do you?" Pramod said. I watched the drunk about-face and weave toward the men crowded at the doorway of the petrol station.

"I guess not."

"Don't worry. We should be home in about two hours. It'll be a beautiful ride."

I followed Pramod to the line of bicycle rickshaws. I wondered how they would take us to Gunjanagar. Pramod had described the village as being some distance from Narayanghat. Except for the two drivers waiting for us, most slept curled under tattered blankets on their seats. We loaded our backpacks in one rickshaw, sat in the other, and wheeled down the main road. On the steep hill leading east out of town, we stepped down and walked. The cyclists pushed their rickshaws beside us. At the top, we hopped back on board. We passed the district headquarters of Bharatpur before turning onto a narrow asphalt road that edged the airport and led toward the villages of western Chitwan.

After leaving Bharatpur, the rickshaw rolled us past shadowy outlines of fields and houses. I caught wafts of fresh straw and manure and inhaled deeply to gather more. I remembered Pramod's stories about not wanting to pick up cow dung as a child. Somehow, it comforted me.

The fog that had enveloped us through the day sank and ribboned along the ground, allowing brief glimpses of starry winter sky. I took advantage of darkness and mist to rest my head on Pramod's shoulder. Then Pramod did what he had hesitated to do in public places since we'd arrived in South Asia: put his arm around me.

After an hour or so, we bumped off the end of the paved road.

"The asphalt only goes as far as the college," Pramod said, point-ing to a sign on the left. A streetlight made the English and Nepali writing visible, but, of course, I could read only the English:

INSTITUTE OF AGRICULTURE AND ANIMAL SCIENCE
TRIBHUVAN UNIVERSITY
RAMPUR CAMPUS

Although I didn't intend to spend much time in Chitwan, I liked knowing my fiancé came from a family that lived near a college campus.

From Rampur, we jolted over gravel and swerved around pot-holes. Since he'd visited the new family house in Chitwan only a few times, Pramod wasn't sure of the way. He stopped and woke residents several times to ask directions. None of them seemed to mind. When we turned off the main road, muddy potholes made pedaling impossible. The two hired men pushed the cycles carrying our luggage. I wondered how much Pramod had promised to pay them and how it could ever be enough for their work.

My running shoes often squished through what my nose told me must be manure. I liked barnyard smells distant, not on my shoes. Calculating each step slowed my pace. Pramod walked with the confident stride of one used to walking unlit pathways at night. He stopped often and waited for me to catch up.

After thirty minutes or so, Pramod paused in front of a two-story, whitewashed cement house that looked like others we'd passed, at least in the dark.

"Could be the place, but I'm not sure," Pramod said to me. Then he shouted toward the house: "Siddhi-dai!"

Thanks to Pramod's stories, I remembered that Siddhi had become the eldest brother after Purushottam's death. He was also the one who had led the family down to Chitwan. The wooden door on the second story opened. A man looked out and shouted back. A few minutes later, people filed out from the door below, wiping sleep from their eyes and wrapping their heads in shawls and scarves.

Pramod walked toward the silent figures and spoke in a clipped, flat tone. I hung back, waiting for joyful shouts and embraces. Hearing none, I figured we still hadn't found the right house and grew impatient to get directions and continue walking. That was my first misunderstanding. Brahman greetings tend to be subdued.

People lined up. Pramod brought me before a petite woman dressed in a red cotton sari with a striped woolen shawl draped over her head.

"My mother," Pramod said. "You can call her Aama."

I didn't know her real name then. I just knew that *aama* meant "mother." I greeted her with folded hands and a "namaste." She returned the gesture and smiled. I stared for a moment, admiring how wrinkles added to the beauty in her calm face.

"And this is my brother Siddhi"—I noted how different he looked from Pramod: shorter, no gray hair, sun-leathered skin, and deep frown lines—"and his wife, Sakuntala." She put her hand over her mouth and laughed.

I'd heard a lot about Sakuntala, how she and Pramod's mother had never gotten along. Pramod sometimes suggested I think about studying that—the conflict in Nepali culture between *sasu* (mother-in-law) and *buhari* (daughter-in-law). No thanks, I said, mortaring yet another brick in my wall against becoming an anthropologist of Nepal. But since I had a particular interest in social inequality and how women fit into various patterns of property ownership and kinship, I paid attention to Pramod's explanation. All Brahman families, he said, have an ideal of a father and his sons living together in one household and holding all property—land, grain, livestock, and buildings—in common. Few live up to this ideal and endure bitter years of fraternal arguments before they separate. The parents often blame daughters-in-law for pressuring their husbands to establish independent households. Pramod always added another twist: many brothers want to separate as much as their wives do, so they let their wives take the blame for breaking up the family.

I would not meet her this trip, but I already knew that Tirtha's wife, Sarada, was the model daughter-in-law, the one with whom Sakuntala and every other daughter-in-law would be compared. Sakuntala had too sharp a tongue and insufficient respect for her in-laws. I had tried to digest these daughter-in-law tales objectively. But talk of women with too strong opinions and bad tongues made me wonder what parts of myself I might have to give up to become a worthy family member.

"And here are our children." From oldest to youngest, Pramod introduced each in turn. Three girls—Sharmila, Pramila, Urmila, and two boys—Suman and Sujan. They all giggled.

Our children. Pramod had reminded me many times that if we married, these five—Siddhi and Sakuntala's children—would be considered our own children: *chora-chori*. (Literally, it means "son-daughter," but in the *ghar*, it includes all the children of brothers and their wives.) Tirtha and Sarada had four more: three daughters—Anubha, Anjita, Archana—and a son—Anjan. We would be expected to love them all as our own and help raise and educate them.

I had little experience around children, so talk of automatically inheriting nine unnerved me. I wasn't sure I wanted to bear children of my own.

"And this is Udaya." He put his hand on a slight young man's shoulder. I tried not to stare at the distorted jaw and cheekbones. Udaya tilted his crooked chin toward Pramod and curled his lips into a lopsided smile. Udaya had never excelled in school and had failed his School-Leaving Examination several times. I knew we would have to help him too. Pramod had made that clear.

I stepped back and scanned the faces. How easy it had been on a walk, over coffee, or during intimacies in Palo Alto to hear stories of politics, poverty, and tragedy. I was so sure then I would overcome shyness as well as language and cultural ignorance and fit right in. I would love the family. They would love me. And then, somehow, I could get on with the real work I'd agreed to in India.

The family gathered closer to stare at me. With my short hair, jeans, and boxy cotton jacket, I may have looked like a man.

They hadn't seen Pramod in four years. The first they'd heard about this visit came from a letter posted from Mumbai two weeks earlier. Pramod had included a sentence about "a friend" who would accompany him but did not mention gender. I worried about this vague approach, but he assured me it would be easier. For a long time, I thought this approach careless. I would learn that it was typical. Relatives the family had not seen for months or years often showed up at our house unannounced. The way we arrived also reflected Pramod's optimistic approach to everything, a sense that you plunge ahead and sort out problems later.

"Let them meet you in person," Pramod had often said. "Then they can accept you for who you are."

I had often tried to imagine how I would explain myself in terms that mattered to Brahmans: ancestry, kinship, purity.

My mother never talked much about how she and my biological father began their brief romance in 1959, though she did sometimes hint at trysts in the Blue Moon Tavern in Seattle's University District. Outgoing and smart, Mom had once hoped to be an artist. From photos, I know she was pretty: light brown hair curled into a flip at the shoulder, tight dresses over girdled curves, a cigarette pinched between her long, lean fingers. She looked both worldly and optimistic like other young women of the time riding toward a crest of new sexual and professional freedoms. But like many others, she fell off that wave early and crashed into a more mundane life. After I was born in 1960 and my father disappeared, Mom settled for clerical work at Boeing, Seattle's largest private employer. With no other options for child care, Mom asked her own mother to move out from Louisville, Kentucky. We all settled into a modest Craftsman home a block off the freeway in the Wallingford District.

Grandmother was not one to bake chocolate chip cookies and apple pies. After coming home from work, Mom still did most of the cooking. When Grandmother entered the kitchen, she sometimes managed a fried egg burnt in butter, but she mostly served TV dinners. And we ate them on folding tables, so she could continue what she did for most waking hours every day: watch television.

Grandmother was shorter than Mom's six feet and wore flowered housedresses, thick stockings, and orthopedic shoes. I always understood Grandmother to be an invalid. But I never knew what made her so. When I asked Mom, she rolled her eyes the way she often did when we talked about Grandmother and said something like, "That's how she wants to be."

Introverted and eager to please, I was an easy child to look after. That freed Grandmother to watch her shows. She screamed advice at soap opera stars. During commercials, she compared the characters to her good-for-nothing ex-husband, lying sisters, thieving cousins, and lazy daughter. I didn't know if she was talking to me or to some phantom edging around the walls. She sometimes took a break from television to stand by the front window and peek through the curtains. If she noted a car parked too many days in one spot or saw someone she didn't recognize entering or exiting a house, she called the police. Words in her accusations lodged in my mind before I understood what they meant: whorehouse, drug dealers. I was too young to know what such activity looked like, but I don't remember any neighbors being taken to jail.

As I grew older and brought friends home to play, Grandmother often interrupted with praise for them: "Look how clever our little Kim is. And Deborah! So pretty in that dress." Then she turned to me: "Why can't you be more like that?" Bob Enslin, my father, came back into my life for short visits after I turned five. An engineer at Boeing, Bob lived on a houseboat on Lake Union, cooked on a woodstove, and had a tiny bedroom lined in scraps of fur. As a child, I didn't consider how all that must have enhanced his bachelor groove. I just thought it made my new father supercool. He soon remarried and gave me a loving, vivacious stepmother and two half sisters. Bob didn't take much interest in me, but my stepmother picked me up once a week after school so I could play with my sisters.

My mother met her second husband in a scuba-diving club. They married when I was eight. He was already balding then. Aside from that, Mom said, he reminded her of John Wayne, her childhood crush. From the movies we watched together, I didn't see much resemblance except for the thin lips, a vague western drawl, and a patriotic swagger. A middle manager at Boeing, Dad had three daughters and a son. During those first few years of blended family life, the step-siblings visited us at times but continued living with their mother.

Our family had never been whole, so I didn't mind having my parents remarry. That's how families grow, I thought, and I wanted a bigger family. Still, Dad puzzled me. I'd never heard anyone use racial and ethnic slurs so freely. Mom had never talked like that. Attending school in progressive Seattle during the civil rights era, I had learned it was wrong to use the N-word or similar degrading terms for Italians, Japanese, and Jews. Yet Dad used such language every day.

But Dad's good qualities grew on me. He was loyal and dependable—just what Mom needed after being a single, working mother for so many years. Dad also helped pull us out of Grandmother's suffocating orbit and made possible our happiest family times. Most weekends, he and Mom took me on outings. My step-siblings sometimes came too. Mom said the outdoors was the only church our family ever needed. She and Dad taught me how to snorkel along the jetty at Alki Beach Park, across the bay from downtown Seattle. Sometimes, I was content to let the adults go deeper in scuba gear while I collected driftwood and shells with my stepsisters or family friends on the beach. Then when the adults returned, we'd help empty their goody bags of sea urchins, sea cucumbers, moon snails. If Dad speared some ling or rock cod, we'd all help filet.

In the fall, we drove to the Cascade foothills and walked miles through rain-soaked salal gathering buckets of chanterelle mushrooms. During summers, we took road trips: Lake Coeur d'Alene, the Canadian Rockies, Yellowstone. After Dad and Mom bought a half acre with a single-wide on Orcas Island, several hours north of Seattle, we had some of our most blissful summers ever: boating, fishing, snorkeling, hiking, blackberry picking, bird-watching, and sharing meals with family and friends around the food we'd gathered.

Most summers, Dad's parents came from Kansas to join us on Orcas. Grandpa whittled wood, sat us on his knee for story time, and often headed up the fishing trips in our fourteen-foot skiff. Grandma wore aprons and made blackberry cobblers. They were the kind of grandparents I had always wanted.

In the late 1960s, my other father quit his job as a Boeing engineer, grew his sandy hair long, cultivated a beard and mustache, took up pot smoking, and became an artist. In his studio in the increasingly hip Fremont District in Seattle, Bob used "a secret formula" to swish multiple colors into abstracts or fill stencils with swirling patterns.

A middle-aged woman I hadn't met yet emerged from a thatched shed next to the house.

"Look who's here," Pramod said. "My Didi, my sister. I didn't think she'd be here."

I remember Pramod telling me that she lived several hours away by bus. I would only see Didi on special occasions after that, but our first encounter stuck with me.

Didi turned to me and spoke in a soft, singsong voice. I had no idea what she said, but her sympathetic eyes and wide smile put me at ease. I like to think she understood what it was to come from so far to meet one's prospective in-laws.

Pramod's mother laid out straw mats for us on the verandah. The girls lit kerosene lanterns. Then they disappeared with all the women except Didi.

"Come sit closer," Pramod said to his sister, patting the mat.

Didi laughed. She pointed to the buffalo shed. Pramod pondered her hint and then turned to me.

"You'll find this interesting," he said, as though we were in a class at Stanford, sharing tidbits from an assigned reading. "Didi is staying in the buffalo shed because she's having her period. She can't cook or sit with us on the cot."

He turned away from me to talk and laugh with Didi.

Calculating the days to my own period, I ignored them.

A tall, elderly man loomed in the doorway and surveyed the busy scene. He did not smile. I knew at once it was Pramod's father, Pandit Kedarnath Parajuli.

It would be several years before I braved addressing Pandit Kedarnath as Bua (Father). He stood before what I later learned was his place—the wooden cot next to the front door on the narrow verandah. Udaya rushed past us into the house, brought out another straw mat and a woolen rug, and spread them on the cot. Kedarnath sat and folded his knees in front. He wrapped himself in an enormous beige shawl, leaving his bare feet peeking out from below. Pramod came forward, knelt and bowed his forehead to his father's feet. Smiling, Pandit Kedarnath touched Pramod's head. Pramod's mother appeared, assumed a similar position long enough for Pramod to touch his forehead to her feet and then hurried off. Pramod exchanged some words with his father and trailed after his mother. I thought about following, but I was too tired and nervous to budge.

Pandit Kedarnath scrutinized me. He always had such a stern face. I later learned how to see what Pramod emphasized: the kindness, compassion, and wisdom behind the serious facade. Yet I never relaxed around Pandit Kedarnath Parajuli, perhaps because of what happened later that night.

Pandit Kedarnath barked something in Nepali. I hoped he wasn't speaking to me, but he looked right at me with what I imagined to be a sneer. Not understanding, I tried to smile but probably grimaced. I looked down and picked at loose straws in the mat.

Cat's got your tongue again. Grandmother used to mock me like that. Whenever the shyness that has haunted me into adulthood takes my voice away again, I still whip myself with those words.

Pandit Kedarnath narrowed his eyes and glared at me for what seemed like minutes. Then he turned away and stared at the rickshaw drivers sitting on the edge of the verandah. The family had invited them to spend the night and return to Narayanghat the next morning. Pandit Kedarnath asked them questions in Nepali. They laughed and said something in return. He turned to me again. I couldn't understand the exchange. I looked up to see Pandit Kedarnath's eyes squeezed tighter. He stood and walked regally back into the house. I glanced around. No one else seemed to have noticed the storm. Perhaps I was paranoid. Eyes downcast, I poked at the mat some more.

Aama brought me a stainless steel cup of hot tea—*chia.* I savored the warm sweetness, realizing how chilled I had become from the two-hour bike ride in the damp night. Aama also offered us some *dal bhat* (lentils and rice). Pramod told her we weren't hungry. I was hungry but couldn't stomach the food, especially in the early morning hours. The rickshaw drivers ate enough for all of us.

Taking my hand, Pramod led me into the house, up some steep, roughly hewn stairs to the second floor and then through a low doorway into a far room. The lantern he set on a wooden table lit up the dingy white walls, the bare cement floor, and two beds.

"Get some rest. I'll talk with the family and come up later."

Almost delirious from exhaustion and minimal food over the last week, I begged him not to leave me alone.

"Don't worry, I'll be back."

Unable to bear the cold of removing my clothes, I snuggled fully dressed under the thick cotton quilt and willed myself to relax. Talk I couldn't understand filtered up from below. Then came gruff shouting and a loud but soothing voice. I wished I were somewhere—anywhere—else.

Pramod returned, sat on the bed, and stroked my cheek.

"I guess you can hear the shouting from here, huh?"

"Yeah. What's happening? Is your father angry?"

"Oh no. Don't worry. Just a little misunderstanding. Daddy's blood pressure has gone up. We'll have to sit with him more to make sure he's all right. He's had this problem for some time and hasn't been taking his medicine. But I don't want you to worry. Mom says she's glad you came." Pramod kissed me and left the room. I listened to his footsteps descending the stairs. Then came more sharp words. I curled into a fetal ball and pulled the quilt over my head.

I woke with a full bladder in the dark. Pramod lay sleeping beside me on one narrow bed. I tapped him on the shoulder.

"Huh?"

"I have to pee," I whispered.

"Go downstairs and outside, in front of the house."

"I can't see."

"Well, I don't have a flashlight."

I groped my way along the wall, found my sneakers, and shoved my feet into them. I opened the double doors. Squinting, I saw a stair railing silhouetted at the far end of a large, open room. I heard varied breathing rhythms to my left—some short and quick, others long and drawn out, some snoring—and wondered how many were sleeping there. I shuffled into the room, trying not to creak the wooden floor and wake anyone. I reached for the stair rail and found it. I braced myself and let my right foot fall onto the first narrow step. I put my left foot beside it. I took another step the same way. Growing more confident, I placed my right foot on one step and the left on the next. Right, left, right, left, right . . .

I can't say for sure what happened next. I have a vague memory of my foot flying out from under me and my body free-falling. Perhaps I screamed. What I remember best is being what Pramod would later call "sent a-flat" on the landing. My elbows and knees throbbed. Hoping to rise, skip down the last few stairs, and rush outside without waking anyone, I grabbed for the railing, but before I could pull myself up, I heard voices and footsteps. A light flashed on my face.

I let go of the railing and shielded my eyes. After adjusting to the glare, I saw Aama holding a flashlight. She looked concerned. From upstairs came Pramod's voice.

"What happened?"

"I fell down the stairs."

Thanks to Aama's light, I found the railing again and stood.

"I'm all right. Nothing broken."

Siddhi appeared by Pramod's side, followed by Udaya and some others. I saw the girls behind Aama. They all watched me and murmured words I couldn't understand. Pretending my elbow and knee didn't hurt, I smiled and repeated in English, "It's okay," and limped to the door. Aama rushed over, undid the bolt, and gave me a flashlight. I walked to the fields in front of the house, squatted, and peed.

Relieved of bladder irritation, I stood alone for a few moments and considered my predicament. Embarrassment and pain were the least of it.

To think I had once planned to walk alongside the pastoral Maasai. That had been my plan when I applied to PhD programs. The Maasai and I would herd their cattle across the savanna. Then in camp at night, I'd ask them questions about how they value cows like money and resist government schemes to settle and become farmers. Seized by radical politics, I turned to other ideas. Maybe I could base myself among guerrillas along the Mozambique–South African border and be on the front lines of smashing apartheid. Then I switched to India, confident I could master language, culture, and history in a year and sit beside women picking cotton or breaking rocks into gravel in the blazing heat of the Deccan Plateau and ask them questions about their campaigns for higher wages and more respect from men.

Now, here I was in Nepal. Without much planning or thought, I'd tripped into this place where menstruating women slept in the buffalo shed and family patriarchs dictated marriage partners for their children. And how did I respond? I lost my tongue, begged Pramod not to leave me, and fell down the stairs. In less than one night, I had shattered every illusion of myself as mature, sociable, and cross-culturally savvy. I wasn't fit to be a tourist, let alone an anthropologist.

I had little interest in Nepal or Gunjanagar, but no matter where I did my fieldwork, I finally realized what should have been obvious: I'd probably spend a lot of time here too. How badly did I want this marriage? How badly did Pramod want me? If Pramod had to have an American wife, he could find one more outgoing, courageous, graceful, and beautiful than I. Even if the family did accept me, wouldn't they always wish for someone—anyone—other than me?

I fought off tears. In a few hours, daylight would move me closer to my future here. Or force me to choose a different path. Back at Stanford in a week, I could tell my dissertation committee I'd made a mistake. I could still make other plans.

It was cold. I pushed my doubts aside and aimed my thoughts and footsteps toward what I most needed in the next few hours of darkness: a warm blanket and Pramod.

Aama stood at the open door. She ushered me back inside, closed the door, and steered me to the stairs. I offered her the flashlight, but she pressed it back into my hand. Trying to ignore all the faces looking down at me, I climbed the stairs. At the top, Pramod took my elbow, led me into the room, and closed the door.

FOG

I woke to the slip-slap of plastic sandals and the slow creak of the wooden door. A young girl poked her head into the room. Her brown eyes gaped and darted around the room, resting at times on me, her aunt-to-be, and her uncle Pramod sleeping beside me. She appeared to be nine or ten. Urmila, I assumed. I smiled at her and shook Pramod.

"*Hazur*—yes?" he said and opened his eyes.

He saw Urmila and sat up. She said something to him, stood for another moment looking at us in bed together, and left. Her warm, curious smile pushed out memories of earlier dramas. The sound of her flip-flops descending the stairs brought them back.

I examined our room. Clothes hung from a rope in one corner. Papers and books rose in haphazard stacks on a small shelf. Paint chipped off the cement wall. Light and the faint smell of wood smoke seeped through openings in the poorly fitted shutters and window frames. In the distance, roosters crowed and buffaloes bellowed.

Pramod opened the wooden shutters to a view of fog and moved to the other cot. Urmila returned with two stainless steel cups of hot tea and then left. I wrapped my hands around metal, grateful for the warmth. Remembering I hadn't eaten much for days, I gulped the brew of fatty buffalo milk and abundant sugar and hoped there would be more. At least my appetite was returning.

Pramod's relatives drifted in and out. They talked with Pramod and did bring more tea as well as small, stainless steel bowls of popcorn mixed with ghee and salt. Urmila and Pramod's two older nieces—Sharmila and Pramila—took turns in the doorway, staring.

Stuffed with tea and popcorn, Pramod and I found ourselves alone for a moment.

"Did you say anything to Father last night?" he asked.

"How could I?"

"Maybe you said something in English. He understands some, you know."

"I didn't say a thing. I felt too shy."

"It must have been those rickshaw drivers. I think what happened is Father asked the rickshaw drivers who you were. They were just joking around. They saw us holding each other in the rickshaw. And they said, 'Don't you know, sir, that's your new daughter-in-law.' So you see, Father thought we'd married already. He got angry thinking I'd marry without telling him. I'll let him know we're just asking for permission."

"Okay."

"He's also worried about caste. What will become of my caste? What caste will our children be? Those things."

I felt the weight of history bearing down. Even though I couldn't have explained the details, I understood the general contours of social inequality on that first visit to Nepal. I pictured the Vedic image of a body divided into castes: Brahman, Kshatriya, Vaishya, Sudra. Where did a foreigner fit in? Or did she?

I knew Pramod's father, like other Brahman elders, still held to basic pollution rules: Don't accept water from those considered untouchable. Don't take water or cooked rice from menstruating women. But Pramod had always stressed how Pandit Kedarnath also advocated kindness and respect toward social inferiors and urged other Brahmans to practice the same. I had counted on some leniency there.

It must have crossed my mind a few times that Pramod's father might raise objections to our marriage, but I couldn't imagine a father being powerful enough to separate us. Maybe I hoped Pramod and I were so hip, exceptional, and passionate about our convictions that we'd transcend Brahman culture and create new rules. Or maybe I counted on falling back to some plea for American exceptionalism and entitlement. I'd hate myself for that, but I'd done it before to get a bus seat, overcome visa hurdles, harangue bureaucrats.

Mostly, though, I didn't understand how the details of inequality and ritual purity imbued every aspect of life in Nepal, even for those who didn't believe in them. Academic knowledge about caste and gender circled my head like an overloaded jetliner unable to get clearance for landing. My body began to absorb the impact long before my mind did.

"Caste. Sure. I get it," I said.

"Good. Mom told Dad not to worry. She understands, you know. She said this to him: 'If Pramod loves her, we should love her too.' She's really open, you know. It's Daddy who's having a hard time."

I nodded. Pramod's habit of using Americanisms, like "Mom" and "Daddy," made me smile.

"Don't worry," he said. "You're just going to spend time with the family; then we'll see what happens."

"If you say so."

I felt calmer. The only snag was getting permission from Pandit Kedarnath, and Pramod didn't seem too worried about that. The rest, I believed, would be easy. Then we would return to Stanford and get on with our lives.

Pramod and I dressed, grabbed toothbrushes, toothpaste, and soap, and stepped out into the large room I had navigated the night before. On one side was an enormous bed where Siddhi, Sakuntala, and some of the children must have slept. Chests, baskets, and metal storage containers were piled up haphazardly around the perimeter. Double doors opened onto a narrow balcony overlooking the courtyard. Next to our room was another of the same size with similar furnishings: wooden beds, a table, and a small shelf. I wasn't sure who had slept there.

Remembering my fall, I held the handrail and took the stairs one at a time. They led down into another large, open room. On the far side, wooden slats held unhulled rice heaped several feet high. Under the stairs, old copper pots topped a precarious drift of household items. Ropes, machetes, baskets, and other implements hung from nails on beams overhead. Dust covered everything.

Two small rooms identical to those upstairs opened off the main room. I learned that Pandit Kedarnath slept in one and Aama in the other.

From the verandah, I scanned the spacious earthen-plastered courtyard. A barbed wire fence lined by sparse shrubs and trees screened us from the pathway. A large two-story shed stood on the south side, with a cooking room nearest the house and the buffaloes farther away. Old straw mats, firewood, and some large pots and pans mounded carelessly under the eaves. The smell of manure wafted by. Too fresh and close, I thought.

On the north side of the courtyard, a few flowers and a small shrine stood out among abundant weeds. I hoped the place would look better when the fog lifted, but the fog hung heavy and persistent.

At the water pump on the south side of the house, I stood on algae-covered wooden boards, brushed my teeth, and spit into scummy water trickling out to the fields. Pramod showed me the trail to the outhouse and the brass bowl I could fill with washing water. I declined the bowl and fetched the toilet paper roll I had carried from India. I tiptoed through the tall weeds overtaking what appeared to be a vegetable garden and found the outhouse—a nearly full pit straddled by three slippery boards and enclosed by old gunnysacks draped over four wobbly poles. I must have come back with a scowl on my face because Pramod said, "Most families just go out in the fields. We're lucky to have a pit."

I was a camper and backpacker, used to digging holes and burying my own waste when necessary. So I felt ashamed at the irrational criticism welling up. But this was not just another stop on my travel itinerary; it was the home of the man I might marry.

Pramod had brought his father a woolen dress jacket from the

United States and a light blue tunic and drawstring pants from India. That afternoon, Pandit Kedarnath dressed in both and added a woolen scarf and *dhaka topi*. The family insisted we take him for a blood pressure check at the health post—a public clinic—in a neighboring village. Pandit Kedarnath marked time with his walking stick. Pramod and I jogged now and then to keep pace with his long stride. I couldn't understand the words he and Pramod exchanged, but frequent smiles and chuckles suggested improved spirits.

Patchy fog enveloped us, but enough sunlight filtered through to brighten yellow mustard and pink buckwheat fields. As we neared the health post, the fog dissipated. For the first time, I saw steep forested hills rising a few miles to the north. But the clouds never did rise off the hilltops. Pramod assured me that one could sometimes see the Himalayas towering over those hills on clear days. When those clear days would be, he didn't say.

I couldn't see it then, but what made Chitwan look bland on that first visit would later intrigue me. Chitwan was part of a trend. Some demographers were already predicting where it would lead. In ten years or so, Nepal would no longer be a country with most of its population in the mountains and hills. The majority would crowd into the plains.

In other parts of the tarai, Shah and Rana rulers cut the teak and sal forests in the 1800s and early 1900s. They sold the timber to the British to build railway cars and encouraged farmers from Nepal's hills to settle and cultivate in the clear-cuts. But they let the Chitwan jungles flourish. Historians note two possible reasons: to prevent the British from invading Nepal and to keep Indians fleeing famine and British brutality from pouring across the border. So trees, vines, soggy marshes, bugs, and wild animals over about 856 square miles fortified the boundary between Nepal and India.

Indigenous Tharu, who had some immunity to endemic malaria, cultivated rice in Chitwan's jungle clearings, fished in the rivers, herded livestock in the rich grasses, hunted wild animals and birds, and gathered greens and tubers in the forests. By the late 1800s, wealthy Nepali aristocrats made the Chitwan jungles their playground in the malaria-free winter months. The Ranas invited Indian and English and German aristocrats to join them in trophy hunts for rhinoceros, tigers, wild boar, and deer.

Hill dwellers north of Chitwan called the region Madhesh (the Middle Country) or Kalapani (Black Water). Monsoon rains, malaria, and heat made the valley a haven for plants and animals and a hell for all humans but the Tharu. If hill dwellers had to pass through to trade, attend school, or go on pilgrimage in India, they waited for the winter months when the foliage died back. Even then, they prayed at holy sites first and begged the deities to steer them around fever waters, kraits and cobras, irritable rhinos, hungry tigers.

In the 1920s, many Nepalis fled hill poverty and Rana rule to seek work in India. No longer fearing British invasion, the Ranas offered land in Chitwan to slow the exodus and relieve population pressure in the hills. But hill dwellers continued to fear Chitwan. The Rana government needed a more desperate crowd, people willing to endure the risks of pioneer life. So it offered amnesty to criminals and convicts who agreed to settle and cultivate land in Chitwan. This seduced a few more takers. I would later hear Chitwan residents laugh about it: "The criminal in the hills becomes the president in Chitwan."

But not many came to Chitwan for amnesty. Wealthy merchants from Kathmandu, Bandipur, and Gorkha and government officials posted to the region skimmed the earliest benefits. They anticipated future changes and recognized good investments. They had no need to settle in Chitwan; they just wanted title to land. During the 1930s and 1940s, they used trickery, forgery, and intimidation to take already cleared and cultivated parcels from Tharus. They also claimed vast estates of "unoccupied" land. Far from being unoccupied, these were the common lands of forests and marshes where

Tharus had hunted, pastured their cattle, and gathered wild foods for generations. In World War II, more than two hundred thousand Nepali men signed up as hired soldiers in Gurkha regiments in the British army. They fought on the battlefields of Southeast Asia, the Pacific, and Europe. There were at least twenty-three thousand casualties, though some sources put the number higher. The survivors returned to Nepal eager for land and new opportunities. When India won its independence from Britain in 1947 and the Shah monarchs regained power from the Rana prime ministers in 1951, many in Nepal saw a future of opportunity. Meanwhile, U.S. president Harry Truman pledged a new global project of peacemaking and integration called "development" and encouraged even more optimism. Like other leaders in the world, Nepal's King Tribhuvan embraced the new trend. Promising to lead his people out of the darkness of underdevelopment, he gained favor with his own people and among other nations, which showered Nepal with development aid. Millions ended up in Swiss bank accounts, making the Shah monarchs among the richest in the world.

With the help of the United Overseas Mission (which would become the United States Agency for International Development, or USAID) and the World Health Organization, His Majesty's Government launched programs to cut down sal forests, spray DDT to kill mosquitos, and build levees and dams to control flooding in Chitwan. Once official schemes of the 1950s and 1960s promised safety and development, hill dwellers migrated by the thousands. And after the low-cost government land ran out, another flood of migrants bought acreage at inflated prices from those absentee landlords who had been waiting decades for them.

Pramod's family had followed a common path out of the hills and into Chitwan. Didi had arrived first. Her father-in-law had claimed land when His Majesty's Government opened it up for settlement in the 1950s. She and her husband later settled in eastern Chitwan. Siddhi and his family followed to western Chitwan in the 1970s. Meanwhile, various uncles and more distant relatives joined the

migration. In the early 1980s, Pramod's parents sold their hill home
in Kahung and moved in with Siddhi in Gunjanagar.

I did not understand more than a few words of Nepali on that first
visit, so I was grateful that many knew English. Pramod told me his
father could understand some, more than he let on. He probably
could have spoken some too, but he did everything with dignity and
didn't want to speak broken English.

All children studied English in school, so I found the younger
generation easiest to communicate with. Pramod's nieces and nephews were eager to practice.

"Do you have a mother and father?" With others squatting
nearby, Sharmila asked me questions in soft and carefully enunci-
ated English. She was the eldest child of Siddhi and Sakuntala. I
was told she best modeled the ideal qualities—fair skin, soft voice,
and gentle manner—that would make a good Brahman wife. Like
her younger sisters, she usually wore a school uniform—a light blue
button-down blouse and a darker blue pleated skirt.

Except for fair skin, I lacked most marks of Brahman wifehood
and felt embarrassed answering questions about family among people who valued it so highly. "My mother and father are divorced," I
said, and then hesitated as usual. How could I satisfy curiosity with
the shortest version possible? "My mother married another man,
and my father married another woman. They're all still alive."

I squirmed on the braided cornstalk cushion and looked around
the cooking room at the earth-plastered walls and a broad shelf at
the far end where Pandit Kedarnath kept his materials for worship—brass and copper bowls and spoons, a bell, incense, and a
conch shell. Nearer to where we sat, stainless steel pots, pans, plates,
and cups lined a low wooden shelf. Underneath it was an earthen
stove with two holes on top for balancing pots and an opening
below for the fire. Some of the smoke from the stove made its way
outside through a small window. The rest filled the room and made
my eyes sting but kept us warm.

I could have gone on to say that my father and stepmother had divorced, and my father lived with his girlfriend, but I figured I had already said enough. Sharmila and the others might think I came from a "bad" family, where husbands left wives—or worse, wives left husbands. And they would have been right, given their understanding of the good and bad in families and in women.

I come from several generations of single mothers—a great-grandmother widowed by an accident in the rail yards of Louisville, Kentucky; a grandmother in Oregon widowed by her young husband's sudden brain hemorrhage; my mother's mother, who had a fling with a race car driver before marrying my grandfather, who later ran off with his mistress.

Then, there were my father and mother. In my twenties, I would divulge all I knew about their relationship: married right before my birth and divorced right after. I'd usually pause there to make sure the listener got it. Then (especially if my audience was male), I might toss back the long hair I once had and chug some dark ale, pretending none of that hurt anymore.

But I didn't share that angle or attitude with Sharmila. I knew that women who deviated from sexual mores—whether by choice or force—could lower the status of an entire Brahman family. Even if this family accepted me, how would others in the community judge me for bringing down the family line with such a long tradition of not only cultural but also family and personal impurities?

"Do you have sisters and brothers?" Sharmila asked.

I don't remember how I responded since I tended to change the numbers depending on how much energy I had to explain. Although two of Dad's daughters had lived with us for several years, I still thought of myself as an only child, the only child of my mother. I could have said "two sisters" to keep it simple and related to blood. That would include Bob and my stepmother's children. Although we had never lived together, I had watched them grow up, and we'd all become friends. I might have complicated things by adding my stepfather's children, one of whom was adopted. Depending on my patience for explaining, my mood, and the sense of self I wanted to create, I had anywhere from zero to six siblings.

"Do you have a grandmother? A grandfather?"

I thought of my paranoid and verbally abusive grandmother. She had died before I went to college. The grandparents I had most enjoyed were Dad's parents from Kansas, but how could I explain them?

"No," I said.

Always polite, Sharmila did not press me with further questions.

During that first visit, Udaya tried to teach me Nepali and make me laugh with funny stories in his broken English. I admired how he volunteered for tasks that others refused and infected family and friends with humor, kindness, and smiles.

The middle daughter, Pramila—a young teen—seemed shy then. I noticed her often by Aama's side, helping to cook or clean. Urmila didn't talk much either. She peeked around corners, caught my eye, and then disappeared. Or she snuck up behind me, tugged my hair, and skipped away, trailing giggles and a black ponytail.

Pandit Kedarnath remained calm for the rest of our visit but still circled around his main fear: Pramod would stay in America and never come back. Villagers dropped by to share rumors about other American or European women who had married Nepali men and lured them to settle outside the country. Pramod translated for me the gist of their concern: *After all that trouble, some of those women leave when things don't work out. What becomes of our Nepali sons and their children then?*

With my family and personal past, I didn't know how to calm such fears. But Pramod said it didn't matter. Then he did what he does best. He pointed toward a grander project, like how we might start a library or rural university in Gunjanagar.

We had so much other work ahead. In India. That was the plan. How could I meet infinite demands on our time, energy, and money in Nepal too?

"I'm not sure I can do this," I told Pramod. "Maybe I'm not strong enough."

Pramod calmed me in his familiar way: "Don't worry. Everything will be fine." To appease demands that we contribute to the community, I agreed we could collect some books to start a library and see about the rest. Pramod also worked out specific plans for Udaya. A relative posted as a government official near Mount Everest had invited Udaya to stay with him. Pramod tried to convince worried family members that Udaya would be fine in such a faraway place. Udaya loved children and could easily find work teaching the basics of reading and arithmetic in a region that experienced chronic teacher shortages. Teaching in a remote village among the Sherpas, an ethnic group known for their acceptance of outsiders, would give Udaya work experience, confidence, and some freedom from family expectations. Pramod argued that Udaya had been faulted enough for his physical and intellectual limitations. He needed to be somewhere where his gifts of practical intelligence, hard work, patience, and kindness could shine. Pramod proposed taking Udaya with us to Kathmandu and buying him an airline ticket to Solukhumbu. Although we had little money to spare, I agreed.

Pandit Kedarnath continued talking about his fears but said he would not stand in the way of Pramod's choice in marriage.

On our last day in Gunjanagar before we left for Kathmandu and then Palo Alto, Pramod and I drank tea with Aama in the cooking room. Short and graceful, she wore her white, thinning hair pulled back into a small bun. She dressed in thick cotton saris and wore no jewelry except for a huge man's watch on one wrist. The only concession to fashion I noted was a small box. Every morning, she took from it a mirror and a kohl pencil and lined her eyes.

Stoking the fire and stirring a pot of something on the earthen stove, she talked, cried, and laughed. Pramod translated what he could of her questions (Do you find enough dal bhat to eat in Amrika? Do you want some black lentils to take back with you?)

and her concerns (What if something happens to you? What if we get a letter like we got for Purushottam?). There was so much more, but what I understood best was the camaraderie between them. As we finished our tea, Aama smiled and clasped my hands and said something in Nepali. Tears pooled. With one hand, she dabbed her eyes with the end of her sari. With the other, she continued squeezing my hand. I looked to Pramod for an explanation.

"She's saying that everybody's worried about how you come from so far away. They think you'll take me to your place, and I'll never come back. But how Mom is thinking is very interesting. She says she was worried too at first. But she's been thinking a lot these last few days. Now she's not worried anymore that you come from so far away."

"She's not?"

"No. She's saying, 'Why should I worry if I have a daughter-in-law who comes from so far away? I don't have to worry. Now the whole world will become my village.'"

KIN

PRAMOD AND I visited my family in Seattle several times before we married. My open-minded, hospitable mom loved Pramod immediately. Pramod came from a culture that respected elders no matter what, so he knew how to win over Dad too. If tensions rose as we talked about President Reagan's trickle down theory or the new federal holiday for Dr. Martin Luther King, Jr., Pramod told a joke or steered conversations into friendlier territory.

Dad had also upgraded his language over the years, perhaps a reflection of messaging in the Republican Party. I couldn't tell how much his underlying attitudes had changed. I liked to think they had. In any case, his views on other cultures seemed to involve ranking—not unlike a caste hierarchy—and Asians fared pretty well in his judgments. Perhaps he saw Pramod as a dark-skinned variety of what some called Caucasian, just as some conservative Brahmans in Nepal would later try to fit me into their world as a fellow Aryan (a term used in South Asia long before the Nazis claimed it).

Ultimately, Dad must have been relieved that I wasn't marrying an African or African American man. I had never told him about those I had dated, but with my interest in African studies he must have had his suspicions.

Pramod and I wed in a secular ceremony in a park in Seattle's Wallingford District on July 14, 1986. We hadn't intended the convergence with Bastille Day, but it fit our rebel personas. I wore a white Mexican wedding dress I'd bought for seventy dollars at La Tienda, a folk arts store on University Avenue. Pramod wore a wrap tunic I'd sewn from Guatemalan cloth purchased at the same place. Perhaps with the garland of flowers I wore on my head, I was still wishing I'd been old enough in the 1960s to be a hippie. Or maybe we were signifying vague revolutionary solidarity in the same way young people would one day wear Che Guevara T-shirts.

My stepmother, who had divorced Bob several years earlier, drove up from Sonoma County with my two half sisters. Bob told me by phone he was busy and wasn't sure he could make my wedding. Not able to count on him, I asked Dad to give me away. At the time, I couldn't explain why I needed anyone to do that. Perhaps longing for my biological father clouded my feminist thinking.

In his usual careless way, Bob appeared at our house the afternoon before the wedding. The next morning, moments before the ceremony began, I locked elbows with both Bob and Dad and had them escort me to where Pramod stood with the judge. Dad had provided for me since I was eight. He'd paid for braces and most of college, and had always made sure I had Christmas and birthday presents. We agreed on little except a love of microbrewed beer and the benefits of regular exercise, but I knew he would always be there for me. Bob had rarely been there for me, but he was the father I loved. I never asked how Dad or Bob felt about their joint task, but they laughed about it afterward.

The judge had a bulbous red nose and stank so much of whiskey I kept eyeing his suit pocket for a flask-shaped bulge. I hoped Mom had gotten a good deal on him. He had us repeat standard vows. They meant little to either of us, and the slurred wording often confused Pramod.

"By my troth," the judge said.

"By my . . . what? Trout? Did you say trout? By my trout? What?"

We flew to Kathmandu in September and made the usual, easy tourist rounds in Kathmandu Valley: Swayambhunath, Budhanilkantha, Dhulikhel, Namo Buddha, Kirtipur, Bhaktapur. At

Nagarkot, we played carrom (table billiards) with innkeepers, and I finally got my panoramic view of the Himalayas, obscured by neither clouds nor smog. Back in Kathmandu, we shared dal bhat and more rum than I was used to with some of Pramod's urban friends, most of whom worked for nongovernmental organizations. We sampled Chicago and New York pizza, enchiladas, yak cheese, and *momos* in Thamel; dodged offers of hashish and ganja in Freak Street; ate lentil patties and chili potatoes and got drunk on local liquor at a hole-in-the-wall in Patan—a place I would never be able to find again on my own. I began to think I could enjoy Nepal. It could be our vacation spot. I fantasized about trekking to Langtang, Annapurna, Muktinath. Pramod and I even dreamed about going farther afield: maybe a trip to Lake Mansarovar in Tibet someday.

But we had to visit the family in Chitwan. I can't remember how we transported it all by public bus, but we carried books friends in the States had donated for a community library and clothes for all our relatives.

I hadn't felt much pressure to learn more than a few simple Nepali phrases in the days we spent roaming tourist haunts around Kathmandu Valley. But over a few weeks with family, I couldn't avoid the task so easily.

I never had much opportunity to use them, but I had studied several languages spoken in African countries—French, Swahili, Amharic—and aced my tests and assignments in them. When I switched my focus to India, I applied myself joylessly to Hindi and Marathi. So I had a dim understanding of gender distinctions, second person formal, and irregular verbs in languages similar to Nepali. All that should have eased my way into speaking Pramod's mother tongue. But maybe learning five languages in the abstract was a tipping point at which my brain shut down. At that point, I didn't think I needed much Nepali.

What embarrassed me most about my dullness was how easy and fun Nepali speakers tried to make learning.

"What is your name?" a local visitor to our house might quiz me in Nepali, smiling and enunciating every syllable.

"*Mero nam* Elizabeth *ho*."

"Oh ho! She's nearly fluent," they'd say (and, of course, someone would translate for me if they said it in Nepali). "Such a smarty! Probably a genius of some sort." On and on they went. I looked for signs of sarcasm. Nothing.

Of course, in those weeks, if the conversation continued beyond beginner phrases, they'd realize my limitations. But they would never take back their hyperbolic praise. They wouldn't shun or insult me or shout at me in Nepali the way English speakers often do when talking to those who don't speak English. They would patiently teach me a few new phrases or words and praise each tiny step forward. Over the years, I would hear them do the same for any foreign visitor.

But I won't be here for long, I kept telling myself. I need to save myself for Hindi, Marathi.

We arrived in Chitwan in time for Dasain, or Durga Puja—the biggest festival of the year in Nepal. It falls around rice harvesttime. To my untrained eye, it appeared to center on animal sacrifice, sprouted barley, and children spinning around on wooden Ferris wheels.

An anthropologist who had properly prepared for fieldwork in South Asia would have studied basic concepts of Hinduism. Even if not interested in religion, she probably would have at least skimmed the Rig Veda, the Upanishads, the Puranas, the Ramayana, the Mahabharat, and its Bhagavad Gita. She would have understood how to interpret art and iconography. She would have read ethnographies of Hindu villages. I had crammed bits and pieces, much as I had memorized words such as *contumacious* and *lucubrate* for my Graduate Record Examinations. Those words didn't stick and neither had much of what I read on Hinduism and Brahman culture in a year and a half of knowing Pramod. And what did sink in tended to come from writings on politics, economics, or Indian feminism.

So I didn't know what to make of the swirl of rituals through the Dasain holidays and would never get that part of Nepal very well. Perhaps that's when I began to skim bits in a book Pramod had recommended I buy at Pilgrims Book House in Kathmandu: *Dangerous Wives and Sacred Sisters: Social and Symbolic Roles of High-Caste Women in Nepal*. Written by anthropologist Lynn Bennett, that book would become my field guide to Brahman rituals.

Through her fieldwork among high-caste Hindus in a village on the outskirts of Kathmandu, Bennett shows what the title indicates: how kin relations, myths, stories, and rituals set up fundamental contradictions in the lives of Hindu women. In their maiti, women are loved and valued for their purity and elevated ritual roles. But in their ghar, they are viewed as subordinate and a constant danger to their in-laws' stability and ritual purity. Many stories and rituals in Nepal hinge on helping women accept these competing roles.

Like most festivals, Dasain works on many levels. What interested me most was how it mapped out and reinforced women's and men's places in complicated kin networks.

For nine nights, families worship the warrior goddess, Durga—often pictured in her form as Kali, with bared fangs, weapons, and severed heads in hand. The part I remember best came on the tenth day—Tika day. Durga had conquered her demons. The skies had cleared. The Himalayas towered over the foothills. We all gathered around a cot in the sunny courtyard. As head of household, Pandit Kedarnath smeared a dab of red rice powder mixed with yogurt—tika—on each forehead and tucked some barley sprouts in hands or under caps. Then the next eldest took his place on the cot and repeated tika for all his juniors—on down the line until every superior gave tika to every inferior.

Dressed in a green, handspun cotton sari I'd bought in Kathmandu, I took my place to receive tika from Pandit Kedarnath; Aama; Pramod's brothers, Siddhi and Tirtha, and their wives; and Pramod himself. Then I sat in the superior spot and gave tika to nieces and nephews. Afterward, we walked for miles to the homes of uncles and aunts—anyone remotely related—for more tika exchanges and snacks.

During all those festival days, I wondered if the family might arrange a Hindu wedding for Pramod and me. I asked Pramod. He laughed nervously about it not being the wedding season. In any case, he said, the family didn't think it necessary. How odd, I thought, considering the ritual obsessions all around us. But I didn't pursue the question.

As much as I struggled with Nepali, there was no way to get through the ten days of Dasain and beyond in Gunjanagar without learning when to refer to individuals by kin names, proper names, or nicknames.

Aama had recently renamed herself Parvati after "a goddess of both virtue and power." But like most Brahman women in Nepal, she was hardly ever called by her new or previous name. She was always Aama, Hazuraama, Bhauju (Mother, Grandmother, Ma'am). Although most daughters-in-law called their mothers-in-law Sasu—often in a derisive tone—I always called mine Aama.

Few spoke Kedarnath's name either. Depending on the speaker, he was Pandit, Bua, Hazurba, Dai (Priest, Father, Grandfather, Brother). If I had to address him directly, I didn't call him Sasura (Father-in-Law). I mumbled "Bua." However, like most daughters-in-law, I avoided addressing him directly. Now I refer to him in my writing as I always saw him: Pandit Kedarnath.

I never heard Aama refer to Pandit Kedarnath by his name or even call him "my husband." It was always, "Your father did this," or "Your grandfather did that." And in moments of disagreement or exasperation, she sometimes called him Budda (Old Man), a form of spousal address I heard more often among Tharu or Tamang neighbors.

Sons and their spouses are often addressed by a term denoting birth order. For instance, Pramod was Saila, or Third Son, and I was Saili. But that practice jumbled my brain as much as wrapping a sari tangled my limbs. So I addressed all my brothers-in-law by their name, and my elder sisters-in-law and Pramod's sister as Didi.

As a married woman in Nepal, I became Bhauju—a respectful form of address, like ma'am. I also became Saili (Wife of the Third Son), Maiju (Maternal Aunt), and Saniaama (Little Mother/Paternal Aunt).

After he resigned himself to my marriage to his son, Pandit Kedarnath tried to bestow Sanskrit names on me: Kalpana, Pratibha, meaning Imagination, Creativity. "To reflect what you'll contribute to our family and village," he said. But those names never stuck. If they needed a name, he and Aama called me whatever variation on my birth name they could roll out on their tongues, usually something like Elizha, with a strong aspiration on the "h."

More often, Aama called me what she called all younger women she liked: Nani. She never addressed me as Buhari, usually spat out in a way that everyone knew meant "that lazy, good-for-nothing daughter-in-law with whom I've been cursed."

After Dasain, Pramod and I went on to Pune, India—best known among foreigners for the ashram founded by Bhagwan Shree Rajneesh but attractive to us for centering a lively regional culture of grassroots organizing among women, workers, indigenous peoples, and Dalits. I had received funding for my proposal to examine caste and ethnic factors shaping women's participation in agricultural labor movements in the region but was waiting for approval on a research visa. We rented and furnished a modest flat and met with local leaders and scholars. But our local sponsoring institution began ramping up restrictions on what we could investigate. We also found it difficult to earn the trust of organizations facing increasing government scrutiny and threats from Hindu fundamentalists. After two months, we decided Pune was not for us. We packed what we could fit into our bags, gave away the rest, and rode a train north for what would be several months of wandering in search of other research sites.

Along the way, we made time for sightseeing. My period did not arrive as expected. The first clear signs of why came at the Taj Mahal. I thought back to a condom that broke one afternoon in our flat in Pune. We hadn't planned on a pregnancy, but we did want children someday. I was already twenty-seven. Was there ever a good time? We knew other anthropologists who had children during fieldwork. Why not? How hard could it be?

Pramod and I moved on to New Delhi, then south. I couldn't hold down more than boiled eggs and potatoes, bananas, digestive biscuits, and coconut milk. Usually a lover of spicy food, I couldn't bear it in those early months of pregnancy. The smells that saturated every corner of India—frying onions and masala mingled with urine, excrement, sweat, and incense—bent me over dirty squat toilets in trains, bus stations, and hostels. And the nausea didn't stick to the morning; it stalked me into lunch and dinner and woke me at night.

I stopped caring about dissertation research. I retreated into habitual shyness and focused on comfort and occasional pleasures. We floated on ocean waves in Goa, walked in the forest and rode an elephant near Mysore. Then for two months, we settled in Bangalore to assess new research possibilities.

Embarrassed by chronic sleepiness, frequent trips to vomit, and a hazy brain that could no longer follow simple instructions, let alone intelligent discussion, I let Pramod buzz around the city to network on his own. I spent entire days between daydreams and naps on the outskirts of Bangalore in a half-built bungalow belonging to an acquaintance who stayed there only at night. Like upended, rebar-legged spaceships, similar unfinished homes spread for kilometers. Ragpickers collected glass bottles, cloth, and plastic along the dusty lanes. Cattle and goats grazed the sparse grass in what might some-day be fenced yards.

I wallowed in self-pity.

Some of my peers had planned, learned languages, and prepared for research for years. Others traveled as young adults or spent time in the Peace Corps, fell in love with a place, and saw anthropology as a way to return. A few studied whatever they could find funding for, while some eschewed travel or the risk of revolutionary violence and chose to work closer to home. Still others ran their fingers around the globe—Bali, Jamaica, Costa Rica, Tahiti, Brazil, Fiji—and chose their destinations by whim.

I had once prided myself on being among those who planned. But I had fallen into what my addled feminist brain saw as the lowliest category of all: I'd followed a man.

Our housemates had a boombox and several tapes. I played "Gracias a la Vida" over and over. It wasn't so long ago, I reminded myself, that I'd helped guide Joan Baez to the microphone near the dean's office in Stanford's quad. She'd given a brief speech on divestment and human rights. I'd never been to Latin America or learned Spanish, but hearing her sing "Guantanamera," "Dos Colores," and "La Llorona" on tape made me cry for home. "No Nos Moveran" reminded me of all I had once hoped to accomplish. Then I looked out barred windows at the rag collectors and realized I had no idea how to budge anything in India. I could barely move my own body.

In a Bangalore hospital, I took a number in the obstetrics ward while Pramod waited outside. I figured I was more than two months pregnant but wanted official confirmation. The clean and orderly appearance and shiny, modern equipment reassured me. I sat among other women on benches in the wide hallway and inhaled the perfume of jasmine garlands braided into their long black hair.

A nurse ushered me into an examination room. There were no magazines, landscape photos, or anatomy posters, but the room included the basic equipment I hoped to see: Q-tips, cotton balls, antiseptic, syringes, needles packaged in plastic, a thermometer, a blood pressure monitor, shiny metal trays for laying out the tools. And it was as clean as any exam room I'd visited in the States.

Dressed in a traditional pressed apron and cap, the nurse told me in crisp English to take off my *salwaar* and underpants, lie down on the bed, and put my feet in the stirrups. I did so and waited.

Soon the doctor—a middle-aged Indian woman with long hair—entered the room. She did not look at me or speak. She wiggled her hands into latex gloves. Still without looking at me or speaking, she thrust two fingers on her right hand inside me and poked around while pressing hard against my uterus with her left hand. I groaned at the discomfort. She removed both hands, peeled off the gloves, and dropped them in the wastebasket. She wrote something on my chart and walked out.

The nurse glanced at the chart. "Pregnancy confirmed," she said, and followed the doctor out of the room.

I had met rude, dismissive, and condescending doctors in the States. Plenty of them. But this seemed more extreme. Were all women treated so coldly? Or just foreigners? I rose and put my salwaar back on. On the way to the reception area, I peeked through an open door and saw the doctor sitting with other women, laughing, smoking cigarettes, and drinking coffee.

"Excuse me," I said. "Do you have a minute?"

"And what is it you want?" she asked.

I had so many questions: Does the fetus seem all right? When will the morning sickness end? Have I lost too much weight? I watched her blow smoke rings and hesitated, waiting for her to look at me. She never did.

"Nothing, I guess." I hurried down the hallway to find Pramod in the waiting room.

Later, I told a friend who worked in the feminist bookstore collective in Bangalore about the incident.

"Perhaps they thought you wanted an abortion," she said. "It's a Catholic hospital, you know. They'd probably assume that about a pregnant American woman."

I wasn't entirely convinced by the abortion angle. But what else could it be? Disdain for foreign travelers getting pregnant abroad and burdening local hospitals? Or just poor bedside manners? Payback for European colonialism and American imperialism? Or just an overworked doctor annoyed at being interrupted by a naive, self-important woman during a well-deserved smoke break? From then on, a confused mix of outrage, guilt, and fear shadowed every decision I made about my pregnancy.

Still in Bangalore in May, I received a forwarded letter from the Indian government. My research visa had been denied. I felt more relief than disappointment—a way out of my latest predicament. I could have switched topics or filed an appeal. But I had grown weary of India, embarrassed trying to explain a research project that had more life in my head than on the ground, ashamed at how little I understood of the language and culture, paralyzed by how I imagined people saw me: naive, ignorant.

I could hear the academic version of "I told you so" from each of my dissertation committee members.

Pramod and I talked for days, weighed the options, and tried to figure out how best to advance both our careers and support my health and the baby's. Together, we reached a decision. We would split up for our research. As a Nepali national, he didn't need a visa to do research in India. He had already become intrigued by Jharkhand, a region in southern Bihar State where corporations, government, and indigenous peoples battled over forests, minerals, and water. Some thought he could gain the trust of leaders more easily there than around Pune. And he could also communicate in Hindi, a language he already knew.

I could go with him but wouldn't be able to do my research, at least not legally. We decided I would fare better in Nepal. There, Pramod told me, rules about foreign research were more relaxed. I wouldn't need a special visa. I could live with the family in Chitwan and figure out a research project for Gunjanagar. Maybe I could work with women or landless people. At least in Nepal, I would have family, clean water, and healthy food. That was the priority; the rest we'd figure out.

Jharkhand was about twenty-four hours from Gunjanagar by bus and train. Pramod could go back and forth. He would help me settle in with the family, head to Jharkhand for a month or two, and then come back to help with the birth and baby in autumn. By December, he could return to India for another month or two of research.

In hindsight, I can't fault Pramod. He didn't coerce me to accept the plan. Maybe I was the one who proposed it. Like Pramod, I often pushed through gloom and fear with a sunny, can-do optimism. But more than that, I had reached a state of mind where I was making odd calculations. I needed to add on to a string of failures in a way that might equal success. That meant upping the ante. I had never had an athlete's motivation to take on daredevil feats: swimming the English Channel, holding my breath underwater for a record number of minutes, climbing Mount Everest without oxygen. I wanted to prove my courage as an anthropologist, world traveler, and political activist. Being pregnant and giving birth in Nepal while learning another language and finding a new research project could be my own test of skill and endurance.

Besides, before I fell for Pramod, I had pondered traveling by myself into conflict zones along the South African border or in Mozambique. How hard could it be to live with a kind family, eat home-cooked meals, and have a baby? Sure, there would be some hardships, but they would test my resolve, my commitment to be one with the people, especially rural women. If I successfully pinned my body to a rustic life in Nepal, I could rebuild some of my confidence.

I would have to learn Nepali. I'd also need to scramble for a new topic, rewrite my research proposal, and win approval from my committee. I knew how they would see me: spiraling down from one poorly conceived project for which I was badly prepared to something even more tenuous. But I believed I could do it and become a better person for it.

PART II
1987–1988

Ripe Mangoes

✦❖✦

ON MY SECOND overland trip to Nepal, we rode the train from New Delhi to Gorakhpur again. Thanks to the Loo—the strong, dry wind that blows heat from the deserts of Rajasthan and Pakistan across the Gangetic plains—I remember the crowded jeep that rattled us to the Nepal border. Like a furnace, the Loo blasted sand through a gap that had once held a sliding window. I had never been so hot before. I had no thermometer but suspect the temperature that day neared its seasonal maximum of 122 degrees.

I don't remember much of the border or the bus or the vehicle that brought us the last few miles to Pramod's village. Only Sakuntala was at home. After we exchanged greetings, she went to work in the kitchen to prepare a meal. Soon, Siddhi returned home from work. After dinner, we all sat on benches in the courtyard and watched the sun blaze toward the horizon. I hoped for a cool breeze. There was none. It wasn't as hot as it had been in the jeep, but sweat still oozed from pores I didn't know I had.

Pramod and I hadn't explained our sudden arrival, yet Sakuntala touched her callused hands to my belly. In her smile I caught a glimpse of the pretty young woman she must have been years ago, before taking on the role of embittered buhari. "How did you know?" I asked in the crude Nepali I remembered. I could see how delighted she was to learn the news before others in the family.

"La, I'm a woman like you. I know these things."

I wasn't aware of it then, but I arrived pregnant in Nepal in time for Chaturmas (literally, "four months"), also known as Night of Vishnu. Among Hindu communities throughout South Asia, it marks the monsoon and harvest seasons, during which the gods and goddesses are said to sleep. Vishnu retreats to an ocean of milk where he once directed other gods to churn out a buttery nectar of immortality. There, he and his consort Laxmi—goddess of wealth—recline on a floating serpent to rest and nap through the rains. Other gods and goddesses sleep as well.

If I'd known more about Hindu deities then, I might have tried for some faith in Vishnu, asleep or awake. The Sanskrit root of his name means "to enter or pervade." He began as a minor solar deity. Over the centuries, people increasingly saw him as a god who takes a personal interest in human affairs. Now, if needed, he is said to appear in one of his many incarnations: Rama, Krishna, Buddha. Or sometimes, in the human heart.

Chaturmas begins on the eleventh day of the Nepali month of Asar (mid-June to mid-July). To give Vishnu and others their cosmic sleep, humans may not hold weddings or male initiations. For mortals so inclined, Chaturmas—much like Catholic Lent—is the time to renew faith through austerities, penance, study of particular religious texts, special meditations. Such activities undertaken during the four months when the gods are sleeping are thought to be particularly auspicious.

While Vishnu snuggled into his serpent bed adrift on the milky sea and his followers began their penance, I settled into life as a pregnant Brahman wife and cultural anthropologist.

Before sorting out my research focus, I wanted some sense of how I would give birth. We decided to visit a Nepali woman doctor in the compound of the district hospital in Bharatpur. Waiting patients as well as relatives of the sick and dying milled around in the dry grass under a few shade trees. We found the doctor's office in a one-story cement building. Dingy and small, the room made me wonder about the quality of the facilities and equipment in the hospital. At the same time, I questioned my sense of entitlement to any medical amenities in a country where most people couldn't afford a doctor.

I asked about options for delivering a baby and learned there was only one: in the hospital, flat on your back, feet in stirrups.

"Can my husband be with me?"

"Of course not."

"Are you sure?"

"Trust me, I'm a doctor. I know best."

She wasn't as rude as the doctor in Bangalore, but she didn't smile much either. She kept looking at her watch as if to remind me she had a lot of work to get on with and didn't have time for frivolous foreigner questions. I suspected Nepal and India had many fine, compassionate doctors. Pramod's nephew, Keshav, was studying to become one, and I trusted he'd be good. But I was losing faith in doctors anywhere to guide me through pregnancy and childbirth. Still, Pramod and I figured we should explore all options. So we bused to Kathmandu to meet more doctors. In the same curt manner as the doctor in Bharatpur, they also recommended flat-on-the-back delivery in the hospital with no friends or relatives present. I returned home more confused than ever, only to collide with the first of many beliefs and stories that would tentacle my womb and half-Brahman fetus. I made the first entry in my field notes the next day.

July 10, 1987
Aama and Bua were worried we returned on the ninth day after we left. Apparently, that means it will rain (which it did, though it's been doing that a lot anyway) and that something bad will happen. They said we weren't to enter the house until the stars came out and

Bua did some mantras or something. As it turned out, the rain came so hard while we were trying to bathe that Aama let us in the house.

At that time, I could see only one other option: return home to Seattle. But that would mean admitting failure. I had been the kind of child who cried over a minus after an A on a school assignment. If I left now, would I ever get back on track in graduate school? And would Pramod come with me? I wasn't sure I wanted to test that. He had worked hard to make it this far and would lobby to keep going. Then there were the friends back home who had warned me about giving up my dreams for a man.

Besides, since we'd believed we would be out of the country for a year or more, we had canceled our health insurance. We couldn't afford to have a baby in my country. Nor could we afford to fly to another Asian country with better facilities.

I let myself be lulled into other scenarios.

"Babies are like mangoes," Sakuntala told me. "When ripe, they fall. You won't need to go to Kathmandu. Have the baby here at home."

A granola-eating, Birkenstock-wearing, organic-food rebel from the Pacific Northwest, I trusted nature. She would be my shield against the trifecta of demons: my wild, suddenly unfamiliar body and the medical professionals and ritual specialists who wanted to tell me what to do with it. If my sister-in-law could give birth like a mango tree, I could too.

Pramod and I agreed that if my pregnancy progressed without complications, we would consider a home birth. Siddhi introduced us to Bhagvati, a local nurse-midwife. With a constant smile on her round face, she beamed confidence and compassion. She agreed to monitor my pregnancy and help us make the decision about where to give birth as the time approached. During the first examination, she talked me through the procedure, made me laugh, and told me what to expect in the months to come. Her friendly attitude and

competence won me over and mingled with happy fantasies of ripe
fruit needing only gravity to fall free of the mother tree.

The Hindi and Marathi I had studied helped me improve my grammar and vocabulary in Nepali. But in the midst of all I had to learn,
I blazed some trails through the new language by first following
words borrowed from English, or, as villagers called it, Angrezi. I
found it comforting to slip into another language with words I could
identify. When someone called out, "*Euta gheelass lyauta,*" I saw a
stainless steel cup appear. After a few more times, I knew *gheelass*
meant "glass," but one made of stainless steel. In English, we might
call it a cup. Slowly, from there, I made out the meaning of the entire
phrase: Bring a cup here.

Many of the Angrezi words I recognized must have trailed after
commodities and social changes. An undergarment I would call a
slip in English became forever imprinted in my mind as petticoat,
or sometimes petti for short. Notebook became *copybook,* polyester pants were *terrycotton paants,* school was *esschool,* and flashlight,
torch.

I slowly became fluent in Nepali by first learning a new kind of
English. But in those early months, I knew myself lucky to be surrounded by many who spoke or at least understood some English.
Didi's sons and daughter, who came to visit from time to time, were
fluent. Most had ambitions to study and work abroad. They read
English novels and science and philosophy books. Siddhi—like
most college graduates and secondary school teachers in Nepal—
also spoke, wrote, and read English with strong fluency. Those more
fluent in English helped me learn Nepali phrases for daily activities, like *puja* (worship), *ghas kattne* (cut grass for livestock), *batti
balne* (light the kerosene lanterns), and for abstract concepts like
samaj (society), *samajbadi* (socialism), *nari* (female), *naribadi* (feminism). They also taught me how to understand the Nepali calendar,
56.7 years ahead of the Gregorian calendar with months following
both lunar and solar phases, much like the Hebrew calendar. So

July roughly spanned the last half of Asar and first half of Bhadao. Brahmans recognized the progression of the moon through its light and dark phases and marked days for particular fasts and rituals.

Pramod oversaw some home improvements: a better outhouse, a new cooking room, a cement platform around the water pump, and a bedroom for us. Construction crews worked every day for several weeks to finish all the projects before the heavy rains arrived.

The new kitchen took on an American flavor that both comforted and troubled me. Pramod assured me others also wanted some modern conveniences: more space, a raised counter, tables, chairs.

On one arm of the new L-shaped cement counter, women arranged pots, pans, utensils, and jars of ghee, mustard oil, and other staples. On the other, they built a traditional earthen woodstove and vented it out one wall. Used to squatting while cooking, Aama often pulled a wobbly table over so she could climb on top and work on the same level. And while everyone gave up the habit of removing shoes now that we were eating at a table, women still sorted rice and grain and chopped vegetables into trays on the floor.

Pandit Kedarnath gained more shelf space for his puja materials and a private table. In that big room, he could eat at the same time as the rest of us without giving up his ritual distance. He smiled at our conversation now and then, but otherwise kept to himself. For the devout, any activity can be a means toward transcendence. So some days, Pandit Kedarnath turned his back on us so he could fully concentrate on the rite of pure eating.

Just as in the old cooking room, the family seated me among those who ate first, usually the men and boys in the family, but sometimes older women who were visiting or girls who had to rush off quickly to school. The women who cooked ladled the food onto our plates. When all others had eaten, they sat down and ate themselves. Aama usually took her place at Pandit Kedarnath's table and ate from his plate, a practice still common among older Brahman wives.

Everyone praised the new outhouse—a simple batch-composting model (*sulabh sauchalya*) that an engineer friend of Pramod's had dedicated his life to popularizing in Nepal. It had two cement-lined pits. When one filled up, the flow could be diverted into the other. After six months, the sludge in the first pit would be compost.

Although I knew I would miss it as my pregnancy progressed, we decided not to install a sit-down commode. Too hard to keep clean and flushed, I agreed. We installed the more common squat toilet: a porcelain bowl with foot placements on either side—and had it connected by pipe and a covered canal to the two pits.

We later regretted our haste in building the toilet and kitchen. The additions made life more convenient but could have been better designed and sited. Added on to a boxy cement house, neither the kitchen nor the toilet received enough sunlight, making them damp and dreary in both the foggy, cold winters and the rainy, hot summers.

With Siddhi and Sakuntala and their five children as well as Aama and Pandit Kedarnath crowded into the house, Pramod and I debated options for our own space. The family offered to clear out one of the four bedrooms, but we wanted more privacy. Pramod suggested we move all the junk in the barn loft over to the side above the buffaloes, nail up some boards in the middle, and make the new empty space above the old cooking room our bedroom. With a wall of bookshelves, a large bed, new bedding, and slats removed to open a view out over the courtyard, the space turned out better than I had imagined. I worried about climbing up and down the narrow ladder later with a full womb (and later, an infant) but figured it would be good for me.

On the way to the outhouse each morning, I often met Pandit Kedarnath coming out, his sacred thread still wrapped up over his right ear. Before washing my hands, I had to wait for him to finish at the water pump. My father-in-law's toilette had the air of high ritual about it, but he didn't dawdle. After his bath, he wrapped himself in a clean dhoti. Then the women of the family took turns bathing. They dressed in fresh saris before boiling tea and cooking the morning snack and meal.

Through all the bustle, Pandit Kedarnath sat in the ritual corner of the cooking area or in front of a small shrine on the north side of our courtyard. Barely visible in the weeds, the shrine held a holy basil plant. Hair wet from her bath, Aama brought Pandit Kedarnath a stainless steel plate of freshly picked flowers, red-stained rice, seasonal fruits, and other ritual tools. He chanted, blew on the conch shell, and placed offerings here and there for puja.

I sensed a detailed rhythm in daily, monthly, and seasonal ritual rounds but took few notes on that. I recorded what interested me more in local religion.

> July 14, 1987
> The Brahman priest (Bal Krishna), who lives across from the temple and cares for it, came to visit Bua today. They talked about how people are losing a sense of caste distinctions. He argues that Pramod has lost his caste since he went to America and married an American. Bua says no; as long as he does good work, he remains a Brahman. A few weeks before, Bal Krishna was arguing that women should not study Sanskrit and can't become pandits. Today, after he left, the family talked about how conservative he is. He won't let untouchables in the temple. One time, Aama said, she led a group of untouchables to claim their worshipping rights. The priest turned them away.

I would slowly learn that the particular shape of caste in Nepal evolved as eighteenth- and nineteenth-century rulers tried to manage and purify Nepal's cultural diversity. Hindu communities in the hills had long upheld caste hierarchy. Through intricate legal codes, Nepal's rulers tried to impose a similar and more uniform caste ranking over the kingdom's many other ethnic, occupational, linguistic, and regional groups. The caste veneer took hold in some regions better than others. The old legal codes were abolished in 1963, but the notions of inequality lingered on.

As in India, caste and class did not fully synchronize, though higher castes typically enjoyed more economic, educational, and political opportunities than lower castes. And the lowest castes inclined toward poverty.

The social hierarchy in Nepal has probably always appeared clearest for the highest Twice Born castes but more debatable among groups ranked at the middle and bottom. Twice Borns are considered so because the boys undergo a second ritual birth when they are initiated and allowed to wear the sacred thread. They include Brahman (Bahun, in Nepali), Chhetri (derived from Kshatriya), Thakuri, and some Newars.

As in other parts of South Asia, Brahmans in Nepal tend to be priests, scholars, and educators, while Chhetri, Thakuri, and some Newars are idealized as rulers, warriors or soldiers, merchants, and shopkeepers. But in rural areas, many Brahmans, like Pramod's family—as well as Chhetri and Thakuri—are also farmers and spend most of their lives in physical labor. In historical times Brahmans had impressive influence in spiritual and educational affairs, while Chhetri and Thakuri wielded political and economic power. But with the emergence of political parties requiring education and persuasive skills, Brahmans have become political elites as well.

At the bottom of the caste hierarchy are Those From Whom Water Cannot Be Taken, or Pani Nachalne in Nepali. Inspired by movements for social justice in India, they increasingly call themselves Dalits. They are Kami (blacksmiths), Damai (tailors), Sarki (cobblers), Sunar (goldsmiths), and many others. The appellations, often used as surnames, refer to communities once associated with particular occupations. But not all individuals in them pursue customary work anymore. For instance, Kamis in Nepal, like many Smiths in the United States, may have blacksmith ancestors but no knowledge of smithing. The difference is that Kamis, like other castes, have maintained an identity as a particular group, often still living in segregated communities and still considered lower-caste because of their occupational ancestry. As in India, many Nepali Dalits have also become low-wage, unskilled laborers.

Most unclear in terms of caste hierarchy are those lumped in the middle, whom Twice Borns and the old legal code refer to as Matwali (Liquor Drinkers). They include groups that speak languages in the Tibeto-Burman family, such as Magar, Tamang, Gurung, Rai, and Limbu, as well as the Tharu indigenous to Chitwan. They trace their ancestry to communities that populated the Himalayan foothills and mountains long before Hindus arrived. Their physical features echo historical connections to groups in Tibet, Assam, and Burma. Many are Buddhists or followers of local, nature-based religions, but some also follow local variants of Hinduism.

The old legal code stated that some Matwali, like Tamangs and Tharus, could be enslaved but others, like Gurungs and Magars, could not. At the same time, Tibeto-Burman speakers usually identified more strongly with their ethnic identity than with an imposed caste status. Although some embrace their superiority over Dalits (Kami, Damai, Sarki, and Sunar), they do not necessarily see themselves as inferior to Twice Borns. And for over 150 years, men from Tibeto-Burman communities have been hiring themselves out as mercenary soldiers in Gurkha regiments in foreign, particularly British, armies. Decades of military remittances have made some families wealthy, or at least comfortably well-off.

I would discover that the same social and ritual practices that lower Magars and Tamangs in caste hierarchies also make them highly valued neighbors. Sneaking off to a Tamang home for some millet beer and buffalo meat is an excellent way to keep impurities out of one's own household.

As in India, caste ranking in Nepal partly hinges on the degree to which groups control their women. At the same time, some communities like Tharu and Tibeto-Burman groups take ethnic pride in resisting high-caste notions of how women should be treated. They uphold variations on more egalitarian ethics: allowing young people to choose their own marriage partners, giving women the right to divorce and remarry, and respecting women's independent earnings in trade or liquor manufacturing.

Despite distinctions of ethnicity and language, all castes, out-castes, and ethnic groups from mountain regions—Brahmans, Chhetri, Tamangs, Magars, Dalits—share a common identity and pride as hill dwellers, or Pahadi. Even hill dwellers who have migrated to the plains retain some solidarity and intercaste social networks as hill-born and take pains to differentiate themselves from communities with ancestral roots in the plains.

No matter what I studied in anthropology, I especially liked investigating those gaps between cultural ideals and actual prac-tices. The caste system in Nepal had plenty. Pramod often pointed to his flat, flared nose, so different from pointy Brahman beaks, as evidence. "Who knows? Maybe one of my Brahman granddaddies slept with a Magar woman." He'd go on laughing about how such noses as well as dark skin and angled eyes sometimes appeared in Brahman families. Other ethnic groups in Nepal took pride in mixed origins, he said, but Brahmans didn't like to admit the possi-bility of impurities in the ancestral line. Still, they happened.

As I pieced together my understanding of Nepal's complex cul-tural diversity and caste system, I missed a key category that some older Brahmans in our village still honored. Old legal codes reserved a special niche for foreigners like me, just a notch above Those From Whom Water Cannot Be Taken: impure, but touchable.

People urged me to explore the village before the monsoon arrived. "It'll be hard to go anywhere after that," they said. I couldn't imag-ine how rain might stop a Seattleite like me from walking. But I accepted local advice and—always accompanied by Pramod, Aama, or one of my nieces—ventured beyond our loft and courtyard. It was impossible to get to know everyone, but I greeted neighbors as I passed and matched faces with homes. Some I wouldn't know by more than passing namastes until after I had been in the village for a while.

I had always imagined a village as a cluster of related households with a clear center, definite edges, and fields beyond. From what I'd seen, that's what they were throughout the Himalayan foothills. But in Chitwan, rather than perching on hillsides, houses squatted in the fields, often widely separated from one another. Our nearest neighbors were Tamangs and Tharus. Visits to relatives—uncles, aunts, and cousins—took us farther afield. When I walked to the health post for checkups with Bhagvati, I learned that I crossed an invisible boundary into a neighboring village, Saradanagar.

Those walks made me wonder about what we all described as *hamro gaon* (our village): Gunjanagar. I gleaned from Pramod that, as in other "villages" of recent immigrants in western Chitwan, it was real estate sales, not kinship, that tended to dictate the sprawl of houses and fields. That explained how paths, lanes, and roads cut through the village on such haphazard grids—like plaid squares quilted together by a novice who had trouble matching lines.

Gunjanagar had multiple centers—a primary school, Ram Temple, the Panchayat building, a big bazaar, and many smaller ones. And some ethnic communities—especially Gurungs or Tamangs—clustered in hamlets along one stretch of a straight lane or around an intersection of lanes and pathways. A few Tharu villages also remained where immigrants had cleared forests and built houses and planted fields all around them. So like an occasional paisley remnant in that quilt of unmatched plaid squares, particular areas of Gunjanagar defied the grid.

Straddling the main road between Bharatpur airport and Tiger Tops resort in Chitwan National Park, Chanauli Bazaar had become the economic center of Gunjanagar. Numerous shops, mostly in two-story wooden or cement buildings, sold consumer goods—tea, sugar, soap, cloth, kerosene, plastic buckets, metal dishes, copybooks, pens, pencils. In 1987, I counted one chemist shop (pharmacy), several tailoring shops, a bicycle repair business, tea shops, an agricultural bank, and an always busy mill.

On small sections of public pasture near their homes, some landowners followed traditional practices from the hills and built *chautari*—shady resting places formed under broad ficus trees such as *swami* (*Ficus benjamina*), banyan or *bar* (*Ficus bengalensis*), and pipal (*Ficus religiosa*). The trees are often planted on raised beds shored up by stone or brick. Although created by individuals to gain religious merit, chautari are considered public places where anyone can sit, meet, play cards or other games, amuse children, or chat with friends.

Aama had built a chautari along the lane in front of our house soon after she and Pandit Kedarnath moved to Gunjanagar. Not yet sturdy enough for children to climb when I moved in, the three saplings were still broad enough to cast some shade.

My language and cultural understanding lagged, but six months pregnant and panicked about my professional path, I had to submit a change to my research proposal to keep my grant. I needed a new focus.

When I switched from Africa to India, I had hoped to base my work in an area where there would be a clear divide between oppressors and oppressed and some grassroots movement welling up from the latter. When I gave up on India and resigned myself to Nepal, I knew the grassroots movement would be hard to find but still hoped for some line between the haves and have-nots.

Studies I'd read on rural inequality and emergent capitalism in South Asia highlighted two different patterns: (1) a nearly feudal system of zamindars (hereditary aristocrats with huge estates) and serflike sharecroppers; and (2) a more modern, Green Revolution style of wealthy industrial farms with wage laborers. Bonded laborers—workers held in near slavery through debt—could be a feature in either. Even with my limited understanding, what struck me most about Chitwan was that neither the zamindar-sharecropper nor the industrial farm—wage labor form seemed to fit. Some Tharus had been evicted from their villages in what was now the national park, and others had been tricked out of registering ownership for their lands. And there were some inequalities in how immigrants had claimed land in the 1950s. Those with wealth and good political connections, mostly Twice Borns as well as some Gurungs or Tamangs with military pensions, got better land and big parcels. And since the 1950s, family partitions, sales, and misfortunes had led to some disparity. But overall, landholdings in Chitwan ran along a continuum, with a majority of residents in villages like Gunjanagar bunched into the middle. Most farmers cultivated small to medium-size holdings for their own subsistence and sold small surpluses now and then. What tended to mark wealth more clearly was off-farm income. Some with very small holdings but good income seemed better off than those with better landholdings but no jobs.

Except for my presence, our family was fairly typical among smallholders. Like any eldest son, Siddhi shouldered responsibility for all the family landholdings. They weren't much, but they produced enough rice in good years to feed Siddhi's large household in Chitwan and Tirtha's smaller one in Pokhara.

Siddhi and Pramod told me my best bet for have-nots would be the *sukumbasi* (landless squatter) settlement five minutes' walk from our house. Knowing my interests, they played up the violent history. Squatters built huts on common pastureland, and then local landowners tore them down. They rebuilt again. After several more rounds of tearing down and rebuilding, police brought in elephants to trample sukumbasi homes and gardens. Then came the national referendum in 1980, in which citizens voted on whether to replace the Panchayat system with multiparty democracy. On both sides, politicians throughout Chitwan bought votes by encouraging

sukumbasi to squat on common forest- and pasturelands and grant-
ing them quasi-legal rights. Democracy failed in the referendum
and Panchayat rule continued, but the race for votes led to perma-
nent sukumbasi settlements. In Gunjanagar, eighty families gained
the right to rebuild their homes and cultivate small kitchen gardens
on former pastureland.

I had met many sukumbasi already. In the weeks I'd been in
the village, our family had hired them to harvest corn, drive the
bullock cart, sew sari blouses, pour concrete for the new outhouse,
build tables and shelves, wash dishes, repair the thatching on the
roof, forge a new hoe and repair some old ones, and cut and weave
bamboo into baskets. Although many were Dalits, they came from
all castes and included Tharus, Tamangs, Magars, and even some
Chhetri and a few Brahmans.

So I had found some possible have-nots, but my proposal for
research in India had been to work with an organization serving
women agricultural laborers and research how the members over-
came caste and ethnic differences to find solidarity as women and
workers. India had a lively enough tradition of women and workers
organizing that such research made sense. In Nepal in 1987, I saw no
parallels. I was disappointed to let go of a clear focus on women, but
for my dissertation committee and funder, I proposed a different
angle on social inequality. Through surveys and interviews, I would
investigate whether sukumbasi families showed any tendency to
move beyond caste and gender differences to organize around their
shared interests as wage laborers.

Siddhi warned me not to expect much around organizing. First
of all, it was illegal to acknowledge party affiliation. In relatively
liberal Chitwan, people did not hide their party loyalties, but they
didn't publicize them either. Aiming for an end to the Panchayat
system and greater equality in landownership and wealth someday,
Siddhi and his communist friends had organized sukumbasi, especially in the lower castes, as party cadres in other areas of Chitwan.

"But these sukumbasi in Gunjanagar just don't want to organize," Siddhi said. "Some are communist. Some are Congress. Some are Panchayat. They don't agree on anything."

It didn't sound promising, but at least I could dig deeper into why people who shared vulnerability in land rights, low wages, seasonal work, and caste discrimination didn't find enough common ground to organize.

I hoped to talk to all the families before I gave birth in late October or early November. Then I'd award myself a few weeks of maternal leave. By December, I'd review the interview information, find some patterns, and figure out where to focus next.

I formulated survey questions to gather consistent information on sex, caste, household size, length of time in Chitwan, birthplace, which generation lost land, whether they had livestock, whether they had land in tenancy and how much, whether they had other land or residences, and current work and past work.

Narrow pathways led between the small huts in the settlement. I expected to see the piles of rotting garbage and streams of raw sewage that lined the slums along the Bagmati River in Kathmandu. But despite the lack of clean water and toilets, the settlement radiated care and pride. Women shook out straw mats and swept the dust from their small courtyards. The mud-plastered houses were small but in good repair—most tidier than ours. Most homes had flowers planted in front. Small kitchen gardens also looked more productive and better tended than ours and, for their size, included an astonishing variety of vegetables and trees.

To help with translations, Sharmila, Pramila, Urmila, or Aama accompanied me on each interview. While chatting with sukumbasi, I also learned new vocabulary and grammatical constructions. But doubts nagged at me every day. I had taken qualitative and quantitative methods classes, passed my comprehensive exams, and received funding, but I had never done fieldwork, not even on a small scale. I'd read how others did it, but I really didn't know how to be an anthropologist. Not anywhere, but especially not in Nepal.

I made charts for each family, clung to the certainties of lined paper and simple questions with answers I could quantify:

> from hills fifteen years ago
> has three chickens, two goats

I had long ago taken the turn toward being more of a word person than a numbers person, but gathering some numerical data steadied me. Slowly, lined pages filled with information. I took pride in the volume and tried not to worry about whether the details would amount to any worthwhile findings.

By late July, I understood why people recommended I explore the village before the monsoons. Storm clouds blew in from the southeast most days. I usually smelled the wet earth first and then looked up to see rain sheeting across the plains. Brown, dusty pastures in front of our house sprouted green. Every day, herders led cows, buffaloes, and goats through to graze the new growth. With the heat soaring over 100 degrees, I longed for the cooling rain. But after a few hours of steady downpour, I found myself hoping for sun again, at least enough to dry out mildewing clothes and moldy shoes. Then the heat made me hope for rain again.

In the dry season, Chitwan had seemed perfectly flat to me. But once the irrigation canals opened, I recognized subtle undulations. Low areas—*khet*—held the water and grew rice. Higher areas—*bhari* or *tandi*—drained well and grew corn and sesame. Although the family owned some higher ground, we lived and worked on a low-lying parcel next to an irrigation canal. When the rains came, our courtyard became a pond and the pathway in front of our house a rivulet. We couldn't walk through the muddy water in our flip-flops without turning up buffalo or human turds.

Sometimes—without having to close my eyes—I found it easy to imagine Chitwan Valley as it used to be: a huge alluvial floodplain teeming with fish, waterbirds, and crocodiles.

I looked for diversions.

July 25, 1987

I cooked vegetables yesterday morning and evening. Bua is having some contradictions now. Apparently, he likes the taste but is still uncertain whether he should eat the cooking of a non-Brahman. He is already criticized by more conservative Brahmans for his unorthodox ways (e.g., giving tika directly on the foreheads of Those From Whom Water Cannot Be Taken). Vegetables aren't as important as dal and bhat. While I was cooking, Aama had to put bhat somewhere else, or cook new bhat, or something (Pramod wouldn't tell me really—no one wants to insult me or make me feel bad, so they do things discreetly). Anyway, Bua probably would never eat bhat and dal cooked by me (okay with me). Pramod says his father is thinking deeply about the problem of vegetables cooked by my hands.

With the rain so relentless and a simple task like cooking so complicated, I spent more time than ever in my room over the buffalo shed. We'd brought books from the United States and Kathmandu—in both English and Nepali—to start the community library we'd promised on my first trip to Gunjanagar. Friends in the States and Nepal had donated enough to fill three long bookshelves the width of our loft with an odd assortment, mostly books they wanted to get rid of. Many young people in the village were fluent in English; some hungered for new reading material. They had borrowed a few of the English books. But more—including our nieces and nephews—came by for the picture books. And they didn't just look at them. They borrowed them for a few hours and brought them back with pages missing. I would later see photos from the books pasted on walls alongside gods, goddesses, and Bollywood stars.

That library may have served me better than it did the community. It pulled me through the rainy season. I mostly caught up on the classics. The Russians—Tolstoy, Dostoevsky—absorbed some of my melancholy. Jane Austen revived my spirits and also fed my conviction that mischief might lie behind social mores. All of them helped me escape to faraway places and times that seemed more culturally familiar than the strange happenings around me every day.

Escapism was my favorite pastime, but I did devote some hours to improving my South Asian knowledge. That's when I began to lean again on Lynn Bennett's *Dangerous Wives and Sacred Sisters: Social and Symbolic Roles of High-Caste Women in Nepal*. I could imagine myself and my peers in a graduate seminar at Stanford, shredding the book. That's what we did in cultural anthropology in the 1980s. We questioned any analysis, like Bennett's, that showed social life as a system of rituals and symbols and failed to describe how people animated it all. Many of us wanted to pierce the surface to find that contradictory consciousness Gramsci described. At the same time, I desperately needed what Bennett offered: rich descriptions and explanations of Brahman culture—what this or that hand gesture meant, how daily and seasonal rituals in a local village fit into a larger picture of the so-called Great Traditions of Hinduism, the stories behind the rituals.

After the family finished planting rice toward the end of July, Pramod left for India to do his doctoral research on social movements in Jharkhand. He planned to return at the end of the rainy season in two months. We had agreed that this would be the arrangement, and I had tried to be brave. But it was all too much: being pregnant and left alone in a place I had never really wanted to be. August? September? How would I get through those months?

The morning after Pramod left, I stayed in my loft and cried most of the day. Aama had hosted a Peace Corps volunteer in the late 1970s and understood that Americans often liked to be alone when they felt sad, but I could tell everyone worried. They delivered food and chia and peppered me with questions in English and simple Nepali: Are you okay? Are you sure? Leaving a person alone in misery must have seemed so wrong to them. I didn't want to be fussed over and tried to stop crying so they wouldn't feel bad, but I couldn't.

That afternoon, I woke from a nap to hear movement and voices through wide gaps in rough wooden slats that separated our loft from a storage area on the same level. Spiders and scorpions escaped my broom by scuttling over there to hide among old pots and pans, broken tools, lumber, and torn straw mats.

I climbed down my stairs and looked up the wobbly ladder next to the buffaloes' feeding trough. It led through a small opening into a dark room. I heard crying and soothing voices.

"What's happening?" I yelled up in Nepali.

Sharmila came down the ladder. She explained in English that Pramila had started menstruating and had gone into seclusion.

"For how many days?"

"For our family, four days," Sharmila said. "Other families, fifteen days. Sometimes twenty-two." Pramila could not come out except to use the toilet, she said. During this first period, she would not be allowed any light. In stricter families, women in seclusion who came out to relieve themselves had to hold an umbrella over their heads so they couldn't see the stars or the sun.

I remembered Didi on my first visit and how Pramod suggested I learn more about that aspect of women's lives. I hadn't done that, but I had seen Sharmila and Sakuntala going into semi-seclusion when they had their periods. They could not cook, but they could sweep the compound, wash clothes, cut grass, and collect buffalo dung in the fields for fertilizer. I never saw secluded women doing any less work than usual, just different kinds of work. Now, I saw that the first period called for special seclusion.

Sharmila went off to fetch something. After Sakuntala hurried down and disappeared, I climbed the ladder. The light that usually filtered in through openings between the wallboards had been blocked off by old blankets. As my eyes adjusted to the darkness, I saw Pramila wrapped in her shawl lying on an old straw mat. The women had cleared a tiny space for her amid the jumble of debris.

"How are you doing?" I asked in simple Nepali.

"*Peth dukcha*. My stomach hurts," she said. Barely audible through her tears, she went on in a mixture of Nepali and English. I didn't catch all she said but understood her meaning. She didn't want to stay in the dark room for the next four days. But she knew there was nothing she could do. She hoped the family would let her finish her schooling before she had to marry. And, of course, Sharmila would have to marry first. But she didn't want any of that to come too soon.

Sakuntala returned with an armful of blankets and stood at the bottom of the ladder.

She pointed to Pramila and said something about flowing blood and then pointed to my swollen belly and talked about women's fate.

"It hurts so much to have a baby," she said, "just like it hurts when women have their period." She went on in simple Nepali. I caught some familiar phrases: blood, women's fate, *dukkha* (pain and suffering).

What had happened to ripe mango babies? I wondered.

I returned to my loft and tried not to hear the soft weeping and low moaning next door. I had not expected such strict following of pollution rules. The family had seemed fairly lax about such things. But clearly, some customs had to be followed. Sharmila and Sakuntala brought Pramila food and water over the next four days and kept her company. I also climbed the ladder and talked to her sometimes, although Sakuntala warned me not to touch her. For her sake or mine, I wasn't sure.

For illumination on menstrual seclusion, I turned to Bennett's chapter entitled "Female Sexuality and the Patrifocal/Filiafocal Opposition":

> The final ritual to be considered in our discussion of menstrual pollution is actually the first one a woman undergoes, the gupha basne, or "staying in the cave" ceremony which occurs at menarche. Gupha basne is a rite of passage that marks the transition of a girl from a

presexual to a sexual being. As such it reiterates some of
the negative ideas about the dangers of female sexuality
with which we are already familiar.

How odd to have my life and my niece's described in such cold,
elevated language. If I had read "with which we are already familiar"
for an anthropology class several years earlier, I would have understood what it meant: Are you with me, Dear Reader? We've been
covering this for several pages now. But sitting above the buffalo
shed with the rain thudding on the thatched roof and listening to
Pramila sob on the other side of the thin wooden slats between us,
I read that "we" in a new way. Negative ideas about the dangers of
female sexuality? Yeah, Lynn. We're familiar with it, all right.

Bennett points to the story of the Rishi Pancami—the Five
Saints—as a cultural explanation for why women have to be secluded
when they bleed. Long ago, the god Indra killed a Brahman man
and asked around for some ideas about how to erase his sin. The
god Brahma advised him to divide the sin into four parts. Then, he
said, throw each part into a different place: fire, river, mountain, and
menstrual blood. Have women carry the polluted menstrual blood
in the womb, Brahma said. On the first day of menstruation, treat
a woman as accursed and damned. On the second, treat her like
one who has murdered a Brahman. On the third, treat her like an
untouchable. By the fourth day, you may regard her as clean again.

I wondered why that fourth bit of sin didn't get tossed into semen
but didn't have the confidence to question thousands of years of culture I hadn't studied. Bennett says women she interviewed talked
about Indra's sin as one reason they might have lesser status than
men, but most didn't feel they personally carried such ancient sin.
And she points out the paradox of menstrual blood in the story:
damned, but also on the same level as the fire, river, and mountain
that also received the sin—and all those are considered holy.

So, I wondered, if first menarche was such a big deal, what would
happen when I gave birth?

My concern merited an entry in Bennett's index: "birth pollution rituals, 52–54." Turning to those pages, I learned that birth is akin to death: an unfortunate, but unavoidable, reminder of how deeply humans are embedded in mortal bodies and nature. Brahmans seeking a higher spiritual plane must distance themselves from bodily processes, especially where nature is most powerful: at the beginning and ending of life.

I read on to learn that by the fifth or sixth month of pregnancy, the embryo is seen as having life breath, and the mother carrying it as having two bodies. From then on, a pregnant woman may no longer participate in religious ceremonies or cook rice for the family.

I was already polluted? That explained a lot. I continued reading and learned my pollution would gradually increase. After I gave birth, I would wallow for eleven days in even deeper ritual pollution. During that time, Pramod's relatives would not be able to participate in any rituals, but they could move around freely and share food.

"Only the mother is untouchable," Bennett writes.

Hoping once again for foreign immunity and hating myself for it, I caressed my bump and repeated Pramod's mantra, "Everything'll be all right . . ."

Bikas

WITH PRAMOD GONE and the pathways flooded, I awarded myself a brief break from research. Some afternoons, I helped Aama, Sakuntala, and my nieces sort the *makai*. We pulled the husks from bug-eaten, runty ears of corn and piled them in woven straw baskets for later decobbing. They would feed the livestock. The better ears we tied in groups of four to hang from the eaves of the shed. Those would be for popping and grinding in the coming months.

Aama and Sakuntala told stories and showed the girls and me how to improve our corn-husking techniques. The girls giggled at my feeble efforts and continued my daily Nepali lessons.

Like most young women who have gone through puberty, Sharmila and Pramila worked hard with serious concentration. A child, Urmila could not sit still for long. She skipped around, sat back down again, halfheartedly decobbed an ear while telling a joke, then flitted off again, snuck up on one of us, and put a bit of grass down our backs or pulled braids and ponytails. "*Nachala!* Settle down!" the women said, sometimes all at once. She did for ten minutes or so, but then she interrupted our conversations again with chatter and squeals.

"*Chup!* Be quiet!" the women said, looking stern for a moment. Then they smiled and shrugged their shoulders.

I played with Urmila but didn't know how to make her stop when I got tired. And I often didn't know how to respond to the games and jokes other children pressed on me.

I had visited my younger half sisters when they were young but had never lived with them. I had avoided babysitting jobs throughout my teens. How would I ever learn to care for my own child?

In Nepal, I saw children and adults with children every day. Women who visited us carried bare-bottomed babies and toddlers on their hips. Older children trailed behind, sometimes carrying more young ones on their hips. Some had black hair slicked back with mustard oil; others had brown hair, either from heredity or malnutrition. When babies cried, women and men cooed: "Bichara (Poor thing). What could be wrong? Are you hungry? Cold?" They made child care look easy. Of course, they had abundant support. Young mothers rarely stayed confined with infants all day long. Going out to cut grass to feed buffaloes and goats or weed the corn, they left their infants and children with mothers-in-law and sisters-in-law.

In Nepal, no child slept alone. They nestled up against a warm mother, father, older sister or brother, cousin, grandmother or grandfather. I thought of the saying "It takes a village to raise a child." It had already become an American cliché attributed to generic African village life, but I still liked it. Of course, it glossed over cultural specifics even in Africa. And children in Nepal were not raised by a village per se since villages were made up of people of different castes. But they were raised by extended rather than nuclear families, watched by caring neighbors, and held by many arms as they grew.

I thought back to child-rearing lessons from my own mother. I could not remember being held by her. Of course, memory rarely takes us back into those intimate years before age five. When people asked, I described our relationship as close. Throughout adolescence and into adulthood, I regarded her as a friend, someone I could talk to. Without consistent child support payments from my father, she had worked unfulfilling jobs to earn money to support me. She encouraged my schoolwork and quirky professional path. But I didn't remember her being motherly, not in the way of mothers I saw around me in Nepal, who blew into baby bellies and—with bare hands—wiped yellow snot from tiny noses. My mother always admitted she enjoyed me more when I grew older, when I could talk and reason. She had never been one to hold infants and rave over them. I didn't feel drawn to that either.

What if I had no desire to hold my baby?

Despite hundred-plus-degree heat every day, Aama nagged me to wear a sweater or shawl to cover my belly and head. Instead, I loosened my sari or *lungi* (sarong) and let breezes fondle my rounded middle. I'd seen Tamang, Gurung, and Magar women expose their bellies, shoulders, thighs, and even breasts in the heat. I wanted similar privileges for myself. More than that, I discovered a perverse pleasure in defying Brahman rules.

In the highly social cultures of Nepal, I longed for more solitude too, some space for my introverted self to gather energy. But on most days, the skies cleared for at least a few hours, long enough for children, women, and men to wade through the flooded pathways to visit.

Dressed in blue school uniforms of varying cleanliness, girls and boys stopped at our water pump to wash faces and muddy legs and drink water on their way home from school. They leaned against the posts by the buffalo shed, watched goings-on in the Parajuli courtyard, and snuck glances up into my loft. Aama and her granddaughters asked after their mothers and fathers and sometimes offered snacks.

Women came almost daily requesting diagnoses and treatments for their illnesses. I had no training in health care, but people reckoned that since I came from a *bikasi* (developed) country and was studying for a Pee Haitch Dee, I ought to give some medical advice now and then.

Skin infections prevailed. Women showed me rashes and sores brought on during rice planting. The skin cracked, bled, dried out, and itched, and then cracked open again. People said there was something in the soil—maybe a fungus or small bug—that "ate" the feet. I avoided walking through flooded areas but had a mild version of the infection between my toes too. I winced with each step during the open sore phase. As the sores dried, I scratched them open again. Many sukumbasi women who planted rice in waist-high water every day had the infection all over their feet and up their calves too. I helped them clean their legs and feet with antiseptic soap, just as I did mine. It didn't help much.

Mothers brought their children with fevers, swollen bellies, prickly heat, infected insect bites, rashes, cuts, and burns. Consulting David Warner's *Where There Is No Doctor* and always reminding people I was not a doctor, I did my best. In broken Nepali and with some translation help from my nieces, I counseled men and women to take full courses of antibiotics, spend money on nutritious food rather than the expensive vitamin water prescribed by doctors, and visit the health post for the most serious illnesses. But I had few illusions about what I was doing. I provided compassion, soap, and water but could not remove the social inequalities that led to poor working and living conditions and illness.

I told Aama about my doubts.

"Even if you can't figure out what's wrong, talking with them will help," she said. "Sometimes women just need to share their problems. Listen to them."

But other visitors urged me to do more. "You and Pramod are going to be doctors from some big American university. Surely, you can do more than give us soap and bandages. Bring us *bikas*."

Development. Both Pramod and I had focused much of our graduate study on what we then called Third World development. In my undergraduate days, I had talked about economic development as a positive force for alleviating poverty, as long as planners considered the cultural angle of the indigenous groups they worked with. But in graduate school, I learned to see the underside.

Although published in 1991, several years after my pregnancy, *The*

Development Dictionary, edited by Wolfgang Sachs, best captures my thinking in 1987. In that collection, Gustavo Esteva describes how, for hundreds of years, development had meant nothing more than growth, evolution, maturation. Just as seeds develop into plants and children become adults, one form of social system can give rise to another. History, like biology, appears to follow natural laws. Feudalism develops into capitalism. Monarchies develop into democracies.

Starting in the postwar reconstruction projects of the 1950s, the word *development* altered to mean something more engineered: a process of social change and modernization linked to economic growth. It no longer meant a neutral organic process of cultural unfolding, of fulfilling internal potential. It meant escaping, uprooting, or destroying what was in order to force participation in the global marketplace. It meant shedding a former identity and becoming more American, more European, more Western. It meant measuring growth only in economic terms and success only as wealth. Tradition became a barrier to economic growth. Indigenous wisdom became ignorance and backwardness. Men and women became labor units. The environment became an economic resource.

Steeped in critical theories of political economy, I understood development as the first onslaught of a capitalist war against subsistence, self-sufficiency, autonomy. The enemies? Those who do not need to buy and sell. Those who grow their own food. Those who have no desire to drink Coca-Cola. The mission? Inspire people to want Coca-Cola and need baby formula. Change their lives so they depend on hybrid seeds, pesticides, and tractors. Better yet, convince them to borrow money to fulfill their expanding needs and desires. Then they will produce and sell even more to pay back their loans. And then keep them and their children and their children's children buying, selling, and borrowing in perpetuity. The result? Growing pools of cheap labor, expanding consumer markets, higher corporate profits.

"Do you want a boy or a girl?" The women who visited our house with health problems always steered our conversations there.

"A girl," I said, knowing I'd provoke a friendly debate. "And Pramod says he doesn't care. Either a boy or girl would be fine with him." Surrounded as he was by so many men and women who advocated for the birth of boys, I wasn't sure I believed him when he told me that. But I enjoyed dangling the idea.

They laughed. "You can't possibly want a girl."

"But I do. Girls work harder and are better behaved."

"Of course, they work hard. Of course, they're better behaved. Everybody knows that. But then what happens? They get married and go to work for someone else. A son will bring a daughter-in-law to work for you. Much better to have a son."

Visitors asked, "What do you dream about? Chili peppers?"

Perhaps I did. I certainly thought about them a lot in the daytime. Bhagvati told me I needed to eat more food for the growing fetus. Since I insisted on being vegetarian that year, that meant more rice, more lentils, more boiled soybeans, and occasional eggs. At every meal, I picked several green chili peppers from the bushes near the house. It was the only way I could swallow a full meal of our bland food. Aama scolded whenever she caught me, told me chilies weren't good for the baby. I scowled at her and continued. Sometimes, I chewed slowly and grabbed another chili from my stash to taunt her. I noticed that Pandit Kedarnath also took bites of green chili with his dal bhat and waved Aama's warnings away too. When one of us caught the other sneaking peppers, we exchanged sly grins.

Eventually I gave up chilies and also sour foods, but not because I feared harming the fetus. They gave me heartburn.

"Yes," I said. "Sometimes I do dream about chili peppers."

"Then you'll have a boy."

Aama also had dreams of a son. Pandit Kedarnath made his predictions through astrological calculations rather than dreams. There would be one male and one female born into the household, he prophesied. One would be born to the buffalo, and the other would be born to me.

On a hot August day, Siddhi and my nephew Anil Bhattarai came to visit. A teenager, Anil was one of Didi's six children. I had met him several times before but did not know him well. Still, I knew where he fell in age order among his brothers: Keshav, Yadav, Anil, Sunil, Dipesh. He also had a sister named Binita. I knew to call Anil *Bhanja* (sister's son), rather than *Chora* (brother's son). I also understood by then that *bhanja* (as well as *bhanji*, sister's daughter) are considered especially sacred among Nepali Brahmans. They are supposed to be present at certain rituals and festivals to receive special gifts and honors. So, I understood that we were about to celebrate something.

I chatted with Anil and Siddhi in the kitchen. They asked if I had heard from Pramod. I said I had received a brief letter. He was in good health and progressing on his research. They explained in English that they had come for Janai Purnima—the full moon day when everyone gets a thread bracelet and men get new sacred threads. They had first received the thin cotton sash at initiation, usually held when a boy reaches adolescence. They're supposed to wear it throughout their lives as a mark of status and ritual purity. Yet some Brahman men rebel against it. Pramod didn't wear his thread anymore. Siddhi told me he continued to wear his to please his parents but didn't believe in it. And he hated the hypocrisy of some Brahmans. They're not supposed to tell lies or eat meat, he said, but many do. Anil nodded in agreement.

As we talked, rice boiled over on the cob stove. Instinctively, I rose and rushed toward it. Aama and Siddhi shouted at me to stop. I did. Siddhi explained that pregnant women should not touch cooked rice. Out of respect for his father rather than for his own beliefs, I guessed, he seemed as upset as Aama that I had almost ruined the rice. I was shocked that two people I respected could be more upset by ritually polluted rice than burnt rice.

"What about after delivery? Can I touch it then?" I asked.

"I'm not sure Bua will like that either," Siddhi said.

I noted my lack of enthusiasm for Janai Purnima in my journal:

> August 9, 1987
>
> Later, Anil put a yellow-colored thread around my wrist as the family looked on. He said it would protect me from evil. He also said I should show it to Pramod, meaning, I supposed, that I am meant to wear it for some time. Everyone got such a bracelet. I hesitated in taking the bracelet from Anil since I was not sure how "Brahmanized" a thing it was. I guess I had had enough of Brahmanism for the morning and didn't feel like being a willing participant in its reproduction. But I could hardly turn it down. It was given with a great deal of affection.

More rain, more sore feet: still, the visits continued.

"Why don't you set up a project for women?" Sukumbasi women asked as they cleaned their feet at the water pump. "We need an income. We earn a little money from rice planting. But when it's done, what can we do? We can't earn enough for the rest of the year. We need money."

Pramod and I had never promised to do more than bring books for a library in Gunjanagar. But I was quickly catching on that villagers made requests for "development projects" to anyone they thought might listen: party leaders, foreigners, locals returned from abroad. And since I had begun asking them questions for my research, sukumbasi women might have thought I would take a special interest in their request.

I did know something about women's income-generation projects, but that knowledge had made me a skeptic. Donors loved the tangibility, the measurable outcomes. Government officials loved how they satisfied calls for progress without challenging the overall balance of wealth and power. Corrupt officials liked the steady stream of money they could siphon from them. And even the poorest villagers in a country overrun by jeeps emblazoned with World Bank, USAID, FAO, or UNICEF logos had heard about income-generation projects and wanted their fair share.

Income allowed women marginalized by social norms—widows, unwed mothers, former prostitutes—to survive and support children. But without political intervention, such projects didn't give women control over land. And in many parts of the world, the inequality in land inheritance laws ensured a steady stream of outcaste women and their children who needed income. Moreover, earning income sometimes added to women's already heavy workload. Women made a few extra rupees, shillings, or pesos by sewing dresses or making baskets. And their income improved the nutrition, health, and education opportunities of children. But that also gave men license to spend more of their money on bicycles, radios, and liquor. When women worked, men sometimes became less responsible about sharing their earnings with the family.

Where women generated income by taking out loans, their lives became more precarious. If their enterprises failed, they usually sold what little property they had or did without food, education, or health care for their children to pay off debt. Oddly, when economic growth is measured by gross domestic product and gross national product, debt becomes a positive. In fact, because income-generation projects always involve exchanges of money and products, they tend to look like successes in the annual reports of development agencies. But in individual lives, they have often led to disappointments or catastrophic failures.

Talk of income generation for women led to more general discussions of women and development. I was already hearing and reading in English—among Pramod's activist friends and in development reports and newspapers—what I would later understand as even more pervasive on radio and in village gatherings in Nepal: stock phrases and homilies admonishing women to develop for the good of the nation: *As long as women are behind, Nepal will be behind. You* women must move forward. You must learn to read and write. You must educate your children. You must work to develop Nepal. You must learn to uplift yourselves and help Nepal become modern. Various development organizations operating in Nepal devoted considerable funds and staff to "women's development." And no political leader of any party could go far without paying lip service to the issue. At times, the whole notion of women's development twisted so far backward that it seemed women should take the blame for Nepal's slow progress, just as dangerous wives took the blame for the dissolution of extended families.

I didn't want to say no to the sukumbasi women eager for income. I was already learning the Nepali custom of saying yes or maybe without conviction. It was considered more polite, and as far as I could see, one was rarely held accountable later on.

"Wait until Pramod comes and I have this baby," I told them. "Then we'll see."

That August, Brahman men also braved the flooded pathways to our house. Some of the more liberal men brought me their sons and daughters.

"Teach them some English. Help them improve their marks in school. Make them bikasi."

I understood the motivation—better jobs (maybe even overseas jobs) for sons, the hope of wealthy husbands for daughters. But I couldn't muster enthusiasm there either.

Unable to say no, I tutored a few girls and boys for a while. The children were painfully polite. But none of us enjoyed slogging through their boring English textbooks, and I didn't have the energy to come up with my own lesson plans. When the children stopped showing up ("too much rain"), I felt so relieved that the subsequent guilt about enjoying the relief passed quickly.

Conservative old Brahman men brought their own burning questions on development to Pandit Kedarnath.

"What will the child of this American buhari be?"

"Can it be Brahman?"

"What caste will it be, if not Brahman? Will it be Chhetri?"

"Can it be Hindu if she is Christian?"

On they jabbered for hours. Their concerns for fetal status reinforced my worries over bikas; there would be no development without someone trying to use it to increase power and wealth. And fighting that tendency would mean challenging those old men.

Eavesdropping on such conversations, I should have been taking notes to dig deeper into why caste mattered, how it might determine the ritual purity and status of my child. But as the object of their discussion, I felt no curiosity. Instead, I raged in silence and plotted clever ways to challenge their entrenched beliefs. But I had little experience to draw on. I knew I'd get no further than the arguments I used to have with my stepfather.

Thanks to Seattle's controversial and short-lived experiment with mandatory busing in the 1970s, the schools in our neighborhood became some of the most integrated in the city. I sponged up the positive message of racial harmony from class and school assemblies and became less tolerant of those who stood in its way. Dad became an easy target. I waited for him to drop an ethnic offense like the N-word. Then I pounced and called him a racist. He called me an N-lover, and on we went. Mother usually put her hands over her ears and called a truce in time for dinner. The best way to keep household peace, I learned, was to stop talking back. But that meant letting racist slurs slide—something I found morally repugnant.

In Gunjanagar, I had more reasons than household peace to be silent. I had to develop and maintain a professional persona: objective anthropologist, open to all ideas. And I was only learning Nepali, had only faint, confused ideas of the stories and concepts contained in the Vedas and other sacred texts. And I had to overcome all that I lacked as a non-Brahman, a non-Hindu, and a relative newcomer to South Asian studies by being the best daughter-in-law possible. All that added up to not confronting elderly men, no matter how much they insulted me or our family. I turned my rage inward. There it mixed with habitual shyness and the loneliness of being pregnant in an unfamiliar place without my husband, and then jumbled with the confusion of being an anthropologist with too many opinions. It all spilled out in depression and tears and detailing tragedies in my journal:

August 24, 1987

Last night, a woman living nearby lost her baby in childbirth. She was eight months pregnant by Nepali counting, which means, I think, around seven by ours (Nepalis count ten months starting from the month of last period). The baby was in a breech position. Some men came last night to borrow Siddhi's bullock cart to take her to the hospital because she was getting weak. I don't know how far they got, or if they even left before the baby came out dead (or died shortly thereafter). Aama says the woman is okay now. She's eating lots of meat. The baby was a boy. Pramila told me how the woman has lots of girls, implying, I think, that the loss was an even greater tragedy for the woman since it was a boy.

August 27, 1987

I found out that the woman whose baby died had sensed some problem fifteen days before. The baby had stopped moving and may have died inside. Siddhi said the guy who came for the bullock cart was "a bit nonsense" and should've taken her to the hospital long before. By the time he reached there with the bullock cart the baby had come out dead. The woman has had twelve babies, six of whom have died either before or during birth or in early infancy.

The festival of Tij diverted attention away from fetal and village development for a while. I'd heard women talking about it for weeks. For insight, I turned again to *Dangerous Wives and Sacred Sisters*.

Celebrated by Nepali Hindu women during Bhadao (mid-August to mid-September), Tij is the festival in which women work through the paradox of being both dangerous wives and sacred sisters. They show off their dangerous tendencies and seductiveness through "shameless" dancing. But at the same time, they control those dangerous powers through purification—fasting and worship.

What struck me most in the weeks before the festival was how giddy women became in planning getaways to their maiti. For several days, they could leave behind work in their ghar and the scrutiny of in-laws and husbands and relax and have fun with mothers and sisters in their maiti. They could once again be the sacred and beloved sister and daughter, not the dangerous wife.

Sakuntala's parents had died, so she left for a few days to spend Tij with a sister. In a silly tone that characterized the atmosphere in our household for several days, Aama said to me, "You should go to your maiti too. Too bad it's so far. You need an airplane." Then she laughed and laughed. I didn't understand what was so funny, but I soon learned anything could evoke hilarity during Tij.

Bennett describes what happens on the morning of Tij: Women gather with groups of friends to walk to the nearest river to bathe. In order to ensure long lives for their husbands, they also shape phalluses in the sand—a reenactment of how the goddess Parvati woos her busy, philandering husband, Shiva, back to her arms.

On the morning of our Tij, I asked the women seated on the verandah what I should bring for the long walk to the river. They all talked at once.

"River?"

"The paths are too flooded."

"And it's so far."

"We'll bathe at home."

"And practice our songs!"

We jostled for turns at the water pump. After bathing, the girls pulled me inside. We put on our best saris, earrings, glass bangles, and necklaces. Earlier that month, Tirtha had brought us all new polyester saris from a conference trip to Bangkok. The girls squealed: "How modern they look, how silky they feel." We combed our hair. Everyone but me smoothed her hair down with mustard oil. Married women also painted a red streak into the part of their hair. Aama's sister, Thuliaama, told me to do the same. I declined. Already wearing my marriage necklace and a wedding ring, I believed those marriage symbols sufficient. Of course, I didn't know how to explain all that in Nepali, but Aama came to my rescue.

If I had studied the appropriate section in Bennett a bit more, I might have given in. That was, after all, the day on which women were supposed to respect their husbands, and a little extra respect—with my husband so far away and me missing him so much—wouldn't have hurt me.

After bathing and dressing, Bennett explains, women gather to dance.

We planned to go to Chanauli Bazaar, but the rain pounded harder.

"We have umbrellas," the girls said. "Let's just go. The dancing has probably already started."

"Hush," Thuliaama said.

"The rain will stop," Aama said. "There's plenty of time. Besides, we should practice our dancing and singing first."

So we crowded upstairs. Aama and Thuliaama knew lots of Tij songs and didn't need any encouragement. Giggling, Urmila started off the dancing. With each song thereafter, women and girls pushed someone forward to dance. She usually rotated a few times, hands miming the words in the song, and then fell back into the cluster of women, laughing and saying, "I don't know how."

In a simple, chantlike melody in a minor key with pauses between couplets, Aama sang a song she described as old:

My husband is bringing a new wife
She will bring a servant as dowry

Father, you must also give me a servant
Or give me a knife to kill myself

One should always give a daughter a maid
But never give her a knife

A queen bird has come flying
She is golden

We sisters, friends since childhood
Have come together for Tij

The marigolds are blooming and fragrant
Bumblebees buzzing around

My mother did not invite me for Tij
So I am very sad.

Finally, Thuliaama, a widow of many years, rose. During her visit, Thuliaama had taken on cooking duties, insisting that no one else in the house, including Aama, was pure enough to serve Pandit Kedarnath. Thuliaama crouched over the fire and growled at anyone who came too near. She chastised Aama for allowing menstruating women in the cooking zone and Dalits near the water pump. The younger women in our family even allowed Kami, Sarki, and Damai friends to sit with them on the same mat or share food together outside. Evil, Thuliaama called it. Evil.

I found it difficult to like Thuliaama. But her dancing revealed an aspect I could admire. None of the others in our group could match her grace or beauty in dance.

She finished and sat down again. "You young girls just don't know how," she said, and smiled wide enough that we could see a few remaining teeth.

"You always were such a good dancer," Aama said. "I'm good at making songs; you're good at dancing."

We all laughed.

I looked up to see Pandit Kedarnath in the doorway. The others stopped laughing and looked at him.

"It's raining hard now," he said. "The clothes you hung out to dry have all fallen in the mud. Someone needs to pick them up."

Normally, Urmila, Pramila, or Sharmila would jump up and do as their grandfather said. And if none of them did, Aama would pick one and say, "Eh, Nani, go on, go get those clothes now." But not today, not on Tij.

"Oh ho!" Aama said to her husband. She tried to go on but gave in to laughter. She held her stomach and leaned forward in a huge guffaw. Tittering, the girls leaned against her. Even Thuliaama chuckled.

"The clothes! Ha Ha! They're … in … ha ha … in … the mud." Snorting and shrieking, Aama sprawled out and rolled on the floor with the girls.

I studied Pandit Kedarnath's face. The scowl seemed to lack some commitment. He knew this was women's day off, but he was not accustomed to handling laundry even on sunny days. And now the clothes were wet and dirty.

Finally, Aama sat up. "We can't pick them up. Can't you see? We're too busy. Ha! We're very, very, VERY busy. Singing!"

She collapsed into another pile of girlish squeals.

Pandit Kedarnath shook his head and went downstairs. Curious to see what he might do, I stood and walked to the window. A black umbrella emerged from the verandah and headed toward lungis, saris, panties, bras, blouses, T-shirts, and petticoats scattered at the side of the courtyard. Pandit Kedarnath picked them all up and carried them inside.

We continued our dancing and singing. The girls pushed me up. I tried a few rounds but imagined myself looking more like a broken windmill than a dancer.

The rain stopped around noon. Our Tamang neighbors arrived and invited us to walk with them to Chanauli Bazaar. We smoothed our hair and saris and set out. The pathway channeled water like a river and reeked of decay. Carrying our flip-flops proved easier than tugging them out of the mud with each step.

We came to the main irrigation canal. There was no bridge over it then. We all knew an easier route, but Chanauli was just on the other side. We could hear the singing and clapping, see the swirl of red. If we took the detour, we'd miss another fifteen minutes. So we hitched up our saris and waded across. The water lapping my thighs reached the waists of the other women. But no matter. We had not braved the flooded pathways earlier that morning to purify ourselves. But we would brave anything to get to the dancing sooner.

On the drier main road, we joined streams of smiling women saried in reds and pinks. They clustered in tight circle, singing and clapping and stomping, glass bangles tinkling to the beat. In the middle of each circle, one woman performed, spinning first in one direction, then in another. She sang a rhyming couplet, which the women circled around her repeated. The dancer's arms undulated, sometimes acting out the words. Compositions often strained phrasing and meaning to achieve clever rhymes. Most songs went something like this:

> The only daughter, so fair and thin
> My eyes were just amazing

> Everyone said to Bua
> Don't wed her there.

> They have no servants
> They have no oxen

Bua sent me nevertheless
I wish I'd jumped off a precipice

The rice is already finished
Eaten by useless guests

Husband has no irrigated land
Sending me here, Father sinned

I have never liked my in-laws
They yell when I don't feed the buffaloes

Then they gave me rice
all dry, stale, and tasteless

Sister-in-law got a sari twelve feet long
But mine was a measly seven

People say such short ones are for the dead
When I complained, Sasu yelled

Oh gods and goddesses
I can't endure more troubles

From my maiti, this village is too far
I want to leave and never return here

Of course, I didn't catch all the lines then. I heard words like
sasu, *buhari*, and *dukkha* often enough to glean themes. I would
later collect pages and pages of Tij songs and look for patterns in
content: how women sang their troubles, their desires, their fears;
lamented husbands and mothers-in-law who did them wrong; celebrated escaping such trouble and enjoying the company of women.
Smiling and laughing, women complained about their married

lives, criticized the cruelty of in-laws, poked fun at the injustices of Hindu society, and warbled about longing for death. Some songs also rehashed current events: famines, earthquakes, major road accidents, elections, arrests, political conflicts.

One morning, I woke to hear some Brahman men talking loudly to Pandit Kedarnath on the verandah. I couldn't usually follow their philosophical discussions peppered with long Sanskrit words, so I was surprised to catch some phrases I could understand.

"She reads too much . . . writes too much."

Did I hear that right? I listened for more.

'Women should be out in the fields . . . working."

"But reading and writing are my work," I heard some braver Elizha shouting in my head. "I'm paid through a research grant to do them. I'm a breadwinner in this family. I bring in more money than Pramod right now."

But I couldn't shout at those men the way I wanted to. So I cried into a pillow.

I could never agree with their reasoning, but I knew some truth slivered through their conclusion. Instead of reading Jane Austen or Lynn Bennett, I should be out doing more fieldwork, the anthropological kind. But I was so tired, so pregnant. And my feet still hurt and itched, the pathways were still flooded, and wherever I went people wanted to talk about whether I wanted a girl or boy, whether I was eating enough, how often I dreamed of chili peppers, when I would bring bikas. And I hadn't decided how or where I'd give birth.

There was more that I didn't want to admit to myself: that I should have been working harder as an anthropologist to understand Nepal, Hinduism, Brahmanism, Vedism. I shouldn't want to shout at these men. I should want to ask them questions and learn from them.

One of the notions that lured me into anthropology came in an essay I had read in my first anthropology class: "The Impact of the Concept of Culture on the Concept of Man" by Clifford Geertz. At last, I thought, someone could explain what had bothered me in literature and philosophy classes—how too many thinkers projected their own limited experiences on the vast diversity of humanity and claimed to speak for a universal human nature. Explanations of human lives as "nasty, brutish and short" or rooted in "a propensity to truck, barter, and exchange" had never made much sense to me when applied to people across centuries and cultures. Geertz did not attempt to define human nature from the limited vision of one cultural viewpoint but insisted that we only become human through the particulars of the culture we're born into, not through general principles. Human nature cannot be isolated from the culture that shapes us.

I grew to love that concept of culture the way I loved my Swiss army knife. If culture, rather than human nature, made us who we were, there was nothing natural or inevitable about racism, hate, war. With a concept of culture, we anthropologists could fix anything, or at least explain it. But too deep a love can disappoint, and that concept of culture had so far mostly failed me in Nepal. Ever since my first arrival, Pramod's family and village had offered a perfect opportunity for intimacy with another culture. My pregnancy offered even more. Even when I didn't plan research there, I should have been more curious. Yet all along disappointment nagged at me: these Brahmans I lived among were not the kind of Others I had in mind when I decided to become an anthropologist.

I needed something more than a conceptual pocketknife to find my way here.

If pressed, I would have admitted even then that part of what had made Africa so appealing was that my first trip had been led by skilled guides—all the fun and meaningful experience without the hassle. I had no idea how it would be to wake among the Kikuyu or Maasai. I'd only woken in tourist lodges, tents shared with fellow travelers, and hotels. I had liked how that put me close to exotic cultural encounters, but not too close. In all my years of classroom and library studies, I could defer the actual nitty-gritty encounter to some imagined future when I was sure I would get everything just right.

I pushed the pillow harder into my face and sobbed more. Even if I wanted to know, I wouldn't be able to ask the questions because I was such a dolt when it came to learning Nepali. What had I been thinking? I should never have come here, didn't belong here. I wanted to go home.

"Women should not read at all," a gruff voice said. The priest from Ram Temple, I suspected. "It says so in the Vedas."

I beat the pillow with my fists and muffled a wail into it. Why hadn't I stuck to Africa? Why had I even gone into anthropology? I should have studied animals. Penguins, maybe. Or pythons. I had no patience for people, didn't like to talk so much, was terrible at interviewing, felt so bad about people all around me who barely had enough to eat. I had plenty to eat, even though it was the same bland food every day, but how could I complain about it? I was one of the lucky ones.

I heard their namastes, then silence. I threw the pillow aside, wiped my face, and looked out. They were gone. I waited a few minutes. Hoping the puffiness in my face wouldn't show, I climbed down the stairs.

Aama knew what crying looked like. I'm sure I didn't fool her. She invited me to sit beside her on the verandah. I could see she was angry.

"Ke bhayo?" I said. "What's wrong?"

In the slow and simple Nepali she used with me, she told me how she had served tea to the old men.

"But they wouldn't take it from my hands. They think I'm too lax with Damais and Sarkis around the water pump. And I let foreigners live in my home."

I started at that, but she put her hand over mine. "That priest is a fool." Her voice rose. "What does he know of the Vedas? He's a know-nothing illiterate. Bua says there's nothing in the Vedas about women not reading."

We sat in silence for a while, looking out at a wall of dark clouds moving in. I had been pondering my situation alone for too long. I had seen Aama fast and go to temple and shoo me gently away from cooked rice. But I'd also heard her talk about the world as her village, women's rights, and the unfairness of pollution practices. She referred to me as her daughter and usually treated me with respect. She had her contradictions, but who didn't? Maybe I didn't have to suffer my anger alone. Nor did I have to see all my irritations, questions, and critiques as a foreigner's reaction to local customs. If Aama could be justified in her anger, I could join her now and then. Perhaps I wouldn't express it all myself, but I could cheer her on.

She gripped my hand tighter. "You and Pramod should teach women to read. That will show the old know-nothings."

I did not see the specifics then, but her idea pierced through layers of theoretical and cultural confusion to the beginnings of an idea.

HARVEST

THROUGHOUT THE MONSOON summer, Siddhi, Sakuntala, and all their children except Pramila sorted their belongings so they could move out of the family house before Dasain. I worried that Pramod and I had crowded them out. No, others said, the tension in our ghar had been building for years.

I witnessed the final few months. Just as Lynn Bennett described, the blame and anger revolved around the dangerous wife, the buhari. Day after day, Pandit Kedarnath yelled at Sakuntala to cut more grass for the buffaloes. Sakuntala yelled back, hid pots, clanged pans while cooking, served rice with too much force, and cached a share of grain that Aama said exceeded her fair share.

Sakuntala had been pushing Siddhi to establish a separate household for years. Siddhi wanted all the family property legally divided among the brothers and their father. But that would have to wait since Udaya was still teaching in Solukhumbu and had not yet married. He would be the most likely candidate to care for the parents when the brothers divided the property, but the family agreed he would need more time to prepare for the role.

By early September, Siddhi and Sakuntala had moved into a temporary house along the main road near Chanauli Bazaar while Siddhi arranged for a new one to be built. Sharmila accepted the move away from her grandparents as graciously as she accepted all the demands put on her as eldest daughter. She was in her last few months of secondary school and hoped to attend nursing school in Pokhara the following year. Urmila and the two boys, Suman and

Sujan, also followed their parents. But Pramila stayed behind. She had spent much of her childhood with her grandparents when they lived in Kahung and had grown closer to her grandmother than to any other adult.

Siddhi and the children cycled to our house several times each week for visits. Sakuntala visited less often, but usually came for family rituals and festival days.

One afternoon, we gathered at the entry to our compound, straining to see what the buzz of a motor across the fields might bring. A three-wheeled tempu turned onto the pathway along the irrigation canal leading toward our home. I recognized the familiar blue-and-gray-striped shirt. Pramod had been gone for two months and had sent a few letters. I had not expected him to return home for another week or so.

Family, neighbors, and children huddled around the vehicle as it stopped at our gate. Ecstatic, I tried to drag Pramod toward privacy. But others demanded his attention. He sat in a chair in the courtyard and let children fondle his new beard and mustache. And then Pandit Kedarnath sat beside him and shared his thoughts and prophecies.

Over the next few days, we found little time for togetherness. Men dropped by to request our support for more projects they said were essential to village bikas. The more conservative Brahman men asked us to donate money for building Hindu temples. They were alarmed, they said, at all the new Buddhist temples in Chitwan. Such groups were secretly organizing to overthrow Hinduism. They were sure of it. If they could just keep pace with all the Buddhist temple building, they could better carry out their dharma and guide bikas. Then, Tamang and Gurung Buddhists visited to ask if we could help them build their temples. They wouldn't just be for worshipping, they said, but would be local centers to rally support for development among their groups. With all the Hindu dominance, this would help bolster pride and trust for bikas.

Some wealthy men arrived one day and asked us to pledge financial and political support for a great symbol of village development, an institution that would foster peace and prosperity and protect private property in Gunjanagar: a police station. They had already asked the village Panchayat to provide a piece of the public pastureland for it.

That's how it was in Nepal. Every project for social change had to be framed in the language of bikas. That was one reason he had chosen to work in India, Pramod reminded me.

Even as they skimmed funding from development projects, the royal family and Panchayat officials waved the flag of bikas to signal their commitment to the common good. On the other side, development provided the only safe language available for underground political parties—both the Nepali Congress Party and various communist parties—to speak publicly about their agendas. No one from any side could argue with an initiative called a "development project." So, of course, those from various sides could make it mean almost anything.

Pramod and I had been discussing the problems with development since we first met. But we also understood the political expediency of bikas in Nepal. And we wanted to help in specific areas: health care, water, food production, education. Pramod often described our situation with his favorite English aphorism, although he often mangled it to something like "caught between the dilemmas of two horns."

Pramod avoided criticizing temples and police stations, but he articulated a firm position that honored our concerns about development as globalization but also respected bikas as the only language available for those seeking real change. We will only support a project, he said, that would be open to all people in the village. And we prefer educational rather than religious or bureaucratic projects.

Disappointed, the men who asked for our help had to agree that education was a worthy goal.

Aama listened in on these numerous conversations and then

unleashed her opinions after the men left. They ran something like this: "How dare they request our money for police stations and temples when just a few weeks ago, some came here and said women shouldn't read? And those police will come put us in jail. Maybe even shoot us for being Nepali Congress. You did the right thing sending them away, but you have to do more. You have to start classes for women. Now. Teach them to read. I'll be a student. If an old woman like me can do it, anyone can."

After that, she badgered us every few days. Hers was the best suggestion we had heard so far on how to respond to bikas demands. Pramod said she had been wanting to learn to read and write for some time but, like other women, preferred the fun and motivation of studying in a group rather than alone. She probably also liked the idea of hitching her individual learning to a broader community purpose. Village Panchayats sometimes offered literacy classes for rural women, but laced them so heavily with propaganda that many avoided them.

When earning his education degree in Kathmandu, Pramod had discovered the writings of Brazilian educator Paulo Freire, especially *Pedagogy of the Oppressed*. In the late 1970s, Pramod went on to work with colleagues in the Society for Participatory Cultural Action (SPACE) to develop a Freirean literacy approach appropriate for Nepal. He taught such classes in Kathmandu and other regions of Nepal and trained others to teach them.

Pramod had considered creating literacy classes for Gunjanagar before but regarded himself as still a stranger to the place. And, knowing the constraints of the Panchayat system, he doubted his efforts would yield much. But since that bombing in Kathmandu, he also sensed a slight shift in the political climate that might make a literacy campaign worthwhile.

We made a decision. If we could find others as interested as Aama, we would host one literacy class for women. Beyond learning how to read and write, women could meet with others and share opinions and ideas—an opportunity rare in Panchayat Nepal. And then women might have a stronger voice in directing bikas in the region.

Women might even begin organizing, we repeated to each other in moments of doubt, although I couldn't imagine what that might look like.

I continued interviewing sukumbasi families but stopped writing in my already intermittent journal after September 24. My last entry:

> Yesterday, there was supposed to have been an eclipse around 8:00 a.m. I didn't notice anything, but it was cloudy. Aama had told me a few days before that pregnant women should not look at it or the baby's eyes will be bad. She rolled her eyes, crossed them, made them look weird to show the things that could happen.

I did not write in October, November, or December. I would not write about the last weeks of pregnancy until three months after I gave birth. And I would write in red pen—page after page of red. Perhaps that was the only pen I could find, but no other sections of my journals appear in red. That pen crossed out many words and phrases, enough to tear through the paper in places, and wrote in loopy, sloppy letters. Part of me must have known I needed to record the details before I forgot them all. But I did not want to dwell there. I had to quickly gush out some memories, then forget again and move on.

Now, I try to reconstruct what happened in the weeks leading up to birth from those pages written in red pen long after the fact.

On Dasain and Tihar, the major festivals of the year, I wrote little except to remember that "if I had given birth within eleven days preceding either festival, the entire family would have had to forgo celebrations that year."

I didn't give birth early, so we did observe Dasain that year. But I find it hard to hook any more memories to make up for the silences in my journal.

I vaguely remember the season: how the rains stopped, the air cooled, the skies cleared. Farmers harvested paddy. And I could finally see Annapurna, Macchupuchare, and Ganesh Himal above the green hills to the north.

I remember the sprouted barley grass and a vague appreciation for that as a symbol of the harvest, of fertility. I remember relatives arriving.

I remember bloody goat heads and men passing by our house carrying plastic bags loaded with fresh buffalo meat, talk of hundreds of water buffaloes and goats slaughtered in the courtyard of Hanuman Dhoka in Kathmandu, and the sound of marrow being sucked from bones and the burps that followed. But I continued my commitment to vegetarianism. Some of my nieces were lifelong vegetarians. They showed me how to push twigs into a squash to give it legs and ears. Then with one stroke of a curved *khukuri* knife, one of them decapitated the cucurbit.

I remember talk of female powers—Kali, Durga, Shakti.

I remember the final day of Dasain: fields burnished in golden harvest light, the rice stalks piled into sheaves, the Himalayas tall and white. I wore a silk sari and the marriage necklace Aama had given me—a gold pendant hanging between twisted strands of green glass beads.

Giggles and jokes mixed with the seriousness of high ritual around a cot in the courtyard. We all took our places at proper times to give and take tika.

I remember exhaustion from so many people and so much talk. I tried hard to understand yet understood little. Those seven pages of charts in Bennett's book on the kin order of Dasain tika and gift-giving illuminated what some sukumbasi women meant when they once told me letters on a page looked to them like little black buffaloes. But like a child directed here and there, I knew enough. Tika and gifts and all the ritual wrapped each one of us in a web of protective kinship. And I was a part of it, proud to take my place as Bhauju, Saili, Maiju, and Saniaama. And soon, I would be Aama, too.

I remember the gooey, oily sweetness of deep-fried rice flour donuts dipped in spicy chutney made from bitter melon and how my first taste of that after months of plain dal bhat made me a glutton.

We walked the now dry lane to Chanauli Bazaar, ate more at Uncle Padma Raj's house, and then walked down another lane to an older uncle's house and ate more.

After Dasain, Pramod and Siddhi prepared for literacy classes. First, they needed to select and train two women as facilitators. Pramila was an obvious choice. She had long stood apart from the conflict between her mother and grandparents and got along well with everyone. She spent many hours huddled with Aama, whispering about poverty and women's rights. Her prominent hooked nose and tendency to mull things over before smiling made her appear more serious than her sisters.

Pramod and Siddhi planned the literacy class mostly for sukumbasi women and hoped to find one to train as a teacher. They offered the job to Pramila's friend Radhika—a smart, sassy Damai woman. Unlike many other sukumbasi women her age—who had to devote their days to field labor—she attended school. She accepted. Pramod worried she might be more interested in the monthly salary—small though it was—than in the broader issues. She clearly spent the money she earned from field labor on nose rings, earrings, felt tikas, and the best fashion she could afford. Still, he wanted to give her a chance and show that our literacy program would support Dalits and sukumbasi in leadership roles.

The idea was to give both young women an opportunity to grow as teachers, grassroots organizers, and leaders. Whether or not they continued as teachers in the years ahead, they would, we hoped, carry more confidence and leadership skills with them whatever they did.

As eager as I was to help plan the literacy classes, I begged Pramod to devote some time to making birth arrangements. Bhagvati worried about my failure to put on much weight but said the baby was in a good position. Perhaps because I had more experience with them, I feared doctors more than I feared Brahman culture. So Pramod and I decided we would try a home birth. We knew labor could begin at any time, so we cleaned our bedroom with disinfectant and decided who could assist when the contractions began: Pramod, Aama, and Bhagvati. With Pramod back and some sense of Aama as a new ally, I grew confident that we could temper any cultural ideas at odds with my own beautiful vision of natural childbirth.

Much to everyone's amusement, we took a bus to Narayanghat to buy flannel to cut into diapers. Many said buying items of clothing before a child's birth was foolish and asked us, "What if the baby doesn't survive?" I had never considered that possibility. Many also called diapers a silly idea and told us good mothers know when their babies are going to poop. Then you just hold the baby away from you over the ground and clean it up afterward.

That sounded good in theory. But in our visits around the village, I had seen babies making messes on women's saris, straw mats, and woven carpets. Those all had to be cleaned. I held to the idea that it was easier to clean a small piece of flannel than a whole sari or carpet. Women laughed. Then I reminded them what "cleaning up" meant in some households where dogs and pigs slurped up human feces. Brahman women insisted they cleaned up *dishaa* long before dogs and pigs ever got to it.

On October 24, the day before my due date, we celebrated Tihar, the ritual that many groups in Nepal emphasize within the more widely celebrated Festival of Lights (Diwali). My red pen would not record much on that.

Everyone expected that we would not celebrate the festival. When someone asked why we had planted no marigolds for the sisters to make garlands for their brothers, our nieces said, "Why bother, since we probably won't celebrate Tihar anyway?" The day passed without event except that Didi could not come to give tika to her brothers because she was menstruating.

What else do I remember from those five days of Tihar? How the nights became cooler, how the days remained warm, and how we could still see the Himalayas against the cloudless sky. There were dogs and cows wearing garlands. And little clay lamps.

Or maybe I saw those at other houses. Or in other years.

More than two decades later, my mind digs for more details. The stars must have been bright on the new moon night of Cow Tihar. Did I notice that? Did I watch the moon grow fuller each night after? Didn't children wake me from sleep, singing in Laxmi's name for sweets and coins?

Someone must have reminded me to take off that string Anil had tied on my wrist at Janai Purnima. Did anyone tie it to the tail of a cow, so that when my time came to die, I might grab it to cross the Hindu version of the River Styx into the underworld?

I'm sure everyone watched me with concern. They knew more than I about what can go wrong in birth, how death takes so many mothers and children.

I must have watched women and girls painting Seven Color Tikas on their brothers' foreheads, draping garlands of globe amaranth around their necks, asking Yama to give them long lives. Did I wonder which side of that equation my child might take someday? Did I wish for a brother of my own?

If someone tried to tell me the Tihar story, I don't remember it: how Yama, the god of death, came to take the life of a young man, how the man's sister begged him to wait until she finished worshipping her brother. Yama agreed. Then the girl carried out such a long and proper puja for both her brother and Yama that Yama let the brother keep his life as long as the puja flowers stayed fresh. The sister kept the flowers fresh for an entire year. Yama was so impressed by the sister's devotion that he let the boy live on, unconditionally.

As my due date came and went, relatives and neighbors badgered me with questions: Does your belly hurt? When will you deliver? I told them I didn't know. I worried but reassured myself with what I'd read in my pregnancy books. Due dates are approximations. Many women miss them.

I woke to cramps in the early morning hours of October 31. By midmorning the contractions petered out. I fell into a grand funk. Siddhi brought me a small pumpkin that evening and, along with others, encouraged me to celebrate Halloween. I understood so little about Nepali holidays, yet my relatives knew it was a special day in my culture and tried to use that to cheer me up. I halfheartedly carved menacing eyes and a spooky smile in the pumpkin and lit a candle inside. My nieces asked me what that meant. I told them about costumes and trick-or-treating. Maybe I also said something about warding off spirits and compared that to Nepal, where eyes are drawn to protect people from inauspicious sights: evil spirits, evil eyes.

Sharmila, Pramila, and Urmila carried the *rakshas* around the village. Neighbors and friends shrieked and ran from the demon. My nieces laughed. It was all a strange echo of the begging songs children had sung for Tihar treats several nights earlier and the pumpkin we had animalized and sacrificed for Dasain.

My explanations satisfied my playful nieces but deepened my blues. I gave little thought then to how my own cultural or biological ancestors carved faces in vegetables to mark the turning toward winter, wondered little whether there might be some ancient connection to the festivals celebrating light and the underworld in South Asia.

At some point, I had come to believe that studying someone else's culture as an anthropologist would be easier than unfolding myself in my own. What I hadn't foreseen was how I might be called to a deeper sense of humanity by bringing a human into the world in another culture. I longed for home, my maiti, for something I might vaguely call my culture. Yet I hardly understood the rituals around a popular event like Halloween. And I was about to bring a child into a culture I understood even less.

I sensed that stronger roots in one or the other place might help me through what would come next, but I was like a ghost fluttering in the dusty corner of a high ceiling.

Details in red pen fill me in now on how my labor proceeded.

Contractions began fifteen minutes apart on November 3 and continued strong. Day and night, Bhagvati came and went by bicycle. She had young children of her own and other clients. On one visit, she told us to call her again after my water broke, which she assured me could happen anytime. With contractions five to ten minutes apart, I labored through another night, hoping at any moment I'd feel warm liquid pooling between my legs. Through every contraction, Pramod rubbed my back.

I have no memory of one strange incident I recorded:

> I ate some oranges. Aama yelled that I should not eat oranges. She considered eating fruit dangerous before, during, and after delivery. She's afraid to eat too many herself at any time. I kept eating oranges in defiance of everyone ...

How pitiful my rebellion had become.

Better than some other details, I remember waking on the morning of November 5. Perhaps the need to make a decision forced some clarity that would later serve memory. I saw worry etched on so many faces, that walk to the tempu through the crowd.

A blur of moments from the hospital: the sensation of an enema, a surreal shuffle through hallways, stopping now and then for a contraction and trying not to think about all the patients and their families crowded along the edge on straw mats, gratitude for a private room and horror at the stinky overflow in the attached squat toilet, and more gratitude that our nephews came from the local bazaar with new sheets to cover the vinyl cot.

What I see best is the tube in my right arm and the drip, drip, drip of pitocin that made my contractions more frequent. I stared at that tube for hours as though it were some torture device. If it would stop the pain, I'd have confessed anything. I might have handed over accomplices and named innocents too. Anything to get off that drip.

I remember being in the hallways again. Did I walk or was I wheeled? I see the straw mats again; the sick curled under thin blankets; family members holding hands, spooning tea into gaping mouths, crying. And then I am in the delivery room. The nurses did not tell Pramod to leave. The doctor who might have scolded him for being with me didn't show until the last few minutes. So Pramod continued holding my hand and stroking my sweat-drenched hair. With all I could muster of my waning strength, I pushed and pushed through the worst pain I've ever known. I screamed through one final push and then felt a sliding out and, finally, relief.

How does such unimaginable agony one moment finds its corollary in joy the next? My memory would circle around that miracle for years to come and try to filter out all the rest.

LITERACY

Our buffalo gave birth to a male, an economic loss for the family. Based on Pandit Kedarnath's prophecy, I should have given birth to a girl. That would have been another economic, as well as cultural, loss for the family. But before the sun set and the full moon rose on the last day of Chaturmas, I gave birth at Bharatpur Hospital to a borderline underweight, but otherwise healthy, boy. My child did not emerge as Mom always described my arrival: quiet and calm. He made himself heard as soon as he found air to gulp in and wail out.

I wanted to hold what still felt like a part of me but could not stop shaking. I let Pramod and the nurses tend my loud newborn and admired them all from a distance. The doctor did not linger, just long enough to supervise the nurses as they measured vital signs.

Back in my room, muscles finally relaxed, I breastfed my baby and then laid him on the narrow bed. I stretched out beside him. Pramod nestled against my back and leaned over me so we could both marvel at our child's sleep: closed eyelids fluttering, tiny pink lips puckering as though still on my nipple. We took turns stroking the fuzz on his head and talked about what people would say: not as much hair as a Nepali baby, but at least it's black. Though tired, I fought sleep for a while so as not to miss a single breath or twitch.

During my regular pregnancy checkups, Bhagvati had often teased in a mixture of Nepali and English that I'd love my baby more than my husband. I didn't believe then I could love anyone—especially an uncomfortable lump in my belly—more than Pramod and told her so. She laughed. "You'll see," she said. Now, I knew what she meant. It was a different love and hard to weigh against romantic or spousal love. And I loved Pramod more than ever for how he'd borne so much with me over the previous days. And he was with me still, waiting for me to sleep before he curled into a nearby chair with a blanket. But within hours of giving birth, I also knew that through the limits of our different languages, Bhagvati had tried to prepare me for a new emotion.

I did finally sleep some that night, the best sleep I would have for months to come. I returned home by Red Cross van the following day. For the next eleven days, I was treated as a *sutkeri*, a woman who has just delivered a baby. No adult Brahman, not even Aama, wanted to look at me or come near. Pramod arranged some compromises: I could sit on a chair, eat in the kitchen, and bathe (but only out of sight behind the house). Knowing how it might have gone—meals on a worn straw mat next to the buffaloes, wearing blood- and sweat-soaked clothes for days, dried blood matted between my legs—I was grateful. I was too tired to be anything else.

I wanted to believe Aama tried to uphold sutkeri pollution rules to protect her husband's ritual purity. I hoped she didn't believe in them herself. I remember searching her face for some hint of doubt there. But I couldn't see it.

Where life is tentative, children often don't receive names until they show strong signs of surviving. In Nepal, the naming ceremony takes place on the eleventh day following birth. But Pramod and I decided on names earlier. For the girl I imagined having, I had already chosen the name Yatri (Traveler). After all, my fetus had sprouted in Pune, announced its presence at the Taj Mahal, and then traveled to New Delhi, Goa, Bangalore, Mysore, and through the hills and plains of Nepal. I had grown so fond of Yatri that Pramod and I decided to keep it as a middle name. For a primary name, we wanted something more masculine and inspirational, something that echoed the idealism that brought us together. Pramod suggested Amalekh. From an Urdu root, the word refers to Nepal's 1921 emancipation of slaves, announced in a town in Nepal's plains that would, from then on, be known as Amalekhganj. I thought it sounded a little harsh, so Pramod softened the *kh* to *sh*, a subtle shift that makes sense in the Devanagari script.

Amalesh Yatri Parajuli, it was.

Like many first-time mothers, I was a bundle of mixed emotions. The euphoria right after birth quickly blurred into a kaleidoscope of wonder and worry. From there, emotions flattened into sheer exhaustion. For so long, the goal had been to have the baby. Now the baby was here and the goal for each day was to get through, keep the baby alive, breastfeed, snatch an hour of sleep here or there. Long used to independence and solitude, I felt trapped by both the unrelenting demands of a new being and the fear that I would lose him and be inconsolable.

My sutkeri pollution ended with Amalesh's Name-Giving ceremony on the eleventh day after his birth. Amalesh is an uncommon name in Nepal, so uncommon that Pandit Kedarnath believed it to be an American name. It is not unusual for a boy to get many names, so Pandit Kedarnath announced he would give Amalesh the option of a more common Nepali name, Purnendu (Full Moon). He had, after all, been born on the evening of the full moon—a significant full moon that ended the four-month season of divine slumber. After consulting his astrological charts, Pandit Kedarnath also chose a *rakhne nam*, a secret ritual name used only during special ceremonies.

Since family members perform particular roles in rituals, a priest not related to the family usually orchestrates. But our family priest sent word he could not make it. He had been suddenly called away to other business in the hills—a euphemism we understood to mean he got jittery about officiating for a half-caste boy. But, of course, he couldn't insult us outright by saying so. Pandit Kedarnath and his brother performed Amalesh's Name-Giving ceremony in our courtyard. They diagrammed the cosmos with colorful powders, built a fire in the middle, and gave offerings: rice, ghee, flowers. Then Pandit Kedarnath wrote his grandson's names—Yatri, Purnendu, Amalesh, and his rakhne nam—on a sal leaf. Despite all those beautiful names, most friends and relatives fell into the habit of calling Amalesh "Babu" when he was young. No matter what gets written on the leaf, it's what most boys are called in Nepal.

After the Name-Giving day, we all settled back into regular routines. I wanted to forget the labor and birth and move on to more practical matters. I needed to return to some work I could call research and slog through the daily demands of motherhood and my increasingly detached feelings for it. I probably suffered from some postpartum depression. Despite the books I consulted on everything else, I did not think to call it that at the time. I believed I should power through, climb out of my blues, just as I'd once hiked mountains or aced spelling tests. Except for those notes gushing out of my red pen several months later, I resisted thinking about or writing down many details of the labor and birth and eleven-day pollution period. I braved a scene here or there at times but didn't dare let memories wash over me all at once. I would not begin to hold all the pieces together in my mind until I witnessed another pregnancy and labor five years later.

Many in our family were eager to get on with community projects. So Pramod, Aama, Siddhi, Pramila, Radhika, and I walked and cycled around Gunjanagar to meet with women who said they wanted to learn to read and write. We asked them why.

"I want to be able to write down my own songs," Aama said.

"We need to read letters sent to us by our brothers and husbands," Magar, Tamang, and Gurung women said. For over 150 years, women in those ethnic groups had relied on letters to stay in touch with their men gone for months or years at a time as hired soldiers in the British or Indian armies.

"We need to read so we don't get cheated," sukumbasi women of various castes said. "We also want to learn adding and subtracting."

"We want to learn to read the Vedas," some Brahman women said. "Then we'll know if the old men are telling the truth or not."

Under the guidance of Siddhi and Pramod, Pramila and Radhika led the first class for about twenty women, mostly sukumbasi of various castes—Tamang, Tharu, Magar, Chhetri—plus two Brahmans, including Aama, from landowning families. The class met in the shed of a Tamang family across the pathway from the sukumbasi settlement.

Women sat in a circle on straw mats. On an easel, Pramila and Radhika propped a drawing of Nepali men and women in village dress laying bricks to build a house. They asked women what they saw. Without hesitation, many shouted the key word in unison: *kama* (work).

"What work do men do?" Pramila asked.

Women spoke all at once. "Plow . . . thresh . . . lay bricks . . . read books."

"Sometimes they help with planting . . ."

"Weeding! And harvesting too!"

"What work do women do?"

"Plant . . . weed . . . harvest . . . thresh . . . winnow . . . carry firewood and fodder . . . milk the buffaloes . . . cook . . . clean . . . give birth . . . breastfeed."

Dressed in the same blue school uniform she wore during the day, Pramila wrote the word *kama* in Devanagari script on a blackboard. She asked the women to copy the word in their notebooks. She then showed them how the word could be divided into two syllables—*ka* and *ma*—and how to change the vowel to form ka, *ki*, *ko*, *ku*, *ma*, *mo*, *mu*. In Nepali, each letter represents a full syllable rather than just a vowel or consonant, so this method works especially well.

"What other words could you make with these sounds?" she asked.

"*Kaka*! Father's brother."

"*Kaki*! Father's brother's wife."

"*Mama*! Mother's brother."

"*Maka*! Fly."

With women shouting them out, Pramila wrote down each word and asked women to copy them into their own notebooks. Then she pointed to words and asked women to read them. They did so with the kind of excitement anyone might feel in those first moments of learning a new skill. Women left the first night having learned to read and write a few words, words they themselves had thought of.

I wasn't sure then whether or how the literacy classes might fit into my research. But since they involved so many sukumbasi women, I knew I had to follow them.

At first, I brought Amalesh to the classes and breastfed him there when needed. Several other women also brought their children. The lessons and the conversations helped me improve my Nepali and also gave me deeper insights into women's lives and their similarities and differences across caste. But the cold, damp November and December nights made it increasingly difficult for all of us with children.

"You can't take him out in this cold," Aama said. Other women agreed. They told those of us with children to leave them at home on the coldest nights.

I tried, but just as the discussion grew rich and lively, a niece or nephew usually arrived to tell me Amalesh wouldn't stop crying. I usually fell asleep back home with Amalesh hanging off my nipple.

Since I could not sit through all the classes, I had to rely on Pramod to tell me what had happened. I cornered him every morning after a class I couldn't make and took notes.

One evening in the literacy class, Pramila and Radhika showed women a drawing of men playing cards.

"*Taas*," the women murmured.

Radhika wrote the word on the board.

"Men spend so much time on cards," someone said.

"It's true," said another. "Men waste money on gambling, drinking. They should use that money to feed their children."

"Or they waste the money, then come home and beat us."

"Or they beat the children."

"I brew liquor and then my husband drinks it or sells it for gambling money," said a Kami woman whose husband often stumbled through the village drunk.

"I brew liquor too," another sukumbasi woman said. "That's how I earn money. It's not so bad."

Most women, especially the few from landowning families, spoke about gambling and drinking in general terms rather than from their own personal experiences. And most agreed that they wanted to stop the worst excesses, especially men drinking and then beating up their wives and children.

Around that time, several sukumbasi women withdrew from the literacy class. Some faced pressure from their husbands, but others didn't like all the negative talk about how they supplemented their meager incomes.

The shed where the class met happened to be directly across from a shop in the sukumbasi settlement where men drank and played cards late into the night. Many men clustered outside the shed, listened in on the women's conversations, and commented in loud voices, disrupting the class. Some were curious or worried about the safety of their sisters, girlfriends, or wives. They told jokes to make the women laugh. Most did not seem to intend any harm. But a few chastised the women or tried to direct the lessons when they didn't approve of the discussions.

With women talking about gambling and drinking, more men gathered around the shed and interrupted the classes. Yelled at by students and their supporters, the disrupters drifted across the lane to the tea shop for a while, but then usually returned.

One night, a man who had urged his wife and daughter to take the class and helped us look for a meeting place intervened. "You should only study *ka, ki, ko, ku*. You better stop having all this talk."

He had a reputation for drinking and beating his wife. After that evening, he forbade his wife and daughter from returning to class. With that, the classes moved to our courtyard. Women no longer faced harassment, and I found the classes easier to attend.

Pramod planned to resume his research in India in early December. I convinced him to stay with me through Christmas. We celebrated with some American acquaintances living in a Western-style house on the agricultural campus in Rampur. I enjoyed a hot shower, chocolate chip cookies, English conversation, and zydeco tapes. But knowing Pramod would leave the next day for India, I stifled weepiness most of the day by eating more cookies and turning up the volume on the tape deck.

In Pramod's absence, I grew more tired and irritable. Amalesh woke several times each night, crying for my breast or exploding goo into his diaper. I had forgotten the satisfaction of uninterrupted sleep. My shoulders and back hurt from carrying him.

I wanted to savor new motherhood, but I also wanted my old self back. I could not think straight. I had become a lethargic, milk-dripping sack of drooping flesh. I knew it was a phase but wished I could get through it with some decadent comforts: a television to pass the time when I had no wits for anything else, pizzas and huge salads, hot and cold running water indoors, a sit-down toilet, central heating.

At the same time, I knew I was getting more help with a baby than I ever would back home. His cousins, aunts, uncles, and neighbors often tugged him out of my arms and soothed him. Women neighbors—some I hardly knew—took breaks from cutting grass and grazing livestock to stop at our house. With rough, soiled hands, they seized Amalesh and bounced him, cooed nonsense words, and blew raspberries on his tummy. I liked the relief but couldn't help worrying. Wouldn't people drop him or spread colds and coughs or worse through their runny noses? I had grown used to sanitation standards different from those back in the States but during those

first few months of motherhood, I could hardly bear my fear of dirt
and disease. Amalesh seemed so small and fragile. I wanted to care
for him by myself but hadn't the strength.

I couldn't walk anywhere without facing inevitable questions: Are
you sure you have enough milk in your breasts? Why do you bring
Babu out in this damp and cold? Shouldn't he be dressed warmer?
Shouldn't he be growing faster? Why doesn't he have more hair?

One day, on my way back from the sukumbasi settlement, a
Tamang woman whose son was a few days younger than Amalesh
challenged me to a contest. She could feed her son only on one
breast since the other had swollen with mastitis.

"This one can make more milk than both of yours," she said. She
lifted her blouse and squeezed the engorged breast. A stream of
milk arced over the courtyard. I laughed. Declining her challenge,
I agreed she was probably right. I fought back envy, wondering if
perhaps I was deficient as lactater and mother. But I had no mind
left to ponder such questions for long. I felt satisfied to get through
each day with a healthy baby.

By January, the mustard bloomed in yellow patches among fields
of ripening wheat. And the winter fog settled into the valley, barely
lifting in late afternoon before nestling back down in the evening.
The literacy classes continued infrequently through the cold season.
Burdened by household duties as well as family colds and flu, a few
more women dropped out. Others came intermittently. Each class
tended to have ten to fifteen students.

Two months after giving birth, I finished my survey of the sukumbasi households and decided to visit Pramod in India. I informed
him by telegram. With friends of a friend, I found a ride to Kathmandu in a jeep. From there I planned to take Amalesh with me on
an Air India flight to Patna and then a train across the Bihar plains
to the town of Madhupur in the heart of Jharkhand.

On the way to Kathmandu, we stopped at a dairy. My traveling companions, both development workers, had to check in on a

project. If I had not been so tired, I might have joined them, but I had no business there and hoped for some time alone.

Five women wandering by with hoes squatted under a nearby tree, puffed cigarettes, and stared at me. I knew from six months of living in Nepal that they expected some conversation. And I was an anthropologist. My job was to talk. Yet with windows rolled down for fresh air, I sat with my baby in the jeep and ignored them.

All I wanted was some space to daydream about urban life only hours away: hot showers, my friend Sita's spicy food, apple pies and cheese sandwiches at the German bakery in Lazimpat, a new *kurta salwaar* (tunic and drawstring pants) to replace my worn village clothes. With a haircut and a hot shower, I might even begin fantasizing about sex with my husband again. I knew I was being impolite, but I hadn't slept for more than a few hours at a time since the night before my forty-eight-hour labor began. I couldn't bear any more advice or questions about hats, sweaters, food, or breast milk production. For a few days, I wanted to be anonymous, invisible, ignored. I couldn't wait a few more hours.

Since I refused to talk, the women talked about me in Nepali.

"Eh! Look at this Amrikan with a baby."

"Is it a boy or a girl?"

"Who knows?"

"Maybe a boy?"

"Look at the black hair and eyes. Just like a Nepali."

"What do you think she feeds him?"

"Probably feeds him from a bottle. All Amrikan women do, right?"

"That's what I've heard. They don't give mother's milk."

"Do you think it's her baby?"

"Maybe not. Amrikan women don't like to have babies, do they?"

"No. Must be someone else's baby. Must be a Nepali baby."

"Such black hair and black eyes!"

I stepped out of the jeep with my child. "This is my son," I said in Nepali, holding back tears. "I gave birth to him in Bharatpur Hospital. His father is a Nepali. Our home is in Chitwan. I breastfeed him and have never needed to give him a bottle."

The women laughed and asked me to tell them more. We might have had a good conversation from there, but my jeep companions returned, and we resumed our journey. The incident troubled me over the next few hours. But once I reached Kathmandu and indulged in sit-down toilets, hot water, and tasty food, I forgot about it for a while. Yet how those women erased me from having anything to do with motherhood shook something loose in my stubborn head and opened me to new lessons over the next six weeks with Pramod in India. Humbled, I learned to allow the baby in my arms to initiate conversation rather than shut it down and to accept small kindnesses that both women and men showed to mothers. And I didn't miss a step in a tribal circle dance in Jharkhand as women pulled Amalesh from my arms and passed him around—his fuzzy yellow jumpsuit a startling contrast to the brown, wrinkled hands supporting his back.

GATHERINGS

I HANDED AMALESH, JUST four months old, to Pramila, stood up, and looked out from the verandah of the Panchayat office. At least 150 women clustered on the grass in the compound for Gunjanagar's first celebration of International Women's Day, an annual March event around the world. Some sat cross-legged. Others squatted, their feet flat on the ground. The Brahman and Chhetri women wore red, pink, and purple saris. The Tamang, Gurung, and Magar women wore T-shirts and flower- and dragon-printed lungis. The few Tharu women who sat on the margins in back wore green, white, and black midriff blouses and drab lungis. Those who could afford it wore their best. Others wore their faded, torn, everyday clothing. Some of the sukumbasi women carried their sickles and hoes with them, ready to return to work after the event.

Shading themselves with black umbrellas and colorful shawls, women squinted at me through the searing noonday sun. The literacy class had raised expectations. I saw hope in the women's faces and wondered how to meet it.

I gathered my thoughts. Pramod and I had returned from India the previous week. We'd met with indigenous activists and their supporters in Jharkhand. In Ranchi, Pramod had narrowly escaped an assassin's bomb meant for the leader he was interviewing. We had attended a women's conference in Patna and heard stories from women activists about saving trees, stopping big dams, and improving conditions for street sweepers and bricklayers. We had marched through the streets of Patna with the same women. We hoped to bring some of our renewed energy back to Gunjanagar.

My stomach fluttered. I held some notes I'd jotted down the day before. I didn't want to make a speech, but the organizers insisted. Pramod backed them. Academic and political activities at Stanford had improved my confidence in public speaking, but I had never considered myself a great orator. I also suspected that no matter how thoughtful and diplomatic, a speech from a middle-class, North American white woman to rural Nepali women would be tinged with imperialism, or at the very least paternalism. Pramod understood my qualms better than anyone but reminded me there was no room for ideological purity. After all, we had met several American and German women—now Indian citizens—giving speeches and working side by side with activists at the conference in Patna. Although I had once dreamed of being that dynamic, I sensed even then that I might need to forge a different path. But I had married into a politically active family in Gunjanagar and was expected to participate and make my opinions clear.

The event in Gunjanagar began predictably. Well-known women in the community—schoolteachers, student leaders, Panchayat officials, and women leaders known to be loyal to opposition parties—came forward to offer flowers to the pictures of the reigning monarchs, King Birendra and Queen Aishwarya, propped on the wooden table in front of the verandah. Some schoolgirls sang the national anthem. Then a half dozen or so women came forward with short speeches about how happy they were to celebrate International Women's Day for the first time in Gunjanagar. Male Panchayat leaders at one end of the verandah smiled and nodded their heads side to side. The event was going as planned.

Most women talked about "leaving darkness behind to enter the light of development." Better understanding Nepali, I was beginning to discern a speaker's political affiliation from other key phrases. For Nepali Congress supporters, the wording was "moving forward . . . claiming rights." For communists, "ending oppression . . . creating a

new world." In other parts of Nepal, where Panchayat supporters
were more powerful, such language might bring threats and warnings. But in Chitwan, where supporters of opposition parties had
become a majority, such talk was tolerated as long as the speaker
kept the rhetoric vague and linked to bikas.

Most Nepali Congress and communists later told me they usually refused to attend events organized by the village Panchayat. Too
boring, they said, with predictable speeches, polite clapping, and
little or no expected outcome except the enhancement of the status
quo. But scanning the faces of political, caste, and class diversity
before me, I sensed that this day might be different. Despite the
satisfied faces of Panchayat officials, I felt some excitement—maybe
even militancy—buzzing through the crowd.

"Women are half the population and do more than half the
work in the world," I began in English. Although I had improved
my Nepali, I did not yet have the confidence to make a speech
in the language. Pramod translated for me and added his own
embellishments.

"Yet for every hundred rupees earned by men, women earn just
ten. And for every hundred bighas (.67 hectares) of land owned by
men, women own just one. For every hour men work, women work
two."

Pausing to gauge reactions, I noticed some women smiling and
nodding their heads more. Others looked puzzled but interested.

"Even in America now, women are the poorest of the poor. Even
in America, husbands beat their wives. In every country of the
world, women are beaten . . ."

I noticed some sukumbasi women just below the verandah on
my left wiping tears from their eyes. My voice trailed off. Had I
reminded them of their own pain?

I rushed through the rest. "In Bodhgaya, women like you stopped
men from beating their wives. Then they fought to own farmland."

Activists in India had frequently pointed to the Bodhgaya movement in the late 1970s and early 1980s as a remarkable example of

women's power. Dalits, agricultural laborers, and other poor in the historic north Indian town had successfully organized a campaign forcing a powerful temple to redistribute its landholdings. Women rallied alongside men in the protests but pushed further to win titles to land in their own names. At the same time, they challenged men to equalize power in the family and end domestic violence.

The sukumbasi in front continued crying. My hands shook; my voice crackled.

"In the Chipko movement in the Indian Himalayas, women hugged trees and stopped men from cutting them down—" I heard my voice rise into a squeak and then fall into a whispery croak.

I rallied for the conclusion. "I don't know much yet about your lives and problems, but I hope you can come together to talk about them and change things. I'm so happy to be here with you celebrating International Women's Day."

Pramod took over and launched into "We Shall Overcome" in Nepali. Pramod and I had heard the Hindi version at rallies, demonstrations, and marches in India. Our family had spent hours the previous day translating the song into Nepali from what we could remember of the Hindi and English versions. Pramod began the song off-key. I joined him to try to regain the melody but could not project my singing voice far. To avert musical disaster, a visiting singer and activist from India came forward and projected his powerful, haunting voice over ours.

The song brought clapping and some cheers. Amalesh fidgeted in Pramila's arms, his face pruning toward a yowl. I retrieved him and sat down. He smiled, blew spit bubbles, and waved his fists in the air.

A heavyset woman with thin white hair pulled back in a tight bun stood and moved to the center of the verandah. She wore a sari customary to widows—white with small green flowers.

Pramod leaned over and whispered, "That's Ishwarya."

He had told me about her the previous day. She was a well-known Nepali Congress Party activist from a neighboring village, famed for her advocacy of women's and democratic rights. Before the event began, many women I talked to told me they were particularly excited that Ishwarya would be attending.

"She gives good speeches," they said.

I turned on a tape recorder I had bought in India. Ishwarya began.

"It is good that at least one day in a year is celebrated as Women's Day. Women can be very powerful. All men are born from women. In ancient times, women had an important role in society. Where there was a war between gods and devils, women were created as goddesses. By worshipping them, gods won battles."

She paused and scanned the nods and smiles in the crowd. The Panchayat officials on the verandah looked alert, but not alarmed. Having such an outspoken Nepali Congress advocate speaking at a Panchayat event was fine as long as she did not mention her party.

"Men cannot do justice to women's problems. For they are themselves afraid that their wives will become too strong. We have to explore our own problems, share and discuss with others what action can be taken. Men have tamed the society by keeping their own women silent. Husbands do not allow their women to come to the meetings."

She paused and looked out at the women again. Most leaned their bodies forward an inch or two, eager for her next words. Except for a few babies gurgling and fussing, people slapping at flies, and a goat bleating in the distance, silence reigned. Amalesh had fallen asleep.

"Here is a proposal for the village Panchayat. All pastureland is being distributed to various interest groups. So let them give four or five bighas (2.68 to 3.35 hectares) of land to women. Then we can start our own organization and a training program. Women's skills are not recognized and their potential is not explored—"

A few shouts and claps of support from the crowd interrupted her. Soon others joined in a thunderous wave of support. Ishwarya smiled and looked over at the male Panchayat officials. They sat on the edges of their seats as if ready to intervene should the crowd become unruly.

The noise died down. Ishwarya continued.

"The money allocated by His Majesty has not trickled down to the village level. It has to come down to our level. People spend so much money on elections but nobody thinks about initiating some program for women. We should exercise our voting privilege and elect better and pro-women candidates. Only when women are united can that be done.

"If women also had land and skills, then at last women could educate their daughters. We should not spend so much money on jewelry and silk saris. Women are half the country. When that half is dark, half of the country will also be dark. Let us work together to develop a women's center in Gunjanagar."

Shouting and clapping, women in the audience jumped to their feet. Ishwarya nodded her head toward them. Eyes wide and heads shaking, the male leaders looked at one another as if to ask: What happened here? We didn't plan this.

Several more women spoke after Ishwarya. Like the first few speakers of the day, they all began by calling for women's development and women's rights. Then each finished her speech to wild applause by echoing Ishwarya's words: "Give us land for a women's center."

An individual challenge had exploded into a collective demand.

At the end of the event, a few men spoke in support of women's development and the need to move forward but gave no specifics. And none responded to the demand for land for a women's center. Each ended his speech to polite clapping and glanced at Ishwarya. She glared back.

The last speaker, a man, ended on a more domestic note.

"There will be a class for all women next Tuesday at Rampur College. You will learn how to preserve food. You should all come and learn to uplift yourselves. Thank you."

The day after the women's meeting, I followed the smell of burning food into the kitchen. Pots boiled over, the drips sizzling and snapping in the wood fire. I rushed to intervene, then stopped. I was no longer polluted by pregnancy, but I would never be a Brahman.

Aama squatted on the bench next to the table, sari-covered legs drawn up in front of her. She hummed softly to herself and looked out the window grills into the sunny courtyard.

"Aama! The rice! The dal! Look!" Hard of hearing, she didn't look up. And since her peripheral vision was also deteriorating, she couldn't see me. I would need to lean over and wave my arms in front of her, but I heard her sing a line and hesitated. She repeated the same line with a different word at the end. "No, that's not it." Then she hummed the first line again.

Pramod had told me that Aama loved composing songs and poems. Over the months I'd been staying in the house, she may have been doing so, but I was too clueless to recognize the activity. So, seeing this now—an old Brahman woman lost in the creative process while our breakfast burned—stunned me.

I had noticed how Aama valued songs she'd already composed. Sometimes when telling a story about her life, she'd sing a fragment. But she couldn't recall most of her songs. "Go find it, Nani. Go find it, Babu," she'd say to whatever granddaughter, son, or grandson sat nearby. It was usually Pramila who knew which copybook to look in. Aama might have one song in Pramila's algebra copybook, another in Udaya's English copybook, and so on: snatches of her creativity scattered in notebooks stacked in cupboards or piled among dust balls underneath beds. When the copybook was found, she would ask someone to read the song to her. Then she would sing it and go on with the story she was telling.

I shouldn't have been so surprised that Aama's mind might wander from cooking. She'd complained about it before, how she didn't enjoy it the way she used to. She wished she had a good daughter-in-law who could do the work. Old men, like Pandit Kedarnath, could let go of the householder role and become ascetics. Why shouldn't she get a break from household responsibilities too? But with Sakuntala having moved out and only Pramila staying on, she often ended up cooking.

Part of me wanted to join Aama on the bench, know what she was singing, maybe learn to make some songs myself. But as a young daughter-in-law, firmly in the householder stage, I had a responsibility to make sure breakfast and the house didn't burn. And, of course, if I touched it, the food would be worse than burnt.

"Aama! Look!" I leaned in front of her and pointed toward the pots on the fire. She saw me and smiled. I pointed again at the stove. She looked past me toward the fire. For a moment, she seemed stuck in some other world. Then awareness dawned. She snapped out of her reverie, jumped up from the bench, and pulled the pressure cooker and pot off the flame.

"I was just making a song," she said, scrunching up her shoulders. She wagged her head and laughed. "Now look. Everything is burnt."

Before sitting down to eat, Pandit Kedarnath broke his usual mealtime silence. "I'm not surprised," he said, smiling. "She's been humming and making rhymes all night. Kept me awake. Must be all the excitement from yesterday." Pandit Kedarnath had not attended but seemed pleased by the event and the women's enthusiasm.

We made faces through every bite of the meal—worse even than weeks of boiled taro leaves the summer before. But Aama didn't apologize. She tried out her new rhymes on us.

I can't remember which song she composed that morning. I like to think it was this one:

> Listen, listen sisters, something I will say:
> I will tell the story of illiterate women.
> We must express our hearts' feeling:
> We are like orphans without writing and reading.

"That's the first part. Does it work or not?"

"Yes, of course, it works," Pramod said.

Bua looked up from his meal and grinned. I sensed some pride there.

"How about this?" Aama sang the next part:

> I took four measures of rice, that I remember,
> But gave a fifty note, thinking it to be a tenner.

We don't know how to do daily dealing.
Even then the old women keep us from reading.

"It's very good," Pramod said. "You must write it down."

We gulped the rest of our food quickly so as not to taste it and then left the kitchen where the burnt smell lingered.

Pramod and I sat on the verandah. Soon, Siddhi arrived. He and Pramod debated the merits of a women's center. Why had that solution caught everyone's imagination so much? Why not focus on inheritance rights? Or domestic violence?

We heard Aama's humming voice, stopping and starting from the kitchen, still working out rhymes.

"Is there more domestic violence in some castes than others?" I asked. I had begun asking the question in various circles. But I tried to be non-intrusive, so I slipped it into conversations only when others brought it up.

"Less among Gurungs, Magars, Tamangs," Siddhi said.

"Why?"

"Notice how women and men walk—" Pramod began.

Aama appeared in the kitchen doorway.

"How about this? Does this work?"

To develop our village, let's go ahead,
Open a night school and always read.
We lose in dealings 'cause we don't know counting.
Without being lazy, let's start reading.

"Yes, yes," Pramod and Siddhi said. "It works. Where's Pramila? Get her to write it for you before you forget."

The day after most literacy classes, I had often seen Aama sitting on a cot on the verandah or in her bedroom, bent over a notebook, her hands slowly pushing a pen to form Devanagari letters, their loops large and uneven. But she tired easily because of arthritic hands and failing eyesight. She might labor for several hours to write one page, but she persisted when she felt compelled. But more often than not, her ideas still outran her fingers and she had to rely on others to write for her.

"I don't know," Aama said and disappeared into the kitchen.

"Back to what you were saying . . . something about women and men walking?" I said to Pramod.

"Right. You've seen it, I think, how Gurung, Magar, and Tamang women walk in front, carrying a small bag. Men walk behind carrying the baby and a larger bag. But Brahman-Chhetri men always walk in front looking smart and carrying nothing. Their women walk behind carrying heavy loads and children."

We laughed.

"What about Tharus?" I asked.

"They're more equal too," Siddhi said. "There's a saying . . . have you heard it? Tharu women give their husbands rice with their feet."

I thought of Tharu women I'd met with their straight backs, pride, muscled legs and arms. I imagined them shoving plates of rice toward their husbands with their bare, field-worn feet—a sure sign of disrespect. I doubt many did that, but I understood what was meant: Tharu women did not defer to their husbands as much as Brahman women did.

"I think Brahman women suffer lots of ideological violence and some physical violence," Pramod said. "Dalit women suffer—"

Aama appeared again.

"Chup," she said. "Be quiet and listen to this part."

> Taking the rest we need, let's work the whole day.
> Let's learn to count up to a hundred this way.
> That I am too old to read, nobody say.
> Let's learn to count up to a hundred this way.

"That's it," Aama said. "That's the whole song. Or do you think I should add more? Maybe something more about the poor? Remember that song about the poor eating nettles? Where's that one?"

Before anyone could answer, she returned to the kitchen. Pramila rode up on her bicycle. She had been talking with other women about yesterday's meeting and wanted to share her gleanings with us.

"Go help your grandmother first," Pramod said, nodding toward the kitchen. Pramila obeyed.

"You were saying . . . about ideological violence?" I said.

"Well, maybe not Aama," Pramod said. "But Brahman women suffer the most violence ideologically. Dalit women suffer less violence from patriarchal ideology and more from physical violence. It's just a theory—"

Aama and other women were eager to follow up on ideas sparked at International Women's Day. But the ongoing wedding season distracted us all for several weeks.

No weddings can take place during the four months of Chaturmas. Then November, December, and January are cold. So by February and March, those families planning weddings are eager to get on with things.

The first wedding I attended gathered guests without much ado. Pramod and I were sitting on the verandah drinking tea. We heard voices approaching, growing louder and louder. We walked out to the path to see a merry, mixed-caste crowd.

"There's a wedding, a Tamang wedding," one told us. Several held half-drunk bottles.

"Join us," they said. "There will be dancing, drinking, maza [fun]." We caught up with the wedding party walking across the pasture. Dressed in everyday clothes, the bride and groom walked side by side. Men carried baskets of plates and food.

We asked others in the procession why we hadn't heard about the wedding before.

"These two have been living together five years. With two children now, they decided it was time to marry."

We gathered at the bride's maternal home. She hadn't been living there, but with her lover and their children on the other side of the pasture, several minutes' walk away.

Men sat in a large circle and feasted on buffalo meat, rice, and *rakshi* (home-brewed liquor). When they were done, women did the same. The bride sat comfortably with a few other relatives on the verandah and nursed her infant.

After the meal, I sat with others and asked about the relations. Cross-cousins, they told me. I recognized the parallels in Brahman kinship terms. It would be like our chora-chori marrying our bhanja-bhanji: children of a brother marrying children of his sister. My mind did the calculations: Like Siddhi's daughter, say, Sharmila, marrying Pramod's sister's son, say, Anil?

I must have internalized enough of Brahman morality—or my own culture's jokes about kissing cousins—to look shocked. The Tamangs laughed the way they often did at Brahman stuffiness.

Their families were strong because they married like that, they told me. And their daughters never lived far from their maiti. Everybody stayed *close*.

"Yote ho," they said, again and again. "We are all one."

The families exchanged no dowry. The bride's family gave nothing to the groom's family. The groom's father presented a shawl to the bride's mother and fifty rupees to her father—bride-price, not dowry. Both sides chipped in for food and rakshi.

After the meal, women sang and men danced. On other occasions, some told me, men sing and women dance. Everyone, including the bride and groom, laughed and shouted for more merriment.

A few other Brahman men and women sat with us. I knew Brahman weddings involved more formalities and asked them what they thought of this Tamang wedding.

"It's fun for us to see," they said.

"But would you marry your own sons or daughters in a simple ceremony like this?"

Responses ranged from "Oh we wish we could, but it's not possible" to "Never" and then they steered the conversation in other directions.

Several days after the Tamang wedding, Vijaya, a progressive Nepali Congress Party activist, invited us to his son's wedding. The bride was the daughter of the mayor of a neighboring village. After festivities at the groom's house, a Damai band played the wedding party on board a rented Tata bus, and then climbed on top and continued the music. The groom wiped dust off the front seat and sat. The rest of us, including Pramod and me carrying Amalesh, piled in behind. The bus lurched over potholes along back lanes and then sped down the road leading toward the national park, though we wouldn't go that far.

Whenever another vehicle passed, we shut the windows to keep out dust. Then we opened them again for cool breezes. Pramod reminisced with others about older wedding traditions with hand-carried sedans and strolling minstrels in the hills. At each village, the wedding party would be greeted by people throwing rice, he said.

Our noisy bus reached the bride's house at sunset. Despite our efforts, we all had a layer of gray on our festive clothing. The band climbed down from the top of the bus and led the groom's party to the courtyard gate. The groom entered and stood to one side under a red canopy. Dressed in a beaded red sari with head bowed and face veiled, the bride stepped out of her father's large cement house. Pouring water from a brass jug, she circled the groom three times and then stopped for him to put a ring on her finger. After the bride returned inside, her family formally invited the rest of in through the gate as the crowd threw red-stained rice.

We sat at a long table for a spicy vegetarian feast. An earlier meal at the groom's house hadn't settled well, so I didn't eat much. After dinner, some men danced. Others headed off to drink and gamble at shops along the main road. The bride, groom, and relatives took their places again for the main ceremonies.

I didn't last long. I had to nurse Amalesh and put him to sleep and try to calm my churning gut. Pramod found a room for me to rest in. I trudged to the pit latrine many times throughout the night.

When at the University of Washington or Stanford dreaming about myself as an anthropologist in some far-off place, I had imagined some exotic kind of belonging but hadn't thought through what the daily work would be like. There are the formal interviews and surveys, like the ones I did with sukumbasi. But the heart of the profession has always been participant-observation. We remove ourselves from the comfort of our own culture and learn to live as closely as possible in another. Mastering the art of hanging out, we spend entire days sitting and watching, learning to read body language and facial expressions and how they match or contradict what is said. We can't always be sure what will be meaningful, so we observe and note it all. If one were to make a movie of what we do for hours each day, it would look like most people's daily lives: dull, unheroic, unworthy of a narrative arc. After a long day of observing, we retreat to our rooms for more tedium. Hunched over a notebook beside a lantern's glow, we write up our observations. After months of such work, there is a payoff. Clifford Geertz called it "thick description." We understand nuances that no casual tourist would ever pick up on. We're in on the jokes. And we learn what to look for and what questions to ask to dig deeper.

My childhood and introverted nature had prepared me well for the wallflower, fly-on-the-wall aspect of anthropology. I found myself reasonably adept at those long stretches of bench-sitting and people-watching. And like many introverts, I was a good observer. But that ability to sit quiet and alone for long periods also gave me a wandering mind, an inability to make small talk (especially in another language), and a distaste for mingling in crowds, especially at night when I was tired. So I became grateful for excuses—a nursing infant, a new mother's need for sleep, and, yes, even explosive diarrhea—that let me leave work early sometimes.

Still, there was something about observing weddings and taking notes on them that made me feel that I had begun to master the art of being an anthropologist. I wasn't sure how weddings related to my sukumbasi research, but I figured they might at least illuminate another facet of gender relations. In any case, they made me feel more like a professional.

As pit latrines go, the one I used during the night of that Brahman wedding was relatively clean. But whether in the States or Nepal, the mess underneath is the same. Before dawn, I made another trip there. Fumbling with my sari, I dropped the flashlight. A muffled splash followed. Knowing the way well after so many trips, I shuffled back to our room in the dark.

At seven, the bus arrived to return us to Gunjanagar. The bride's brother carried her to the bus. Underneath the veil, she wept loudly. Men loaded dowry items atop the bus and secured them with ropes.

As we pulled up to the groom's house, relatives and neighbors swarmed. Men arranged the dowry items for show in the courtyard: a wooden bed, a woven mat, a thick mattress, a sheet, a quilt, a pillow, two wooden chairs, a modern sofa set with red brocade upholstery, stainless steel dishware (plates, cups, water jugs), cooking pots, a pressure cooker, a thermos, one wooden wardrobe with a mirror, and a cow (though the latter didn't come by bus).

The bride was led to the sofa, where she sat with her veiled head hanging down. Female relatives of the groom as well as curious neighbors inspected her and all the dowry goods. Those closest to the groom (aunts, sisters, sisters-in-law) bent down and peered closely, then commented loudly on her features and jewelry.

"If the bride isn't beautiful, the dowry should be more," someone whispered in my ear. "If she's beautiful, then it can be less."

I didn't know enough about dowries or ideals of beauty to know where this bride fell in the calculation and didn't join the other women for a close-up view. Soon the groom's mother came out of the house and welcomed her new daughter-in-law inside. The crowd dispersed. Pramod, Amalesh, and I walked home. I had sleep to catch up on, and my stomach cramps were getting worse.

Before I knew something of Brahman weddings, I had vaguely expected Pramod's family to sponsor some ceremony for us in Nepal. With both rituals and weddings being popular in Nepal, I assumed local nuptials inevitable. I wondered why there was never talk of a wedding for us, mostly to myself, but sometimes aloud. Family members, even Pramod, averted their eyes and steered the conversation elsewhere.

Unconsciously, I think I knew the reason, but I must have dropped a few too many hints. Finally Pramod said, "Listen. The family accepts you and loves you as a Brahman wife and daughter-in-law. But they will never, ever perform a *kanyadan* for us. And they are too polite to say why."

So, of course, I wondered why, especially after attending a Brahman wedding. I turned once again to *Dangerous Wives and Sacred Sisters*.

The part of the wedding I had missed seeing was the climax: dan—the central ritual exchange. Dan can be any religious offering given by a human to a god or by a lower-status person to a higher-status person. What's most important is that the gift be pure. In marriage, of course, the gift is pure only if it is virgin—*kanya*. Since I was not a virgin when I married Pramod, the family could not perform kanyadan for us.

Dan takes place in the early morning hours at the groom's house. All relatives, in their descending relation to the marriage partners, give money and jewelry to the bride and wash the feet of both bride and groom. The foot-washing water is considered *prasada* —a blessed substance. Touching it transmits a small portion of the divine merit the bride's parents earn by bestowing their virgin daughter.

The bride attains her highest ritual status immediately before and after the gifting. Water dripping off her feet will never again be so valuable. After, the groom gives his bride makeup, saris, jewelry. Then, through more rituals and recitations, the father formally hands over his daughter. Ritual games follow and provoke increasing intimacy between husband and wife.

In 1988, Brahman parents still arranged most marriages I heard about in Nepal. In some cases—mostly in urban, educated families—they facilitated meetings and let the young people weigh in and choose. But more often—at least as far as I could see—young people only met a few times, if at all, before the wedding. So those ritual wedding games compressed courtship into an hour or so. Some friends who fell in love with their spouses through arranged marriages later told me they felt the first sparks of affection and passion during those games.

After ceremonial flirtations, the groom places a vermilion tika on his bride's forehead. Bennett calls it a symbolic defloration. Immediately after, the bride touches her husband's feet and takes her new place at his left—the less honored position. The next day, when she sits among the dowry items, her symbolic subordination to the entire family is sealed.

"What are you writing?" Aama flipped off her sandals and squatted beside me and Pramod on the cot on the verandah.

"Some notes on Vijaya's son's wedding," I said. "I'm listing all the things the bride's family gave in dowry."

Several days had gone by, and I had to catch up on my notes. Still queasy, I had diagnosed myself with giardia and bought some metronidazole at a chemist shop in Chanauli.

"For my wedding, Father gave six copper pots, three water jugs, one cow for my dowry, and a gold ring for your bua . . ."

I finished the sentence I was writing and began jotting down Aama's commentary.

"There was no cash involved in those days," Aama said.

"That was a good dowry then," Pramod said.

"For *pewa*, he gave me five measures of gold jewelry."

"Pewa?" I asked.

"That's separate from dowry," Pramod said. "A gift the parents give to the bride. It's her own personal property."

"That was a good pewa. And then when Father and my brothers divided the family property into separate parcels, he gave each of us daughters another hundred rupees. That wasn't by law or custom. He was just generous."

"It's good for women to have pewa," Pramod said.

"Sure is," Aama said. "I sold some of my gold jewelry later to buy more land for the family in Kahung. That was my choice."

"We needed that extra land," Pramod said.

"I wanted to do it," she said. "The things to give for dowry or pewa are cows, gold, copper—things that last a long time and increase in value."

"Like those copper pots you keep locked in the cupboard?" I asked.

"Yes. They'll go to my grandchildren when I die."

She paused and then continued. "These days, the dowries have no lasting value. By the time the sons separate, the items will be worn-out."

"So true," Pramod said. "It's all these middle-class values coming in. People are showing off prestige and status."

I hadn't heard of dowry deaths occurring in Nepal. When we were in India, activists often talked about the growing numbers of women being killed by in-laws for not meeting dowry demands. Although the media often blamed the deaths on backwardness and ignorance among the poor, some scholars documented patterns linking them to the rise of the middle class. With more emphasis on throwaway commodities, women had become another disposable item. Kanyadan had long ritualized the subjugation of women, but the way it had been practiced traditionally at least equated them with a valuable, long-lasting wealth rather than with the disposable riches of the new global economy.

That afternoon, Vijaya shuffled into the compound. He always walked stooped over with a cane and had to peer closely at things to see them, even through wire-rimmed glasses. But that day, he seemed slower and more bent than usual. We hauled some chairs into the shade so he could light a cigarette away from the house.

"My wife and others complain the dowry is poor. 'Where is the gold chain for the groom?' he said, mocking his wife's screeching voice. 'Where is the gold ring for me?'"

He paused and coughed. "As for me, I wish the bride's parents had not given so many useless things. I asked them to put some money in the bank for their daughter. But no one listens to my opinions. Everyone in my family argues with me. My wife is so materialistic. And others are looking for dowries like this."

He listed names of some prominent Brahman families, counting each one off with a curled finger.

And, he told us, his wife and older buharis had already started riding the young daughter-in-law harder than he liked to see.

A good friend of the family, Vijaya had always struck me as more progressive than other Nepali Congress men of his generation. He and Pramod agreed on most issues. Vijaya talked often about his idol, Mahatma Gandhi, and described a future Nepal where equality would reign among castes and genders. And he had always been kind to me, as if to make up for the judgments of conservative Brahmans in the village. Still, his bitterness surprised me. By then, I had met many women and men who talked the progressive talk, but I could usually predict where their limits were. Siddhi was actively looking for a husband for Sharmila and asking around for Pramila too. Tirtha had married his eldest daughter, Anubha, in early adolescence, even though she had begged to go to college in India first. She gave birth to a daughter around the same time I had Amalesh. But Vijaya was one of those rare men in the village who continued to surprise and delight me with his views and actions.

He went on to share his thoughts on land rights and how the dowry system should be abolished and replaced with a more comprehensive system wherein women would have legal rights to pewa, which would include not only money but also land.

After Vijaya left, I asked Pramod why such a well-respected, progressive man had so little say in his own family. Pramod reminded me of Vijaya's wife. She was one of the loudest, bossiest women I had met in Gunjanagar. She flew into rages at him, her daughters-in-law, and her sons. She didn't support Vijaya's dreams of reform and equality. Yet it was her skill and energy in running the household that freed him up to spend his days talking about social change. And so, on family matters, Vijaya bowed to his wife.

As the wedding season continued, women who had attended the International Women's Day celebration dropped by and shared opinions and stories. Many agreed with Vijaya about the problem of escalating dowries and the devaluing of women. Women should have more rights in property, they said. Having a women's center would give women a place to talk about and fix all that. But talk of politics always petered out, and we returned to the wedding gossip: Who was next? Where was the wedding with the most fun?

One afternoon, I described to some visiting Brahman women how I had slept through a kanyadan and gotten sick. I felt better after taking medicine but still tender. They laughed, slapped me on the knee and shoulder, and said, "You know a wedding is good when people get the runs."

"There's another Brahman wedding soon," someone said and rattled off the names of those involved. I didn't recognize them.

"Don't worry," another said. "You can be our guests. And this time, skip the kanyadan and come for the real fun: *ratauli*."

Women in the groom's party—family and friends—stay at home when the men of the family headed off to fetch the bride. All night long, they celebrate the wedding taking place elsewhere by dancing and singing. Women's giddy anticipation of ratauli reminded me of the atmosphere around Tij. They dressed up in their finery

and shooed the men away. Yet while men could skirt the edges of
Tij festivities, they were not allowed near a ratauli. Some of my
male relatives claimed they had never seen a ratauli and could
not tell me what women did there, although they shyly acknowl-
edged it was very sexy. Women and girls giggled about ratauli but
wouldn't describe specifics either. Even if those usually modest
women had described it, I wouldn't have believed it without seeing for myself.

I dressed in a sari and walked with Aama and other women to
a home about twenty minutes from ours. As night fell, women lit
kerosene lanterns in the courtyard and milled about for a while.
Finally, someone began a song. Others joined. Soon one woman,
and then others, danced.

I didn't follow all the lyrics, but as the night wore on, the moves
translated clearly. Women swayed their hips more than at Tij and
undulated their bellies, bared between midriff blouses and saris.
They pulled me up to join in.

I had long considered myself a good dancer. I'd taken folk-
dancing lessons as a child, performed in a folk-dance troupe at
Stanford, and was often one of the first on the floor at graduate
student parties. By that spring, I had developed a passable inter-
pretation of generic Nepali dance—some pivots with alternating
snake arms and wrist curls. I danced like that through one ratauli
song while other women shimmied and swayed around me. Then I
tried to stand on the margins to watch, but several strong women
pulled me into another dance. They pushed me toward a large Brahman woman I didn't know. By day, she'd be the kind to frown and
shoo me away from cooked rice. But now she circled me with come-
hither looks and smiles. Another woman handed her something I
couldn't see in the dark. She put it between her thighs, sashayed
closer, and—boom—thrust her pelvis at me on the beat. *Boom.*
Boom. Twirling this way and that, I backed away from her large
saried hips moving ever closer. She kept thrusting. *Boom. Boom.*
Boom. At one point, she pinned me against some other women

and—*boom*—pressed whatever it was she had between her legs toward my crotch. I swiveled at the last minute so it hit my thigh.

Women howled and ululated.

The music stopped. The large woman took the object from between her thighs and showed it to me: a dry corncob. She squeezed my arm and laughed. The music started again. She danced off toward the others. I saw other women with corncobs strutting toward me and looked for an escape. I saw some older women sitting on the edge of the compound in chairs. I rushed over and sat down. Others urged me up, but I feigned exhaustion.

As the night wore on, the sexual role-playing escalated. Some women dressed as men and gently seduced or tried to force themselves on women. Some playing women succumbed, resisted, or rejected the men. Others chased after the "men" and offered their breasts, breast milk, and pelvic thrusts.

It's all in good fun, women told me. We make fun of men, they said, but we also show our enjoyment of . . . well, you know. Some of the older women told me they didn't like how women got carried away with corncobs and rude gestures. From time to time, they shouted at other women to cut out the silliness, dance more decently, sing morally uplifting songs. But other women laughed them off. The sexy dancing continued throughout the night.

I shook my hand, sore from writing, and tickled Amalesh, who lay beside me on the verandah cot. He smiled and cycled his arms and legs.

After another full day, I rushed to finish my March 21 journal entry: "This should never have happened . . ."

Girlish chatter. The first students walked through the gate, pulled straw mats out from under the eaves of the shed, and arranged them in a semicircle facing the verandah. Pramila set up the chalkboard and an easel in front. Radhika lit kerosene lanterns and set them around the circle.

Copybook in hand, the only other Brahman student besides Aama walked through the gate. Sanumaya moved with that combination of peasant solidity and grace I was learning to admire in Brahman women. She usually wore a faded, red cotton sari frayed by fieldwork. I hadn't talked to her much before, but couldn't stop thinking about her now.

She had come by earlier that morning to show us a dog bite on her leg. Back from India for three weeks, I'd been pushed again into my daily role as local health advisor. Watery eyes, glaucoma, cataracts. Undefined coughs, bronchitis, pneumonia, tuberculosis. Fevers. Diarrhea. Bowel movements like goat turds. Itchy fungus infections, foul-smelling vaginal secretions. Too few periods, too little blood. Too many periods, too much blood. Burns: first-, second-, third-degree. Children's heads covered in pus-filled sores. Scabs. Impetigo. Compared to all that, the wound on Sanumaya's leg didn't look too bad. It was several weeks old. She told me the doctor had already ruled out rabies and cleaned the wound. It was healing well with no redness or swelling.

We talked about the dangers of feral dogs in the village, how one should be careful walking at night. In my American way, I wondered to myself why Sanumaya had come. Was this an excuse for visiting? Sanumaya must have sensed my question.

"My leg is nothing," she said. "It's my daughter. She almost died. Can you come see her?"

Pramod and I went that afternoon. Indira lay on a cot on the verandah, wrapped in a shawl, shivering.

"She's better than she was, but she's still not well," Sanumaya said.

Indira sat up and unwrapped the shawl to reveal a white patchy rash on her neck and chest. I hadn't seen pellagra before but had read about it in *Where There Is No Doctor*. Her skin was sunken between her facial bones. Haunted and hollowed out, Indira lay back down again.

Sanumaya told us the story. Indira had delivered her second girl three weeks earlier. Like most Brahman woman, she had given birth in her ghar, attended only by her in-laws.

Like every Brahman mother, Sanumaya worried about her daughter giving birth but accepted that she could not be there. Then the news came: six days after giving birth, Indira had developed a fever. So Sanumaya traveled by bus and foot to her daughter's ghar.

Less than a year in the village, and I knew the rest of the story. Everyone did. My midwife, Bhagvati, had told me how common it was. Brahmans and Chhetris often denied food to a woman who had given birth to a girl, especially a second, third, or—goddess forbid—fourth girl. And they denied medical treatment for infections. Later that spring, we would hear of a Gunjanagar woman, about the same age as Indira, who died in similar circumstances.

Indira looked like she had been malnourished long before she gave birth. Sanumaya said her ghar was not poor. They had plenty of food.

Sometimes, they were the worst, Bhagvati had told me.

"If I hadn't gone to fetch her, she would have died," Sanumaya said. "I'm sure of it, the way they mistreated her."

Sanumaya had taken Indira and the weak newborn to Bharatpur Hospital. I shuddered to think how difficult that trip must have been on foot and by bus. But that's how villagers had to go, even when feverish or dying. Sanumaya showed us the medicine the doctor had prescribed: some ampicillin, a painkiller, glucose, and a large bottle of tonic, the main ingredient being sugar plus traces of iron and vitamin B.

"They told us to buy this," Sanumaya said. "They didn't explain anything. I brought my daughter back here to care for her. She might have died in her ghar."

The baby slept in a small cradle hanging from the rafters. Very small, she glistened from the mustard oil many villagers rubbed on infants. Unfortunately, the oil attracted dust in the dry season. Pus oozed out of her eyes. Her stomach looked full, though Sanumaya said she was worried that Indira was not lactating well and the baby was too weak to drink much buffalo milk.

We suggested the usual for Indira: better food, including plenty of protein such as eggs, milk, and dal, plus some nonsugary iron and vitamin B supplement. After several weeks of that and more rest, she would be well enough to return to her ghar.

"Just seventeen years old," Sanumaya said. "I wanted to educate her, but my husband married her off at fifteen. And now she has two daughters."

At class that evening, Sanumaya set her things down on a straw mat. Other women already sat cross-legged and had opened their copybooks, ready to begin. Pramila and Radhika put a drawing on the easel.

"Wait," Sanumaya said. "I have a song to share. I wrote it this afternoon." She sang in a confident voice.

> Sisters! Let's march ahead united.
> Subordinated for so long, how can we endure it?
> What is left to bear? We have borne everything.
> United, let us end women's oppression.
>
> This sinful society does injustice to women,
> Always subordinated, always in sorrow, always in chains.
> In our house of birth, brothers remain
> While we leave for another's dominion.
>
> For our brothers, our father's wealth,
> For a daughter, leaving her maiti, which house?
> Children of the same parents,
> Sons and daughters are the same.
> But when the daughter goes away,
> The son remains.
>
> Like cow-gifting, kanyadan is animal-like.
> Add to that child marriage—curse these customs!
> Kanyadan purifies mother and father of sins,
> Or so they say,

But you see,
Kanyadan is for their own gain.

She dabbed tears from her eyes. Listeners wiped theirs too. Hearing her strong voice, more a raspy Maybelle Carter than a warbling Joan Baez, I vaguely remembered her dancing at Tij. With chipped fingernails, cracked heels, and rough cotton saris, she was the opposite of what people called *nakli*—fashion-conscious. But singing and dancing transformed her into the kind of woman others moved aside for.

She told the class what had happened to her daughter, what we had seen earlier that day.

Amalesh fussed. I closed my journal, put him to my breast, and reminded myself to ask Sanumaya for a copy of her song.

MEETING SPACES

SEVERAL WEEKS after the International Women's Day celebration, over one hundred women finally found time between
weddings to gather at a chautari between our house and the main
road. The public resting place was modest, with trees too young to
cast much shade and the earth underneath not yet mounded high or
buttressed with stone. But since the day was cloudy and the season
still relatively cool, that chautari was enough. Off the main lanes
through Gunjanagar, it also gave us some seclusion.

A few Brahman Nepali Congress women spoke. Women need
more than these chautari, they said. They need a proper women's
center for meeting and training. The challenge will be to get the land
for it. Let's petition the village Panchayat to set aside a small parcel
of the public pasture for us.

A breeze that swayed the branches at the beginning of the meeting amplified during the speeches. Pramila and I had planned a
moment to lead women from the literacy class in singing "We Shall
Overcome" in Nepali. But midway through the meeting, black
thunderheads surged toward us. Women in the crowd stopped
listening to watch the clouds loom darker, larger, and ever closer.
Some women stood, gathered their belongings, and opened the
black umbrellas they carried as sunshades. Wind gusts flipped their
umbrellas inside out. Knowing how quickly a hard rain turns the
pathways to rivers, women hurried away.

In the chaos, a sukumbasi woman, Dilmaya Sarki, shouted. "See, everyone! This is why we need a meeting place. We have no place to take shelter from the wind and rain. Don't run away yet!"

Middle-aged Dilmaya had features Brahmans could have admired: a pointy nose, high cheekbones. But unlike most Brahmans, the Dalit woman had skin as dark as any I'd seen in Nepal.

Some women turned back to join her.

"She's right," a Tamang woman said. "We need a place to meet. Let's take the land by force. We sukumbasi know how to take land by force."

I tossed the word *sukumbasi* around the way others in Gunjanagar did, as a shorthand for "landless." But I had recently caught nuances that gave me greater appreciation for the expressiveness of Nepali and helped me understand the full force of Dilmaya's message.

Sukumbasi comes from *sukum* (dried up) and *basi* (inhabitant). Thus: one who lives in a dried-up or unproductive place. Hanging on to land is so important in Nepal that even the word for landless means inhabitant of some place, even if that place is insufficient. In the history of conflicts over land and political constituencies in Chitwan District, *sukumbasi* came to mean something even more complicated: those of various castes with tenuous rights to land and shelter who work mostly for wages doing farm or other kinds of low-paid labor.

Sukumbasi contrasted themselves to hukumbasi. *Hukum* means "royal decree or order," so *hukumbasi*, I was told, means "those who live in a place from which they can eat and give orders." Even though most landowners in Chitwan had relatively small parcels of land and were not especially wealthy, sukumbasi recognized the power differentials between those who had some land and those who squatted on land and had to sell their labor in order to live and eat.

The wind died down. The dark clouds lumbered by without shedding rain. About twenty women regrouped under the trees. They all spoke at once. Dilmaya outshouted the others.

"We need a women's center on Panchayat land. They have so

much. Why shouldn't we have some too? We sukumbasi took the land by force. Women can too!"

"You sukumbasi cry too much and disturb things," an elderly Brahman hukumbasi woman said. "You always want more land for yourselves."

"No!" the Tamang woman said. "We don't want land for sukumbasi. We want it for a women's center, the same as you. Just because we're sukumbasi, you hukumbasi women don't listen to us."

The hukumbasi women ignored further sukumbasi outbursts and made plans for the next meeting at a chautari beside the common pasture.

I walked home with the sukumbasi women, eager to hear their ideas and better understand the fissure that had opened up.

"*Mero man dukcha*," Dilmaya said, tapping her chest. "My heart hurts. Those hukumbasi misunderstood me. They thought we sukumbasi wanted more land for ourselves. But I don't. I want it for women. Women have no place to meet without getting rained on and blown away by wind."

"*Ho ta ni*," other sukumbasi women walking with us nodded and murmured. "Yes, yes . . . so true . . . indeed . . . that's how it is."

"At other meetings hukumbasi women say, '*Kushi lagyo*—I'm so happy,'" Dilmaya continued. "Kushi lagyo," she said again, imitating their fake smiles. "They are too slow and polite."

"Kushi lagyo. Kushi lagyo." Others said it the same way I'd heard Nepalis making fun of Americans saying, "Have a nice day."

"I wanted to speak out before at other meetings," Dilmaya said. "But I couldn't find the words. Today I could speak!"

I wondered if Dilmaya and other sukumbasi women consciously chose that moment of foul-weathered chaos to speak. What would happen under the blazing sun and clear skies of the months to come?

For her literacy students, Pramila showed a drawing of a woman carrying a bundle of firewood on her back.

Daura. DAU-RA.

Firewood: that mundane word inspired conversations that burned steadily over the next weeks. In singsong Nepali cadences with different voices chiming in, they all began to run together in my mind.

"... collecting firewood. So much dukkha, especially in the hills."

"... all that uphill-downhill. *Ukalo-uralo.*"

The way the women said "*ukalo-uralo*"—elevating and stretching out the *aaaah* on the first word and tumbling it down on the second—echoed the steepness of Nepal's terrain and the heavy breath of exertion needed to traverse it better than any English word I knew.

"But what fun we used to have. We sang songs, gossiped, had a few hours away from our nagging mothers-in-law and old husbands ..."

"It was like that gathering leaves and grass to feed the buffaloes and cows too. True even for how we used to walk from our high, high villages down to our fields so low in the valleys. We had more time to get together with other women then. What *maza*! What fun!"

With that, Aama often told a story about sneaking off with a friend for a forest picnic. They told their in-laws they'd be spending the day doing *parma*—cooperative labor—on distant fields. She would help out on her friend's family field, and then her friend would help her. They took some rice and ghee from their in-laws and set out. They worked in the morning and then cooked a leisurely meal in the afternoon.

"How we enjoyed our freedom that day," Aama said, her eyes misting.

"It was more than picnics," other women said. "Remember how we shared cigarettes, songs, and stories too?"

"We sukumbasi women still work in teams like that. That's why even though we're poor, we don't mind wage work when we can work together. But working alone? No fun at all."

"But now in Chitwan, look. We have no spaces like that anymore.

No forest to go to. We can't find firewood. And finding grass is so hard, such a chore. We have to go alone. And then we have to cut in dirty places where people poo and pee ...."

"And our pasture—look what's happened to it. All dusty. No grass left ..."

"And wherever we go now, men bother us more. Remember how they disturbed the literacy class? And remember how they harassed us when we walked to class?"

"'*Kukurlai Kasi?*' Are dogs going to Varanasi now?' That's what they shout at us."

"That's why programs the Panchayat started for women a few years ago shut down. Remember? All those *naramro mancheharu* making *hala*. Bad men making trouble. It comes with all these roads, cars, bazaars. So much dust. So much hala. So many naramro mancheharu ..."

"But we still have our Tij and ratauli. But even there, bad men are causing trouble ..."

"Did you hear about that rape in Rampur? A security guard ... a twelve-year-old girl."

"And that movie shown in Narayanghat? Eight women raped."

"Is it true?"

"We weren't there, but that's what people say ..."

"And at Tij last year, a thief cut off that old woman's earlobes to get her big gold earrings ..."

"Where was that?"

"Some village ..."

"That's why we old women like our Tij at the temple, not in Chanauli Bazaar in front of all those bad men who just come to see us dance *lajnamanne*—dance without embarrassment, without shame ..."

"And women dance less now, seem more afraid. Husbands discourage them, scold them, accuse them of trying to earn money dancing. But we should still dance at Tij ..."

"What about that ratauli the other night? That gang of boys ..."

"Such chic haircuts!"

"Such fancy clothes!"

"They busted in, pushed women around, threatened to beat them up . . ."

"Was anyone hurt?"

"Oh no. Not too much anyway. The men left. Women continued dancing, of course."

"You can't stop a ratauli, you know."

"But in the morning, what did they find on their doorstep?"

"A dead goat!"

"Throat slit, blood everywhere . . ."

"And we sukumbasi are shooed away from Ram Temple, from the Panchayat office."

"It's why we need a women's center," everyone agreed.

The women in the literacy class were so inspired by the first discussion on daura that they worked together over several nights to compose a song. "Garam Bhayo" ("It's Hot") became the anthem for the women's campaign, sung at every subsequent meeting I attended that year.

> It's hot. Sweat is dripping, dripping.
> Trees let's now go planting.

> Listen, everybody,
> It's hard to get firewood and fodder.

> There's no forest. There's no shade, no shade.
> There's no cold spring water.

> Listen, everybody,
> It's hard to get firewood and fodder.

> There's no forest on the Chitwan plains, the Chitwan plains.
> Now we must go to Nawalpur hills.

Listen, everybody,
It's hard to get firewood and fodder.

Tree planting. Let's all do it, do it.
Let's not worry about fodder and wood.

Listen, everybody,
It's hard to get firewood and fodder.

There's no cool breeze, no hills to make shade, make shade.
Now let's take out our hoes

And plant trees
To make cool shade.

With trees, there'll be a nice breeze, nice breeze.
And it stops floods and landslides and is good for all.

We won't worry about firewood and fodder.
Let's all understand this now.

Until women began discussing firewood and fodder, I hadn't been aware of women's particular environmental concerns. Pramod and I would investigate that topic years later. What struck me in 1988 was how often conversations about trees circled back to women's sense that they needed a social space of their own. With my introverted American sense of wishing I could take a solitary walk in a forest, I had often felt suffocated by the Chitwan landscape before. But after the daura discussions, I saw how women also experienced that same sense of nowhere-to-go—but from a more social perspective.

At least several times a week, women showed up at our house with sickles in hand and deep baskets strapped to their heads. Often arriving in the early afternoon, they set their sickles and empty baskets aside and told stories, asked me questions, had some tea and a snack, asked Aama for advice, complained about in-laws. Then around four or so, they'd hop up as though they'd forgotten and say: "*Ghaas katna paryo.* Must cut grass." They'd strap their baskets back on their heads and make their way home, presumably cutting a basketful of grass on the way.

I imagined the in-laws back home asking them: What took you so long? Why so little grass? And the women would complain about how little grass there was, how far they had to go.

I started to watch how women mapped out their livestock-tending and grass-cutting expeditions. They usually included at least one social stop. Best choices: the open pasture by the school or a chautari where they could hang out with friends. But of course, those were the first places overcut and overgrazed. So then women would work the ditches and berms along a road or irrigation canal that would take them past the house of a friend.

I learned to recognize in women's faces and voices those grim days when they had to buckle down and cut grass more seriously. Those sad but determined frowns. The complaints about exhaustion, aching muscles, filthy places, the hot sun.

And I remembered how Pandit Kedarnath had scolded Sakuntala the previous summer before she and Siddhi had moved out. He pointed to the buffaloes and told her to cut more grass for them so we could have more milk. I imagined what it must be like to have to work in the fields right next to your house, within eyesight and earshot of the in-laws. How that must grate.

Pramod and I planned to stay in Nepal until early June. Before then, he would make one more trip to India to finish his research. After we left Nepal, we would write up our dissertations over a year or two and earn our PhDs.

I had gathered plenty of data on sukumbasi and continued following up on questions about families that had lost land through illicit marriages and female transgressions. But I could not see a dissertation growing out of that. I didn't yet know where women's organizing was going but thought it looked more promising than my formal research. I didn't want to submit a new proposal to my committee, so I decided to hang loose and let events unfold. My professors at Stanford had warned us about the dangers of sticking too tightly to initial research questions and not opening up to local developments. Like most anthropologists, I would take notes on everything and make sense of it all later.

Yet still hoping to trace a few relevant connections back to my formal research, I decided to test the consensus on the idea for a women's center by talking to some of the hardest-edged women I knew: the sukumbasi women who cried during my International Women's Day speech. All widows, they lived in one corner of the sukumbasi settlement and kept to themselves. Unlike most villagers, they never smiled at me as I walked by, as I often had to do since their huts faced the lane that cut between the sukumbasi settlement and the Panchayat and temple compound. They had been reluctant to talk to me before and answered survey questions in clipped answers that ended up in my notes like this: "came from Gorkha, works as wage laborer, had two sons, lost one, husband died, no livestock."

One morning, I found them all at home, sweeping their small yards. One of the women laid out a straw mat for me and called the others to join. They lit cigarettes and sat with me. They were thin, missing teeth, and dressed in faded lungis and blouses full of holes and stitching where holes had been mended.

"I was so happy to see you at Women's Day," I told them.

"Yes, yes," they said.

"But I'm sorry I made you cry. Seeing your tears, I felt so sad."

"Don't worry," one said. "We weren't crying for ourselves."

"Really?"

"No," another said. "Remember how you said women were beaten in Amrika?"

"Yes, I said that."

"Well, we felt bad for those women."

"Yes, we thought wife-beating happened only in Nepal. Thinking it happened elsewhere—and in such a bikasi country . . . see, it made us feel bad."

"So we cried."

I thought I had dredged up painful memories for them. Their explanation was so different from what I expected to hear that I couldn't speak for a moment. I searched their faces for some sign of teasing, mockery. There was nothing like that.

They asked after Babu, whether I had enough milk, how much he pooped—the usual questions. They cooed about the difficulties—cleaning up all that poop, all the crying.

Yes, yes, we all agreed. Raising babies was hard.

I asked them what they thought about Ishwarya's idea to have a women's center. There were no Brahman or Chhetri women around, so I figured they might give me a more critical view from a sukumbasi, Dalit, widowed women's perspective. But they repeated what I'd been hearing from many women I'd talked to in Gunjanagar: women needed a space to meet.

Hali. Pramila wrote the word on the blackboard. Women—about twelve by then—sat in the usual semicircle in our courtyard. Although daytime heat lingered, women wrapped shawls around their heads.

Pramila had matured as a teacher. She needed no help from Pramod or Siddhi now to lead women through lively discussions. More and more, she wore to class a simple, cotton kurta salwaar rather than her school uniform. She projected an air of confident professionalism. Radhika stood beside Pramila in front of the class but had become too distracted by agricultural work and talk of marriage to do more than assist. Pramod's initial sense that she was most interested in the income had proved true. After this class finished, we doubted she would take another.

The students knew the script well by then.

"Hali," they said in unison. "HA-LI."

All women there had been on one side or another of that contract. Since slavery had become illegal in 1921, hali had filled the
gap, allowing landowners to purchase the labor of an entire family—usually from a lower-ranking caste without much land of their
own—year-round. They paid them in grain, gifts, loans, some char-
ity, and an occasional feast rather than cash. Whenever they needed
it, they called on the men for the heavy work of plowing and driving
bullock carts, and on all the women—wives, daughters, daughters-
in-law—to help with planting, threshing, and winnowing. In many
cases, the hali family lived on the property of the landowner.

The discussions in the classes echoed those in my sukumbasi
survey. Some remembered good hali contracts and all the security
that meant for the families—the certainty of having food to eat
every morning and every evening, protection from the government
and other landlords, generous gifts: extra grain to brew rakshi, a
small garden plot.

And, of course, the two hukumbasi women—Sanumaya and
Aama—commented on the challenges of smallholders. It was
hard to find labor—and expensive! They themselves didn't lord it
over hali, they reminded the group. They often worked alongside
them. And even with that, they barely had enough hands for all
the work.

Sukumbasi women remembered the bad times of hali: scoldings
. . . beatings . . . lousy food . . . insufficient food . . . not enough gifts.
They remembered landlords who broke hali contracts with a family when the children were small—when the family most needed
the support. The family would have to make it through those lean
years—and sometimes lose a few children—before they were hired
again when the surviving children had matured to working age.

Without much explanation—because in that crowd, no explanations were needed—sukumbasi women remembered children,
sisters and brothers, mothers and fathers who had died as hali.

So much dukkha. So much hardship.

Yet those in the literacy class echoed what many of the sukum-basi had told me: they were the lucky ones. They had avoided or found some way out of the worst of hali. And what was the worst? Debt. If a family entered a hali contract because of debt or incurred debt while in hali, then all of them might be trapped in something worse: *kamaiya* (debt bondage). They might as well be slaves then because they'd never earn enough to buy their freedom.

Women, as well as the sukumbasi I interviewed, mostly talked about hali in the past tense—a *purano chalan*, an old custom, part of bygone days and those remote hill areas they had fled to seek better opportunities in Chitwan.

Integral to Freire's literacy method was problematizing immedi-ate social realities, so the words chosen to teach reading and writing also became key words for framing discussion and social action and for revealing fault lines.

As usual, women made other words from the syllables in hali: *hala, hawa, kali, lila*. Noise, wind, black, drama. But discussion veered toward another word. Pramila added it to the list on the blackboard. Women read it aloud: *KHE-TA-LA*. Wage labor.

The transition from hali to khetala was a theme that had popped out of my sukumbasi surveys too.

Aside from stories about how they had lost land—and, of course, questions about Babu—it's what many sukumbasi talked to me about. Most described a gradual change over the last ten to fifteen years. They hinted at motivation for the change coming from both sides. Landowners wanted the flexibility of hiring only the individ-uals they wanted rather than supporting entire families. And in the expanding and competitive labor market of Chitwan, sukumbasi could make a better living selling their labor for the highest price than by locking themselves into hali contracts. Women complained about men still drifting into hali. Landowners contracted individual men—or sometimes a few men in a family—for whatever work they needed for a season but refused to support whole families. When they needed women for planting or weeding, they might hire women of the same family for those days, but there was no guarantee.

Every sukumbasi family had to make some calculations about the benefits of khetala, hali, and sharecropping given the size of their family and the ages and abilities of children and elders. Khetala work was seasonal, and the times in between were lean. Some men figured they could relieve the burdens on the family better by serving as hali. They didn't bring in wages, but they earned their meals elsewhere and could share whatever gifts the landowner deigned to give them.

Women complained that the partial hali contracts deprived the family of incomes and took brothers, husbands, or fathers away from the household for extended periods. Some sukumbasi went so far as to call brothers, husbands, or sons who went into hali lazy good-for-nothings. They talked of their pride as khetala—free, independent workers.

Some wept about men going into hali as Aama had wept when Siddhi moved out, moving ever closer to a breakup of family and property. And I understood what that crying meant: for sukumbasi families, labor power was their property. It was all they had. And they felt some honor in holding it all together. Surrounded by relatives and friends, any work—even work for others—could become more *mela pat*—more festive—than solitary drudgery.

The next women's meeting took place at a chautari across the pasture from our house. It was one of the older chautari in Gunjanagar, with well-crafted stonework and mature trees that cast shade far beyond the raised platform. Nepali Congress women opened the meeting by haranguing a group of communist women from a distant hamlet for being late. They went on to explain their plans for writing and submitting a petition to ask the village Panchayat for land.

Communist women interrupted and said they resented being scolded. They had come from far away, had dal bhat to cook, children to look after. It was not easy to come to meetings.

Congress women shouted down their complaints: "*Jai* Nepal! Long live Nepal!" Everyone knew that was the Nepali Congress slogan.

"*Lal salaam!* Red salute," the communist women responded.

"*Jai nari!* Long live women," Aama shouted. Several other women repeated the chant.

"*Lal salaam!*" the communist women shouted again. They told me later that although they appreciated the attempt to build unity around women's issues, they didn't like the tone of "Jai nari." "Too much like 'Jai Nepal,'" they said.

Some Congress and communist women who had remained silent during the sloganeering hushed the crowd and asked women to leave their party loyalties at home and work together as women. Grumblings of reluctant agreement swept through the crowd. Outbursts of chanting died down, and women made plans for the next meeting.

"We'll assemble at the Panchayat building," a woman married to a prominent Nepali Congress Party leader said. "Then we'll show them that we have a place alongside men there."

"No!" a communist woman said. "Not all of us are allowed there. Sukumbasi women are always chased away." With sukumbasi women mostly silent at the meetings, communist hukumbasi women shouldered the responsibility of speaking for the poor and landless.

"We'll have it there anyway," the Congress woman said. "We have nothing to fear from the Panchayat or from men. All will be welcome." Other Congress women shouted their support, but without any more sloganeering.

Dissenting hiccups from among the small minority of communist, Dalit, and sukumbasi women stopped.

The meeting ended. I walked home. Some sukumbasi women caught up to me.

"The meeting should not be at the Panchayat or temple," said a woman whose husband was the only Kami in the sukumbasi settlement still blacksmithing. "Those hukumbasi never let us in the temple. I went once to offer fruit to the gods, but the priest said he wouldn't take it. Not from me. Those members of the temple committee tell sukumbasi not to come into the compound. They say we are too dirty."

"Yes," said a Damai woman who had sewn some blouses for me before. "Once I looked in the window of the Panchayat building to see what they do there. A man came out and chased me away. He told me sukumbasi had no business there."

Other sukumbasi women shared similar stories of being scolded and turned away from public meeting places in the village.

"Maybe sukumbasi women need their own place to meet," I said. "Separate from other women."

"No, that wouldn't work," Dilmaya Sarki, who had been so outspoken at the earlier meeting, said. "Whether rich or poor, women share many of the same problems. We want a meeting center for all women. We sukumbasi women will help get the women's center. Then maybe we'll get more respect."

I wanted to question their faith in the unity of women but held my tongue.

I wrote in my journal: "March 28—Pramod left for India yesterday. Babu rolled over for the first time this morning."

During my pregnancy, I might have spilled a whole pen of ink on my feelings after opening like that. But now, those personal issues barely registered in page after page on meetings, weddings, painting gentian violet on an infected finger or toe, the family response to some plea for help.

I had finally become a full-time anthropologist.

My journal went on to describe what had happened the evening before Amalesh rolled over and Pramod left for India.

The women from the literacy class met as usual. But they didn't take their places. They milled around and talked about the latest news: a Tamang neighbor had beaten his wife. Pramila and the older women in the class wanted to do something.

I wasn't sure which Tamang neighbor but, along with Pramod, followed the women down the lane toward the sukumbasi settlement. As we passed by the small huts on the left, some of the younger class members disappeared. Aama, Sanumaya, and a few others stayed on and turned us right, into the courtyard of a Tamang family. It was where we had held the first literacy class.

Some other women and men plus a few Tamang relatives had already gathered. A few Tamang women from another village showed up after we arrived. The beaten woman stood among her relatives in the courtyard weeping silently into her shawl. Despite her best efforts to hide it, I could see a gash on her forehead. The husband sat alone and silent on the verandah.

We newcomers sat on straw mats in the courtyard. The woman stayed close to her relatives. The husband rose and went inside the house.

"We've come to support you," Aama said to the beaten woman.

Someone asked what had happened. Several of the woman's relatives spoke at once. The night before, they said, her husband had come home and chased the children around. She asked him to stop and then stood between him and the kids. He grabbed a metal-handled fishnet and whacked her head. Word traveled quickly, and some relatives came and stayed the night to keep the peace.

After a long silence, the beaten woman spoke to tell us she was happy we had all come.

Aama asked the assembled women whether they should organize a sit-in like this next time a husband beat a wife in the village. If so, who would commit to being there? Sanumaya, the beaten woman, and a few others consented. Aama reminded women that she had organized similar sit-ins in her hill village and forced husbands to sign papers vowing never to beat their wives again. A few more women promised to join the next time they were needed.

We hoped the husband might come outside to apologize. But he didn't, so we all went home. The next morning, Sanumaya came by to tell us he had promised his relatives that he'd never beat his wife again and if he did, he would submit to public punishment.

Over the next few days, women in classes talked about violence. Since the topic had opened naturally, I pried more.

Did men in some castes beat their wives more than others? Treat their wives more disrespectfully?

Women shared examples of gentle, respectful men they knew: Brahman men, Tharu men, Chhetris, Newars, Kamis, Sarkis. I understood what they meant. I'd met many men who defied all stereotypes I might conjure about the violence of Nepali men, of Brahman, Tamang, Sarki men, of liquor-drinking men.

As a vague indicator of male enlightenment, I had been taking notes on men I came across who helped with cooking. Pramod's elder brothers often helped their wives with cooking and prepared delicious meals. On our occasional visits to the mountain town of Pokhara, I'd been especially impressed by how Tirtha and his wife Sarada divided domestic chores so both could teach full-time. I had also admired Magar neighbors of Siddhi's in Chanauli Bazaar. When we arrived, the man—a pensioned police officer who had worked in India—was cooking a vegetable dish with neem leaves ("good for the blood"). He cooked the entire meal while his wife sat with us and talked. Throughout our visit, they often gazed at each other with affection I'd rarely seen between long-married couples in any culture. They showed off their small home and tidy garden and talked about how they couldn't have sons, but loved their daughters more than anything and planned to give their house to the eldest when they died.

But there were other stories: a woman whose shoulder had become paralyzed after a beating . . . a Tamang woman whose arms and legs had swelled badly after a beating . . . a Brahman woman who'd jumped in the river and floated downstream until pulled out, barely alive, by a fisherman . . . a sukumbasi Magar woman who'd run away from her husband's constant scolding and hidden for several days in a haystack.

A Tharu woman told me how her father used to beat her mother. He beat her when she was pregnant, and then the fetus died inside her and she miscarried. Once the children grew up, they protected their mother.

"If Father beats her now, I'll beat him," she said.

"Do Tharu men usually beat their wives?" I asked.

"Oh no. They wouldn't dare. But after drinking too much, some do. Men are like that after drinking."

But I also heard stories of men who drank and didn't beat their wives and men who didn't drink and still beat their wives. I would need more than casual conversations and anecdotes to discern patterns.

Six months earlier, I had despaired of ever finding a single interesting thread to follow in my research. Now, with talk of domestic violence, hali, khetala, liquor, cards, literacy, women's spaces, and women's songs, I wondered which thread to hold on to. I saw some of what I had planned to study when I switched to Nepal: issues that brought sukumbasi together and issues that divided them. But I had little time for reflection. I barely had time some days to brush my teeth and hand Babu off to some niece or nephew before heading off to the latest meeting, wedding, or crisis. I just kept writing everything down.

As agreed, Nepali Congress women from Gunjanagar and neighboring villages gathered at the Panchayat building for another meeting. They waited and waited for communist and sukumbasi women to show. Then word came that the other women refused to come to the Panchayat building. They were meeting at the same chautari as last time.

The Congress women discussed their options, hoping to hit on some way of enticing the other women to come. Most gave up and walked to the chautari.

At the chautari, Ishwarya lectured on the need for women's unity. Although Nepali Congress and not above shouting "Jai Nepal" now and then, she had the powers of oration and persuasion to create fragile moments of unity, as she had on International Women's Day. So under her influence, most communist and sukumbasi relented and agreed to join a procession to the village Panchayat to hand over the petition for land for a women's center.

Back at the Panchayat building, women sat in their factions, with communist and sukumbasi women on the margins. Ishwarya delivered another speech, this time directed to the Panchayat. A Panchayat official spoke briefly, telling the crowd the petition would be considered.

By mid-April, the wheat and lentils had been harvested, the fields plowed, and the corn sown. Pramod returned from his final trip to India. Since we planned to leave Nepal in June to return to Stanford, we felt a sense of urgency to complete our work in Nepal.

Pramod found a funding source in Kathmandu for more literacy classes. He, as well as Siddhi and Pramila, traveled to neighboring villages or hosted delegations from them to talk about literacy classes. Pramod trained more literacy teachers for new classes in Gunjanagar and neighboring villages and also taught Pramila and Siddhi how to train teachers when needed.

In meetings and the teacher trainings, the issue of a space for women came up again. With women growing more powerful, would police or hooligans try to break up the classes? Would the Panchayat leaders stop them? Would drunken gangs harass women walking to class at night? Or would they hang around and interrupt the classes? Pramod and Siddhi made sure each class had a local committee with plenty of sympathetic men willing to provide security if needed. Luckily, enough men in each locale stepped up to the challenge.

A black-and-white drawing of a hill-dwelling woman with a chunky nose ring, several necklaces, bangles, and earlobes drooping from the weight of earrings rested on the easel.

Guha. GU-HA.

Pramila led the women through the usual discussion, how old women in the hills used to wear such heavy things: all that gold . . . and those Lahoris (foreign returnees) with so much jewelry, back from Hong Kong. *Ameeei!* So beautiful! So heavy!

"That was our pewa," women said. "But you don't want to go around wearing all that jewelry in the towns these days. So many thieves."

"Remember that woman who lost her earlobes? Now we wear these small, cheap things. But we like to go to Narayanghat where the stores have better selections."

I watched Aama perk up. I knew what was coming. Pramila probably did too. Maybe they had colluded to make this a topic for a class. Everyone there had probably heard the story more than once. Aama especially loved telling it with an audience of young girls. No way could she resist telling it now. I'd been living in Gunjanagar less than a year, and I'd already heard it so many times, I'd written several versions in my notes. Everyone in the family—and many of Aama's friends—could have told some version of the story:

> Long, long ago, there was a matriarchy. Women ruled the land. They made all the decisions and told the men what to do.
>
> All was well. But then some very clever and shrewd men felt dissatisfied. "Why do the women have all the power?" they grumbled. They gathered together and began plotting how to take power away from the women.
>
> They went to consult a famous priest. "Guruji, is it possible for us to take power from the women and gain control for ourselves?"
>
> "If you are clever enough, then it is possible." That is all the guru said.
>
> So the men went to the old mothers and said, "Oh mothers! Oh mothers! It is becoming so difficult for you. You must be tired. Let us rule for a while. Give your throne to us."

"What? Give our power to you? You must be crazy. We won't give it up."

"La, if that is how it is, then we will have to fight," said the men.

So there was a war. The women lost the war. Maybe their breasts got in the way. Maybe their saris got in the way. Anyhow, the men were better fighters, so they won the war.

After the men won, the old women went to them and said, "Okay, so now you've won the war. Now you have the power. So bring us some sweets. We'll all sit down and eat them."

The women all sat down and ate sweets. They enjoyed not having to work so hard. The men didn't know what to do. They found that they couldn't do all the work in the fields and in the houses. It was too hard. They couldn't keep up with it. They had to find a way to lure the women back to work.

"La, what kinds of clothes would you like to wear? We can bring you beautiful silk saris. What kind of jewelry would you like to wear? We will bring you gold necklaces and bangles."

"We do like to wear jewelry," said the women.

"Fine, we will make sure you all have gold jewelry. But you must stay at home to work."

The women were dying to wear the jewelry. So they agreed. They pierced their ears. They pierced their noses and began wearing gold jewelry. Some wore so much they could hardly even walk.

And this is how women became oppressed.

The story spoke for itself, but Aama couldn't resist driving home her point. "And that's why you girls should spend your money on books and pencils, not jewelry."

Aama pointed to the empty hole in her nose, the empty holes in her ears, her unadorned neck. She twirled the single bangle on her wrist and said that was enough to honor her husband. And then she pointed out the heavy man's watch on her other wrist.

"At least this has some use. And it's big so I can read the numbers."

Then there was the inevitable discussion. The unmarried girls in the class, including Radhika, giggled and fingered the posts or rings in their noses and ears. They tinkled their bangles.

"Where did you get such ideas?"

"Are they foreign?"

"How can you go around looking like a widow?"

"Yes, of course, we want women to be educated, but what harm does a little jewelry do?"

"We must respect our husbands."

"You don't need jewelry to respect your husbands," Aama always said. "It's better to have an education. We should be models for that."

Women from various villages met at the Panchayat again to deliver their demands. This time, communist and sukumbasi women showed up without having to be coaxed.

Ishwarya opened with a fiery speech in which she proposed details for women's demands: enough land for a combined meeting, training, and health center plus a water pump and latrine. Other speakers followed: Sanumaya, Aama, some communist women from a distant hamlet, a Dalit sukumbasi woman. The topics were familiar. Women should stay united in their campaign for their own space. Pramila and some women from the literacy class sang "Garam Bhayo." Sanumaya sang the song she wrote after her daughter got sick and reminded us how she had nursed her back to health. I led the crowd in our Nepali version of "We Shall Overcome."

A delegation walked up the stairs of the office building and knocked on the door of the Panchayat office. The clerk allowed Ishwarya, Pramod, and Sanumaya inside.

I left to nurse Amalesh.

Later, Pramod summarized the outcome for me. The village mayor didn't take the request seriously. He said there was no land for a women's center. He also scolded Pramod for running literacy classes without informing him or getting permission. Pramod understood what was behind the displeasure. The mayor had tried to set up literacy classes for women the previous year and failed. He didn't like that Pramod could be so successful. In a voice dripping with sarcasm, Pramod dramatized how he had responded to the mayor: "So sorry, sir. I didn't mean to cause you any trouble. I know how busy you are, how overworked. You must have so much to do. I didn't want to bother you with our very small literacy program. In the future, we will, of course, come to you and humbly ask for your permission."

Over the next few days, women visited our house to grumble about the Panchayat decision and figure out next steps.

Nepali Congress women circled around one question: how could our men betray us like that? Communist women circled around another: how could you Congress women ever believe your men would support the women's center? At first, I too couldn't understand Congress women's sense of betrayal. There were Congress men in the village Panchayat, but they'd never come out in support of the women's center. Had the Congress women really expected the Panchayat to approve their petition?

But I also saw that—whether they believed the petition stood a chance or not—they had to begin there, test the limits of the system, and try to wrest away from the Panchayat the one concept that all could agree was good: bikas.

Men on all sides, including those loyal to the Panchayat, talked about the benefits of women's development as though they had invented the idea. Some men, like Pramod, Vijaya, Siddhi—and even Pandit Kedarnath in his conservative way—believed that men and women should move the nation forward hand in hand. Other men used the jargon to build power and attract foreign funding. Brahman and Chhetri women, especially Nepali

Congress supporters, wanted to push men in their own party and beyond. How could men uphold the patriotic project of women's development and deny such a simple request?

The Congress women discovered what many communist and sukumbasi women had tried to articulate: some men would express support for women's development only when they could define, control, and benefit from it. No doubt, at least a few men saw opportunities for siphoning aid into their own pockets. With women defining their own direction and taking control, most male leaders refused to support them.

Soon news leaked that would anger women even more: the mayor and other Panchayat leaders planned to give a plot of the common pastureland to the police to build a new station. This was the same plan that a few men had asked Pramod and me to support months earlier.

"They won't even consider a women's center for their sisters?" women repeated to each other in disgust. "But they'll give land to police who will come to beat and arrest us?"

Communist and sukumbasi women agreed to future meetings at the temple and Panchayat compound if their dignity could be assured. Nepali Congress women said no one would be turned away because of poverty or caste.

LONG LIVE WOMEN'S UNITY

❖

APRIL 28, 7:00 a.m.: that was the time Pandit Kedarnath had determined to be auspicious. I cradled Amalesh on my lap, his young spine strong enough to pin him upright for a while. He wore a new daura suruwal, custom-made by a local tailor. With that, a dhaka topi, and his huge brown eyes and black hair finally growing out, he looked, as everyone said, just like a Nepali.

Family members sat around a big sal leaf plate spangled with small mounds of boiled rice, yogurt, stir-fried greens, potato and chickpea curry, orange wedges, banana slices, and rice pudding.

Turn by turn, Pandit Kedarnath put his right fingers into the different foods, mixed each with rice, and pushed them into that six-month-old mouth. Amalesh took the first bites eagerly.

Aama took her turn and fed Amalesh more. Then came Pramod, then me, and then all the other relatives and visitors. After a few rounds, Amalesh squirmed, closed his lips, and spat out the food. So many fingers, so many new tastes. By the end, he arched backward and screamed every time someone touched him.

But the ritual had to go on. At least the First Rice Eating was lighthearted and joyful for everyone but Amalesh.

Women called for another meeting. This one, they said, would take place under the shade of the new aluminum roof next to the Ram Temple. At the scheduled time, we approached the gate to the compound and saw over one hundred women, many children, and a few men on the dusty path.

"Why is everyone outside?" Aama, Pramila, Pramod, Siddhi, Pandit Kedarnath, and I murmured among ourselves. "What's happening?"

Some women crowded around us and talked all at once.

"The gate!"

"It's padlocked ..."

"Some went to ask for the key ..."

"But the key keeper won't give it ..."

"It's the temple committee ..."

"Those rascals!"

"They made secret decisions ..."

"About some people ..."

"Just some people?"

"Yes, just some ..."

"Some are no longer allowed in the temple ..."

"They can't even enter the gate ..."

It was midmorning. From the sweat drenching my blouse and petticoat, I knew the temperature had already reached the high nineties. In another hour or so, it would rise into the hundreds. Some women took cover under umbrellas and shawls. Most of us clustered in the shade of small bushes. Children sat quietly, only raising a hand now and then to swat a fly. Some dozed off, heads lolling in their mothers' laps. I didn't recognize them as the same mischievous beings who chased goats across the pasture during cooler hours.

The sun arced toward its zenith. Although we would never hear a clear explanation, I assumed that the temple leadership felt threatened by women's new militancy and had locked women out to make a point.

Aama stood, picked up a large stone, and stepped to the gate. She grabbed the heavy lock and said to the crowd, "Let's smash it. We built this temple with our sweat. It belongs to us, too."

"Bring some wire cutters," another woman said. "We'll cut through the fence."

There was a lengthy discussion and then a consensus: no violence or destruction. We would sit in the shade and speak about injustices against women.

"It's a fundamental violation of Hindu ethics," Vijaya said. "Public temples, public shelters, and public resting places should be open to the public. Hot, weary travelers should never be denied water or a place to rest." He had become a regular attendee at the women's meetings, one of the few men besides Pramod and Siddhi. At every meeting, he calmly urged unity and told women he supported their campaign for a meeting place.

We shifted positions to follow the shade. I had not expected to be gone so long. Worried about feeding Amalesh, I started home. After a hundred yards or so, I saw a figure rushing toward me: our nephew—Didi's son—Anil. And he carried a wailing infant in his arms. I took Amalesh, put him to my breast, and walked back to the women's gathering. Amalesh suckled so hard, the milk dribbled out under his cheeks. He stopped now and then to gasp for breath. I returned to my patch of shade. After draining one breast, Amalesh drifted off to sleep. The leaked milk stained my blouse and soured quickly in the heat.

The speeches continued. Fervent discussion followed each.

At one point, Pandit Kedarnath raised his hand and pulsed it, palm facing outward. The crowd quieted.

"No person in the community should ever be kept from the temple," he said. "The Vedas tell us that is wrong. Evil." His voice grew louder and harsher. "Women supported the building of the temple along with men. They should not be kept from it. It's inhuman."

Aama looked at her husband with a kind of pride I hadn't seen for a while. "Now everyone can see why women need a women's center," Aama said to the crowd.

Like his friend Vijaya, Pandit Kedarnath had begun attending women's meetings to show his support and distance himself from more conservative Brahmans. But he still expressed some reservations. He supported women's education and wanted them to have a safe place for it. But he also worried about young girls like Pramila becoming outspoken and disrespectful. Although he'd done his share to open schools in disadvantaged communities, he had never been an activist for change the way Vijaya was. He preferred books and discussion on Hindu reform. But what I was learning to appreciate about Pandit Kedarnath that spring was how he leveraged his community standing in critical moments to advocate for justice.

The next day, about seventy-five women and men gathered at the big chautari across the pasture from our house. Leaders stood on the stone platform under the trees. Followers spread out on the grass nearby. Some prominent Congress Party men swaggered onto the platform. I hadn't noticed them at previous meetings.

"Why don't you submit a petition?" one Brahman man said to the crowd. "It's not right that you were locked out. The temple is for women as much as for men. Women worship at the temple to ensure family honor and well-being. You have a right to complain. But you must do it in the proper way."

The crowd did not applaud. Other men lined up to make speeches. Women leaders, including some communists, waved them aside and took over.

"We want to do something now," said a Congress activist and a teacher at the elementary school. "We've had enough of petitions. Nobody pays any attention to them."

In pairs and small groups, women began talking all at once and drowned out the official speeches. Some stayed on topic, debating the merits of petitions versus demonstrations. Some reiterated what all could agree on: the need for a women's center. Others listened to speeches with one ear and lent the other to whispered news: deaths, births, weddings, the cruelty of mothers-in-law, the laziness of daughters-in-law. They scolded, then laughed at children running through the crowd. They shushed crying babies, not out of respect for the speakers, but because crying babies needed comfort. The hum of voices mingled with the dry rattle of ficus leaves.

Finally, a strong, clear voice emerged from the din: "Let's march to the temple."

The crowd hushed. A few questions rang out.

"What if no women will follow us?"

"What if the police come and arrest us?"

"What if they shoot us?"

Women grew quiet and somber. Despite press censorship, everyone had heard stories about what happened in other parts of Nepal where Panchayat leaders had more local control: arrests, torture, police blocking exits and shooting into crowds.

"Let's not worry," one elderly Brahman woman said. "Let's go to the temple together and lock the gate with our own padlock."

"Yes, how can they arrest us for that?"

"Or shoot us."

"It's good to claim the temple for ourselves," someone said. "But we don't want to lock others out as they did to us. A temple should be open to all."

"Let's not lock anything," Aama said. "Some sisters have talked about planting trees. We need more trees in the village. We need trees by the temple. Let's do that. Plant trees."

Aama's idea swayed the majority. Chanting slogans about women's unity and women's rights, we proceeded together through the village to the temple compound. On the way, we passed the sukumbasi settlement. Landless women ran to their huts for hoes. They shouted for others to join.

On the final stretch before the temple, more women and a few men fell in with us. The gate had been left unlocked, so we streamed into the compound and sat under the aluminum roof of the meeting area. More supporters arrived and swelled the crowd to over 150.

Two men who had earlier urged the petition idea tried to dominate, but women silenced them and took over.

Aama gave a speech.

"We must continue fighting for this land for a women's center. But we must also fight for control of Ram Temple and this meeting place. We helped to raise money for them; we helped to build them. We should also decide how they will be used. And women should read religious texts themselves. We shouldn't trust the pandits to tell us what the Vedas mean. We must find out for ourselves. I've heard there are passages that will show the rightness of what we're doing. The Vedas teach us respect for women in their homes and the community. We must see this for ourselves. And the temple committee must go. We need one with more women and lower castes. We are all members of this community. Those of us who are Hindus, we should all decide how the temple will be used."

The men responsible for locking women out were not present. Women didn't expect them to be. Still, they spoke as though they hoped their criticisms would be relayed.

After many more speeches on the injustices of the previous day, the women ended their meeting with triumphant cheers and clapping. We gathered at the compound's edge, where women envisioned their future meeting center. With hoes brought by the sukumbasi women, each of us took turns digging holes. We would have to wait another month to plant the trees, but holes dug in the dry season would collect early rainwater and be ready by monsoon season for saplings. The trees would not add much to village firewood and fodder supplies, but they were a customary method of laying claim to land.

A taste of success spurred more action over the next few days. Men outraged that Brahman women had been excluded from the temple joined with Aama and other women to demand dissolution of the existing temple committee. The priest remained, but he became accountable to a new committee, with a majority of women and Nepali Congress Party men. Under this new committee, Dalits felt more welcome in the temple, at least for some time.

Still, the question of land for the women's center remained with the village Panchayat. To divert women's attention from the temple and administrative buildings, Panchayat leaders offered women another option: some remnants of public land along an irrigation canal near the main road connecting Bharatpur to the national park. The hitch? Win the support of residents nearby. Although they preferred a meeting place in the village center, women accepted the challenge.

The rally was scheduled several days before Pramod and I planned to leave the village for Kathmandu and our flight back to the States. We arrived early at the roadside chautari. Under black umbrellas, women came in pairs and groups. Once they reached tree shade, they folded their umbrellas, mingled, laughed, and shared the latest news. Despite the conflicts of the previous months, the participants reflected village diversity: Nepali Congress, communist, sukumbasi, hukumbasi, Brahman, Chhetri, Magar, Tamang, Gurung, Sarki, Damai, Tharu.

I wrestled with my own excitement, that familiar thrill of people coming together for a common cause. It had been over two years since I'd left Stanford and the daily stimulation of campus divestment rallies and meetings. What about the leadership here? What would happen when Pramod and I left? This movement—if you could call it that—was dominated by Congress women from landowning families. Even if women got their center, how would the interests of poor women or Dalit women be represented? Any movement could build unity in the face of opposition. But if and when they won a victory, how would this movement work for all women?

I silenced my internal critic and gave myself to the moment, a moment led by others. What I had hoped to research was in front of me now. I would soak it all in and consider contradictions later.

I noticed an unprecedented number of men arriving. Some I recognized as supporters. Others I knew to be conservative Brahmans who opposed the women's campaign. But what about those men who paced around the edges of the group and cast disapproving gazes at the women? I had never seen them before. They looked Tamang or Gurung, but I couldn't be sure.

Over 150 women sat in the broad shade of mature trees. Male supporters walked among us and scrutinized the men brooding on the margins. I set up my tape recorder and turned it on.

Women's speeches repeated now familiar themes: the value of

women, their need for a center, injustices against them, success achieved so far. Some men also gave supportive speeches. From the back, the men I didn't recognize interrupted now and then.

"Pramod is trying to win votes," yelled one. "He's going to run for office. He's using you women. Be careful."

"Pramod and that American buhari are converting women to Christianity," another shouted. "Is that what we want? Do we want our wives, sisters, and daughters to become Christian? They'll make this women's center into a church. Then they'll take over our temples. They've already got a new committee at Ram Temple. You wait and see. There's no end to it. They're trying to make us all Christian."

Women in the crowd murmured: not true . . . absurd . . . ridiculous. Some laughed as though the accusations didn't merit any comment. The volunteer security guards hushed the angry men and asked them to respect the speakers.

I'd been hearing the Christian proselytizing rumor for several weeks. According to some of the stories, I'd been seen in a white sari with a cross around my neck and a Bible in hand, prowling the village for converts.

Proselytizing was a punishable offense in Nepal then. Once at the district Panchayat office in Bharatpur, I had overheard an American woman defend herself on such charges. A missionary working in the region for many years, she admitted to handing out Bibles and holding Christian gatherings for those who had already converted. "But I've never tried to win anyone away from Hinduism," she said. "I only serve those who have received the gospel on their own." The distinction didn't appear to impress the interrogating officials.

Both outraged and somewhat fearful of the rumors circulating, I rose to make a brief speech. The men on the margins scowled and muttered angry words I couldn't catch. Some edged closer.

The absurdity of the accusations comforted me. Some of the men who didn't know me may have believed the rumors, but most present knew the truth.

As usual, I didn't want to make a speech, but the women had

insisted. I said what was expected: dispelled rumors, wished women well in their campaign, congratulated them on small victories. I also said my public goodbyes and thanked those in the village who had welcomed me with such kindness and generosity.

I spoke in English. Pramod translated and added his own flourishes. A commotion from the back interrupted him.

"How do we know what she really said?" a Brahman priest said, pushing his way through the crowd. "You put words into her mouth."

"I have done my best to translate Elizabeth's words," Pramod said. "Those of you familiar with us know I have no need to do otherwise."

Women shouted their agreement and nudged the priest back to the edges of the crowd.

"Stand up, everyone," Pramod said. "Let's show our solidarity." Without hesitation, women and some men rose.

"*Jai nari ekta!* Long live women's unity!" Pramod said.

"Jai nari ekta!" the crowd roared. Even the communist and sukumbasi women joined in.

Pramod took a deep breath to belt out another round of the chant. Some young men—the ones I figured must be Tamang or Gurung—pushed through the crowd.

"We'll never let you have land here. You'll have to fight for it."

Pramod tried to ignore them, but they kept shouting and shoved closer.

"Please respect your sisters here. Don't make trouble like this," he said directly to them. Then turning to the crowd, he cried, "Jai na—"

The men lunged forward, swinging their arms. A group of women blocked them.

Pramod clenched his fists and tried to lunge through the female barrier. "Come on," he said to the young men. "Hit me. Hit me, if you dare."

I'd never seen Pramod like this. A few women tugged him back. Other women surged forward to broaden the barrier between him and the young men.

The attackers fell back and faced an angry line of women. Each side shouted at the other. I stood my ground next to Aama near the front, adrenaline feeding my excitement for battle. Aama and others raised their umbrellas and aimed blows at the heads, necks, and shoulders of the rudest men. The men ducked away from the thrashing, but the angry women nosed around them and allowed no escape. To stop the fight, some men gently pushed Aama and other women back. The women acquiesced but not until they landed a few more blows.

The clash ended with bruises but no serious injuries. Opponents continued hurling words.

The meeting could not go on. A large group of women surrounded Pramod and me and escorted us home. Some of the youngest antagonists chased us down the road or ran for their bicycles. Other men and women blocked their way. After thirty minutes or so, we reached home in peace.

The next day, four sukumbasi women came and sat in our courtyard.

"We're worried. Men might attack again," Dilmaya, the outspoken Sarki woman, said. The others agreed.

Had they come to protect us? Or were they eager for another confrontation? The sukumbasi women had always said they wanted to take land by force, not petition. Perhaps they hoped further excitement would erupt at the Parajuli household.

"We also want to hear the tape," a soft-spoken Damai women said. "We saw you making it yesterday. We want to hear the speeches again."

I brought out the tape recorder. The women listened and chattered throughout. I replayed several sections to elicit their interpretations, especially during the battle.

"I know how it happened," Dilmaya said. "Someone started a rumor. Remember when Pramod shouted, 'Jai nari ekta'? I think someone started a rumor that he said, 'Lognemanche murdabad!' Death to all men! That's why they became so angry. But we know he wouldn't say that. He's also a man."

"Maybe they used that as an excuse to attack," I said. I didn't hear any words remotely like "lognemanche murdabad." How could a rumor like that take hold?

"No, I think some really heard that," Dilmaya said. The others agreed.

I didn't understand then that they perceived something so strange about the men who attacked us that they had to grasp at explanations. We wouldn't have the information to solve the mystery until many months later.

"We don't want that land for the women's center anyway," the Damai woman said. "The village Panchayat wanted us over there so we wouldn't try to get the land by the temple. They're clever."

"The men were angry because they didn't want to give us land," said the Tamang woman who had once challenged me to a breast-milk-squirting competition. "But we felt united yesterday. Now, we know who supports us and who doesn't."

The next day, Pramod and I loaded Amalesh, our luggage, and ourselves into a tempu to begin our journey back to the United States. We didn't know when we would return to Gunjanagar.

PART III
1988–1992

THE NEWS

❖

BACK AT STANFORD from 1988 to 1990, Pramod and I settled into daily routines. In our graduate housing unit, we tapped our dissertations out on keyboards, changed diapers, prepared lesson plans for teaching. We cleaned up pesto Amalesh threw against the walls, tended earaches and fevers, served time in a cooperative day care group. We worried over checking accounts, clapped at Amalesh's first crawl, scheduled endless car repairs, filled out forms for student loans. Like many parents, we argued over who would do which chore. At the end of most days, we sprawled in front of a thirteen-inch television and tuned in to the nightly news: another speech from Soviet president Mikhail Gorbachev, demonstrations in Romania and Czechoslovakia, a lone figure before a tank in Tiananmen Square.

In our own lives and the world around us, we felt uncertainty mixed with hope. Yes, we agreed, this was all hard work, especially the child rearing. On playgrounds and at birthday parties, we commiserated with other graduate students who had children, talking about how to make it work. Pramod and I had gone through so much together, we felt confident we could get through the next few years. We'd finish our dissertations and then find jobs—hopefully at the same university.

On days when Amalesh went to child care, I worked on my dissertation. I still intended to write about sukumbasi, but as I read through all my notes, I found the women's organizing and critical discussions more compelling. Yet I wasn't sure at first how to frame all the information I'd gathered. A small women's campaign for a meeting space in a forgotten corner of the world? It fell wanly into the camp of liberal feminism. Nepal? Compared to what was unfolding in Eastern Europe, the country seemed insignificant.

I crunched numbers from the sukumbasi surveys and worked from memory and my journal to profile individuals and describe the family, the village, and its conflicts. I wrote out the entire story of the women's campaign. That work of laying out the most objective "facts" gave me more confidence when patterns emerged. I realized I had enough information to show what I'd wanted to study in India: women's resistance to oppression and how caste and class differences made it hard for them to organize.

I had spent so many months in Gunjanagar looking for, and mourning the absence of, organized protest against inequality and injustice that I'd missed more subtle sounds and gestures of rebellion. Luckily, I had taken notes on them: Aama composing songs about the rights of women or the corruption of the Panchayat system; Sakuntala clanging pots and pans in the kitchen to express anger at her in-laws and hauling chests and grain-storage containers into her room to prepare for the time when she and Siddhi would have their own household and land; Pramila inviting a Damai friend to sit in her grandfather's place. None of those seemed like much at the time, but taken together they showed a strong gendered undercurrent that I could trace back into history and compare with tidbits in other ethnographies and historical accounts.

We longed for letters from Nepal. When they arrived in crumpled airmail envelopes, we read them over and over. Some arrived a few weeks after being mailed; other news took months. Some probably disappeared altogether.

Several months after we had left Nepal, Siddhi wrote to explain more details about the young Tamang men who had disrupted the meeting at the roadside chautari. They apologized in public and said conservative Brahmans had hired them to feign drunkenness and provoke a fight with Pramod. They felt great shame for what they'd done, they said, and pledged to support the women's center.

More letters. In March 1989, women in western Chitwan rallied for International Women's Day once again and celebrated a victory: the village Panchayat awarded them a plot of land next to the administrative office and temple. That had always been the women's first choice. And although winning it had been hard work, it had taken less than a year.

The activist in me wanted to glorify the achievement. But the academic urged caution. Now that the organizers had satisfied a broad desire for meeting space, wouldn't they argue about whose needs were most important and who should be in control? Where would they find common ground?

Amalesh gradually grew into that loud wail he gave at birth. His large brown eyes gazed at the world with such wonder, friends called him Little Buddha. I knew the other side. He was what parenting books would later call willful or spirited. I called him stubborn. He stopped breastfeeding once he learned to crawl, before his first birthday. He wanted his milk in a bottle to go. In the playground near our unit, he would wait for me to turn my head, then push a handful of sand into his mouth. I'd rush over and scrape it out. He'd laugh and squirm away. Then I'd turn my head again. We'd repeat the game until I scooped him up and returned home to look for other diversions to pass the hours until Pramod took over.

I often called Mother for advice. She had no idea, of course. I had been quiet and well behaved, she said, never needing much discipline at all.

At parties, Amalesh crawled away from Pramod and me to charm and entertain others. It was as though he was making up for the loss of his extended family and the unconditional love lavished on children in Nepal. I dreaded taking him to restaurants or shopping malls, where he climbed where he shouldn't and screamed loudly if I interfered.

Exhausted by parenting, I found myself missing something surprising: Nepal. How easy it had been to hand Amalesh over to someone and head off to a meeting or wedding at a moment's notice. If I brought him with me, women and men helped carry him, comfort him, lull him to sleep. When I returned home, I found my clothes washed, dried, folded, and smelling of sunshine, and then I'd be invited to sit down for a hot, home-cooked meal.

In February 1990, Pramod and I began to catch news of political unrest in Nepal. Although inspired by global rebellions of the previous year, Nepal's pro-democracy movement never did capture headlines like the falling of the Berlin Wall, Chinese protestors in Tiananmen Square, or Czechoslovakia's Velvet Revolution. Nor could it compete with the big news from South Africa in the same month: Nelson Mandela's release from twenty-seven years of imprisonment and the beginning of reforms to dismantle apartheid.

For Nepal, we gleaned what we could from sparse radio, TV, and newspaper reports.

On February 18, the Nepali Congress Party and a coalition of communist parties known as the United Left Front led demonstrations to restore multiparty democracy. The movement spread quickly and gained wide support, especially in Kathmandu Valley, Pokhara, and tarai districts such as Chitwan.

We worried about women activists and family members like Siddhi and Anil who were outspoken supporters of opposition parties. Since the U.S. media had not covered the movement in Nepal much, we gained most of our details from Nepali friends in the Bay Area who had fax machines. Over those weeks of rallies and government crackdowns, we waited for those machines to unfurl messages on shiny paper that seemed too flimsy to hold the weight of the details. Police shot into crowds and ransacked houses, rounded up community activists and forced them to write statements in favor of the Panchayat system, beat those who refused and applied electrical shocks to their genitals, raped and knife-scarred many women activists and even cut the breasts off some.

The resolve of protestors continued.

Pramod phoned friends in Kathmandu to ask about the family in Chitwan. No one knew for sure. Finally, we received a letter from Siddhi. He confirmed atrocities nearby but assured us everyone in the family was fine.

The movement climaxed on April 6. Army forces opened fire on a procession of over two hundred thousand pro-democracy demonstrators headed toward the Royal Palace in Kathmandu. Reports estimated that the death toll from that massacre alone exceeded two hundred. Unofficial reports from various human rights organizations in Kathmandu figured another eight hundred had died over the two months of demonstrations. That pales in comparison to insurrections and massacres in other places, of course, but such open attacks on citizens were unprecedented in Nepal at the time.

Facing threats from international supporters to cut off development aid—the source of much of the wealth among the ruling class—King Birendra had to cede some power. He lifted the twenty-nine-year-old ban on political parties and dissolved the Panchayat system. An interim government led by a fragile coalition of leaders from the Nepali Congress Party and the United Left Front took power and formulated plans for free elections and a new constitution.

I remembered that spring five years earlier when Pramod and I had fallen in love and talked of bombs. His predictions had been right, but even he was surprised at how quickly King Birendra gave in to pro-democracy demands in 1990. Activists around the world were riding global momentum to press local demands. What had seemed so entrenched a few years before—apartheid, the Eastern Bloc, the Panchayat system—finally cracked and gave way.

That same spring, Amalesh learned to use his potty. We'd been encouraging him on it for weeks, with no results. One afternoon, we took a family hike into the Stanford foothills, where Pramod and I had walked so much during our early romance. The same sight that prompted Pramod to launch into his story of picking up dung with bare hands caught Amalesh's eye. He circled a fresh cow pie in the middle of the path and then squatted on his short legs for a closer look. He said nothing and soon toddled after us as we continued up the hill. But he stopped and inspected a few more cow pies near the path on our way.

Back home, he wiggled out of his pants and diapers, sat on his plastic potty, and made a deposit. And that was that: the end of diapers. From then on, he used his potty and, soon, the adult toilet. I wished I could understand the connections he made in his young mind. It was as though he decided to turn away from his animal-like baby nature and align himself with those who control where they poop.

On that afternoon of Amalesh's first successful potty use, I called Mom and various friends to give them the news.

In a box of memorabilia, I still have the pass that allowed me into the Stanford Quad on June 4, 1990, to hear Mikhail Gorbachev speak. I don't remember what he said. I'm sure it was a version of a speech we'd heard many times on the nightly news. What seemed important at the time was how his presence marked the end of a world with a Soviet Union, a Berlin Wall, a Panchayat system—and the beginning of something new that seemed so hopeful at the time.

After Gorbachev's speech, I cornered the last member of my committee to sign off on my dissertation: "Gender, Class, and Caste Conflicts in a Women's Campaign for Meeting Space in Chitwan District, Nepal." Working with historian Joan Scott's definition of *gender* as both a basic "element of social relationships based on perceived relationships of power" and "a primary way of signifying relationships," my research showed how gender permeated social and economic differentiation at every level in a village in Nepal. It wasn't the masterpiece I had hoped for (they rarely are, I was told), but it redeemed something of my false starts and misdirections. I neither romanticized nor diminished women's victories. If nothing else, I figured I had shown the value of gender as a lens for social history and anthropology in Nepal and hoped other researchers might use it to turn up new insights in ethnicity, nationalism, legal codes, out-migration, bonded labor, land rights, and agricultural production.

Pramod finished his dissertation the following month. That fall, we moved to Iowa City, where I had a postdoctoral fellowship in women's studies. The following year, we moved to Syracuse, New York, where Pramod landed a tenure-track position in anthropology at Syracuse University.

On some vacations in between, we visited Mom and Dad. They spoiled their grandson with outings, gifts, and special foods. On other vacations, we took long camping trips through the redwoods or into British Columbia. Amalesh embraced life with gusto, climbed higher and higher into trees, terrified us by wandering away at zoos and aquariums as though he had nothing to fear from crowds, and then pouted for hours when we thwarted his desires.

Throughout our time in Iowa City and Syracuse, more letters arrived.

We learned that women in Gunjanagar had registered with the government as an official organization, which they called Nari Jaga-ran Samiti (NJS), or Women's Awareness Organization. Ishwarya became president. After Pramod and I obtained grants from sev-eral foundations, Pramila and Siddhi used the money to purchase supplies such as lanterns, chalk, chalkboards, and notebooks and to pay literacy teachers they were training. Siddhi worked with NJS leaders to hire a contractor to build a two-room cement building.

We also heard family news. Pandit Kedarnath had frequent bouts of weakness and sometimes couldn't talk. Udaya had returned from Solukhumbu, married, and moved into the family home in

Gunjanagar to care for his parents.

Pramod wanted to spend more time with his father before it was too late. He also hoped to help Udaya and get to know his young wife, Sadhana. I wanted Amalesh to have that rich sense of family only Nepal could give him. When I saw photos of Udaya and Sadhana and their baby girl, Sebika, I felt an even stronger pull. Most of Amalesh's cousins in Nepal were so much older. But here was one who could be like a younger sister—the younger sister I doubted I would ever give my son. I did not want to go through another pregnancy and birth.

I had still not fallen in love with Nepal as deeply as I thought I should. While finishing my dissertation, I had toyed with a fantasy of returning to East Africa and even applied for fellowships and grants that might take me there. But nothing panned out. At the same time, I also wanted to try Nepal again on better terms. I spoke reasonable Nepali by then and, while finishing my dissertation, had caught up on more history and ethnography of the region. I was invited to speak on Nepal at conferences and had become recognized as something of an expert on women in Nepal. Yet because of how I had landed in the country, I lacked confidence in my success. I remembered my research filtered through the haze of poor planning, pregnancy, sleeplessness, and mild postpartum depression. I felt some obligation to have another go at it, get it right, work harder and with better presence of mind to earn the success.

The demise of the Panchayat system and the women's victories in Gunjanagar made a return all the more enticing—for both of us. As long as Nepal had been under the Panchayat system, Pramod had refused to spend much time there. But now, he saw possibilities for shifting his own research on grassroots organizing there. And so, as though it were inevitable, Pramod and I began preparing research projects that would take us back to Nepal.

Ever since that day when Aama let the rice boil over while she composed a song, I'd been mulling over a project on women's life stories and songs. Remembering the subversive singing at Tij and at women's meetings, I wanted to prompt her and other women involved in NJS to share songs and stories about their lives. So I wrote and submitted a grant proposal, imagining a process patterned on the Freiran literacy classes, in which women would get together and share stories and songs to identify their problems and find solutions to them. I hoped the legalization of political parties would free women to speak more openly about their aspirations for change. I also hoped the process would strengthen NJS, inspire new leaders, and clarify goals.

At the same time, Pramod and I wrote and submitted some proposals to get funding for an even grander project inspired partly by women's songs: researching gender, caste, and class differences in how people use natural resources (fodder, firewood, soil, water) in Chitwan and developing a curriculum based on our findings.

By the summer of 1991, we received word that both my project and our joint proposal would be funded. Because of Pramod's teaching duties, we planned to make some trips back and forth and space out our research. Pramod would accompany me and Amalesh to Gunjanagar in December. He would stay for a few weeks and then go back to the States after the new year to resume teaching at Syracuse. Amalesh and I would stay in Nepal for six months to carry out my life story–and–song project. Then we would rejoin Pramod in Syracuse. Meanwhile, he would make arrangements with his employer for a leave of absence so all of us could return to Nepal the following winter or spring for a longer research stay.

ON TAPE

I SURVEYED THE debris sprawled on the riverbank: human feces, orphaned sandals, cloth scraps, plastic bags, whiskey bottles, candy wrappers, condoms, banana and tangerine peels, leaf plates— all remnants, I assumed, of Magh Sankranti parties ten days earlier. Falling several weeks after the winter solstice, the festival goes by various names throughout South Asia and celebrates winter's end and lengthening days. People travel from all over to trade and carouse.

I hitched up my silk sari and blazed a trail through the refuse.

This was my first visit to Devghat, a holy place where the Kali Gandaki and Trisuli Rivers tumble out of the foothills and merge into the Narayani, which then meanders for several hundred kilometers toward the Ganges. Hindus of central Nepal observe major life passages at Devghat, and pilgrims from farther afield arrive every day by the busload.

The fog lifted enough to reveal the terrain: banana trees and cultivated fields on one side, steep cliffs on the other. Two dugout canoes stacked high with hay bales appeared around a promontory. The boatmen shouted words of caution to each other and then shot through rapids below. Their laughter echoed over the calmer waters as they drifted downstream, toward where mourners burned their dead.

I looked around and saw no other people nearby. As good a place as any, I thought, and put my soap on a smooth rock.

Pramod might have helped me find a more private place. But as planned, he had returned to Syracuse several weeks earlier. I missed him, but after six years of marriage, I was enjoying time apart too. I wanted to get to know Nepal and his family better on my own terms, without mediation. That, I figured, would strengthen our marriage and my place in the family.

My sari had become soaked during the dugout canoe ride across the Trisuli River. It was one Pramod had bought for me in Banga- lore. I'd worn it for Amalesh's Name-Giving and First Rice-Eating ceremonies. I untangled myself from the silk and spread it over a piece of driftwood to dry. Spilled breast milk, tears, bananas, and rice pudding had all washed out, but red tika powder had stained like blood and mingled with the magenta flowers.

I pulled my petticoat up over my breasts, cinched the drawstring tight, and removed my sweater and blouse. Soap in hand, I walked down to the river. Shivering, I dipped a toe into the glacial water, flinched, and hopped back.

A memory surfaced: Pramod's voice calling from the loft for someone to bring a tub of water: "It will help her relax and get things moving."

Then Aama's and Sakuntala's voices scolding him: "What are you thinking? A bath for a woman in labor? It's too dangerous."

Then my voice in awkward Nepali: "It's very good for a woman when she's in labor to be clean."

"But it'll make you cold."

Exactly, I remembered myself thinking. That's what I wanted, along with more freedom to do whatever felt good.

Since my return to Nepal, physical sensations had been stirring up memories from pregnancy. My mind still slid over the moments closest to birth but surged nearer. Compared to all that, I thought, entering the Kali Gandaki should be easy. I put one foot and then another into the water and let them go numb. Then I walked thigh- deep and dipped down quickly.

I might have bathed in the holier place where the rivers met. That was where the ascetics, pilgrims, and local priests dipped each day. That was where the other women in the family had already purified themselves. But I didn't trust my skills at untangling and rewrapping a sari enough to bathe in front of the others. So I bathed upstream where no one could see.

I lathered with soap, rinsed off with a few more quick dips, and then jogged back up the sandy bank.

Within minutes, all my female relatives could pull a petticoat up over their breasts, unwrap a sari, quickly dip in the water, pull a dry petticoat over their heads while dropping the wet petticoat to their feet, and then, using both hands as well as their teeth, drape a clean sari over the top of their body, drop their petticoat down to their waist, and wrap the sari.

I'd felt prouder earlier that morning. Wrapped in clean, dry silk and without Pramod to facilitate, I had helped load food, pots and pans, ritual tools, and family members into an old Land Rover and ladyhandled the overloaded hulk through the crowded streets of Narayanghat and over the potholed dirt road leading to Devghat.

Now the wind whipped one end of the sari out of my hands and flew it like a flag of foreign clumsiness. At least there was no one to see that.

Dressed like a Brahman's wife again, I walked back toward the peninsula tip that separated the two rivers. I heard Amalesh giggling and chattering in Nepali with his cousins. For a moment, I worried about how close he was to the swift water. Then I saw how his older cousins hovered, making sure he stayed on shore while skipping stones. If he slipped and fell, someone would catch him.

I rejoined the rest of the family setting up for a nephew's initiation ceremony. The women, including Didi and Aama, prepared the food. Some of the young men took turns recording the event with my new camcorder. I waited for instructions on my role. As maternal aunt, I would soon need to give coins and handfuls of dried rice—symbolic alms toward a boy's education.

With initiations and other festivities over for a while, Amalesh and I settled back into family routines. In the familiar cement house, Udaya and Sadhana and Sebika slept in one downstairs bedroom.

Aama and Pandit Kedarnath had the other. I took over the upstairs bedroom where Pramod and I had slept on our first visit in 1986. Amalesh slept wherever he pleased or wherever he dropped in exhaustion: in my bed, in the room next door with visiting cousins, downstairs snuggled up with Sebika, or with Pramila and her friends in my old open-air loft above the buffalo shed.

With a few gray hairs and an easy smile, Udaya exuded more confidence than when I had first met him. He still limped and deferred to his older brothers at times. But the years teaching near Mount Everest had served him well. He had already proven he could support a family, look after his parents, and manage the farm. He had planted more trees for firewood and fodder and also installed a simple biogas plant so that livestock and human manure could be converted to cooking gas. He also had the house wired for the electricity newly available in Gunjanagar.

A teenager, Sadhana laughed a lot and carried out her daily chores with efficiency and good cheer. She had strong opinions but voiced them gently. I sensed Aama was happy with her youngest daughter-in-law.

Pramila still taught literacy classes and lived with us. Urmila lived with her parents and commuted to Bharatpur by bus for college classes. Sharmila had finished her nursing degree, agreed to an arranged marriage with a kind biochemist, and had a baby. She and her husband shared housework and child care so she could work at a hospital in Kathmandu.

Within weeks of our arrival, Amalesh spoke the same singsong, childish Nepali Sebika used. The two became inseparable. One afternoon, we found them squatting near the outhouse, seeing who could make the biggest poops. Another day, they gobbled chili peppers to see who could eat the most. When we called them to come for dal bhat or chia, they often hid in the upper branches of the trees Aama had planted on the chautari in front of our house. They argued over food portions, which cup they'd drink water from, or which bowl was better for popcorn. They wrestled for the same spot on chairs, benches, or straw mats on the ground. One morning, Amalesh threw a stainless steel plate at Sebika and sliced open her earlobe. After we patched it up, the two resumed playing . . . until the next argument.

Every day, Udaya and Sadhana invited Amalesh and Sebika to help shake papayas out of a tree or cut fodder for goats, and made the chores fun. When the children transgressed, the adults scolded for a few minutes and then laughed and hugged them as if nothing had happened. It looked like contradictory messaging and indulgence to me, but the system turned out some of the politest teens I'd ever met. My greatest worry was how uncles, aunts, and neighbors spoiled Amalesh more than other children because of his American mother.

Sebika was as willful as Amalesh but shyer. She often turned or toddled away from any but immediate family when they asked her questions or tried to pinch her cheek. I felt honored when she first climbed into my lap. From then on, I became one of her inner circle. We found time for a cuddle most days, often after my son had pummeled or insulted her.

Sebika had her mother's pretty face and short, light brown hair that often stuck out every which way. Sadhana told me her own hair had also been light brown in childhood and darkened only in adolescence. When I walked through the village with Sebika and Amalesh, women and men teased us. With that hair, people said, Sebika must be mine. And Amalesh—with his hair so black—must have come from someone else. Amalesh usually laughed. He craved attention of any sort. Sometimes Sebika didn't mind the teasing either. She squeezed my hand and smiled. Other times, she sat down on the path and pouted for a while before agreeing to walk again.

Since Aama had inspired my project on life stories, I figured I should begin with her. For several weeks after the Devghat trip, Aama pestered me: "When can we begin?"

When I told her I was ready, she said, "Wait until Sadhana gets back from visiting her relatives. I'll have more free time then." When Sadhana came back, Pramila went traveling. Then Aama said, "I can't now. I need Pramila to help find my poems and songs." Like Aama, Pramila had started writing her own songs. Perhaps because of that as well as her experience teaching literacy, she had more patience than other family members for writing down her grandmother's new songs and rifling through copybooks for old ones.

Didi's son, Anil, left a well-paying job at Nepal-Arab Bank to become my research assistant. Among his siblings and cousins, he showed the most interest in the work I planned. He had finished his bachelor's degree, knew English well, and hoped to pursue graduate studies in the social sciences. By helping me interview, record, transcribe, translate, and interpret, he could gain some practical experience in research methods and social theory.

A budding intellectual with a strong rebellious streak, Anil often went for months without cutting his hair. A mop of black curls obscured his brown eyes. Childhood ear infections and botched surgeries had left him deaf in one ear. Straining to hear, he usually leaned to one side. That spring, he became a close friend and confidant. He also became an astute critic. He challenged my assumptions about what people's actions meant and motivated me to look deeper. With his deep intelligence and cynicism, he fed my own doubts about doing anthropology—gathering information on the lives of others to serve the interests of Western academia. But he also supported my work in practical ways—helping me take care of Amalesh, accompanying me on trips around western Chitwan, and providing the English conversation I sometimes longed for in Pramod's absence.

Amalesh never gave in to sleep easily. If I turned my head, he sometimes wandered off. Or he whined or sweet-talked me into one more drink of water, one more story, a bite to eat.

One evening, I read Amalesh a story in English in a bed upstairs. The slowly dimming electric lightbulb overhead lured moths and

other insects. As they hurled themselves against the bulb, green-
ish brown geckos darted across the wall to catch them. Aama came
in and squatted on the edge of the bed. I tucked the thick cotton
quilt around Amalesh and kissed him goodnight. Eyes wide open,
he squirmed halfway out from under the quilt and let loose a stream
of toddler philosophy in Nepali and English: "It's night because a
monster is holding his breath. We should tell him to breathe again.
Then when we wake up ...." Over his lilting voice, Aama droned on
about her day.

How would I ever get my son to sleep?

I pulled out a tape recorder with big colorful knobs I had bought
at a Syracuse shopping mall. I didn't use it much but thought it
worth trying that night. I inserted a Raffi tape and pressed Play.
"Baby Beluga" began.

"Badmash! Rascal!" Aama said. She raised her hand playfully as
though to strike me. I flinched.

"What's wrong?" I asked.

"Why are you recording what I'm saying? I'm not ready yet. I'm
just talking now."

I looked at the machine and understood. She hadn't been able to
hear it playing. I turned it off.

"This? It's for Amalesh, to help him get to sleep. I would never
record your stories without your say-so."

She laughed, shrugged her shoulders, and continued telling me
about her day. I turned the tape back on. Amalesh's eyes slowly
closed to the soft hum of Raffi songs and his grandmother's stories.

LIFE STORIES

ONE EVENING, Anil and I translated women's songs upstairs. Through the open windows, we heard Amalesh's giggles from the loft above the buffalo shed where he was spending the evening with Pramila and one of her friends.

Visiting for a few days, Anil's twin brother, Sunil, had come up with Udaya around eight o'clock. They brought Udaya's tape deck, a bottle of local rakshi, and some stainless steel cups. Anil and I stopped work and played a Paul Simon tape. Sunil poured whiskey and Udaya launched into corny jokes and funny stories.

I had to visit the outhouse before relaxing into our party. Downstairs, I passed Aama sitting alone on the cot on the verandah. As always, bats winged back and forth overhead, nearly colliding with us in pursuit of bugs near the bare lightbulb. Wrapped in a shawl and rocking, Aama sang softly to herself. She tried out one word at the end of a line, then shook her head and repeated the line with a different ending.

"I'm making a new song," she said and laughed nervously as though I might think it a silly thing to do.

"Let's write it down," I said.

She didn't say no, so I made for the outhouse, and then rushed back upstairs.

"Your grandmother's mind is racing with a new song. Come quickly," I told Anil.

Udaya and Sunil rolled their eyes, poured more rakshi into their cups, and smiled at some private joke. I knew they didn't like being dragged away from pleasure to write down another of Aama's songs, some of which they found naive or old-fashioned. Anil doubted his grandmother was ready. But he downed his drink, grabbed some paper, a pen, and my small tape recorder, and followed me downstairs.

"I'm making a ratauli song," Aama said.

The wedding season would begin soon. Using the characteristic dancing rhythm of a ratauli song without the sexy content, Aama sang about women being behind and having to march ahead for their rights. Anil wrote down the words, and then we recorded Aama singing it. As soon as we turned the recorder off, Aama launched into another song fragment and a story.

"Wait," I said, fumbling to turn the recorder back on. I feared I would never hear that story told so well again.

"No," she said. "I'm not ready." She seemed to be composing a rough draft in conversation with us that she didn't want preserved. Anil and I insisted it would be good to record the stories as she remembered them so that they wouldn't be lost again. But Aama said she didn't want us to record her stories until she could get them right.

I had the same trouble with photos in Nepal. Whenever I raised a camera, adults asked me to wait. Then they disappeared to edit themselves—put on their best sari or jacket, oil and comb their hair, line their eyes with kohl. Finally ready, they stood, stiff and unsmiling, waiting for the camera to record their perfected image.

With the tape recorder off, Aama reminded us of the many poems that had been lost when she and Pandit Kedarnath moved from the hills to Chitwan. She tried to remember some. Anil wrote them down line by line. She stopping often, saying, "They're not coming; they're not coming."

When writing the project proposal back in the States, I had planned for a one-way process, with "authors" telling me their tales and me—the editor—recording, transcribing, translating, and editing to finally produce a written version of oral speech. But I could already see that for Aama, the boundaries among writing, remembering, and storytelling would not be that clear. Given South Asia's rich regional traditions of both oral and written expression, I shouldn't have been surprised. As priests, Aama's father and husband had been well versed in both oral and written traditions. They had to be. So Aama had always known the value of writing even if she had not, for most of her life, been able to read or write herself.

Aama did not want us to record her songs until Anil had written down the fragments of songs she remembered. Then she pieced them together and tried to sing them. Anil cued her with the first few words of a line if she forgot.

"It's enough for today," Aama said after we'd worked through a few songs. "We'll do some more another day. No more is coming now." Anil and I gathered our notebooks, pens, and recording equipment and started upstairs. Then Aama remembered some more and called us back.

Shivering from the cold and damp, we moved into Udaya and Sadhana's room downstairs. On one of the narrow cots, I cuddled next to Sebika sleeping under a cotton quilt.

Clothing hung from a rope stretched from one corner of the small room to another. Cutouts from magazines and old calendars, featuring idyllic nature scenes, Indian and Nepali movie stars, and Hindu gods and goddesses, covered the flaking whitewash and chipped plaster on the walls. A few tattered photos cut from books we'd brought for the community library years ago remained.

Aama brought three cups and a thermos of tea and set them on a bamboo table covered with a red flowered cloth made in China. Squatting on the edge of the second cot, as she would when sitting on the floor serving a meal, she poured and handed us each a cup.

Anil and I had agreed beforehand that we'd let Aama talk and not interrupt her with questions, except for clarification. We wanted to hear the story as she chose to tell it. Aama drew her striped shawl more tightly around her head and shoulders and tucked her red, homespun sari under her bare feet. Thinking she would begin right away, I turned on the tape recorder. But Aama sipped tea in silence. I turned the recorder off. Anil and I waited without talking.

Finally, Aama upended her cup, plunked it on the table, and launched without warning into her story. I fumbled with the recorder.

"... we were fourteen children: nine daughters, five sons. I am the youngest. After I was born, Father became an ascetic. He was bored and left everything and began living with the renouncers—the celibate yogis. At that time, there was a hill a few miles from our house by the River Madi. He built a hut and started living there. At that time I felt so sad. I brooded and composed some poems:

> The spring water is far for one pot full of water.
> You want to keep us in your house or take us to your hill?
> Saying this, the daughters-in-law hold a grudge.
> If you do this, who will fill the water?
> Small, two-leafed banyan tree in the chautari.
> Father, come back home now.
> Don't stay there, you have to come back home.
>
> In the monsoon, many cornfields everywhere,
> Centipedes and snakes wriggling on the way.
> In winter, dal bhat to eat,
> And in the monsoon the leaves of taro.
> Let my father leave, oh celibate gurus.
> Other yogis, celibates, let my father leave.
> Let him go.
>
> Ink and pen in hand, to scribble on the paper.
> The daughters-in-law will look from up and down.
> The fish lived in the land and birds in the forest.
> Curse this life, my mind says.

"The house of First Daughter-in-Law was on this side. The house of Second Daughter-in-Law was on the other. Over there was Youngest Son's house."

Aama gestured with her hands to show us the layout of homes.

"Mother had to pass in between them. Mother did not have time to stay with Father. She always had to go to Father's to prepare food for him and then come back home. Thinking that Mother might have felt sad in her soul, I made this poem ..."

Curse this life, my mind says.
This big house of my father, the way is too long.
Mother had to pass through the lanes.
Now you are in disillusionment.
You have to go to the unknown, leaving everything.
You have done so much prayer, staying at the mound.
You don't have energy to walk down to your house.
In Father's fireplace, there was a three-legged grill.
The eldest brothers are estranged;
The youngest knows nothing.
Whatever there was, the elder sisters took with them.
When I was to be given away, you went to the mound.
I did not wear homely clothes in my childhood.
For me, the youngest, there was no support.

"Composing all this," Aama said, tears welling up in her eyes, "I had it written down and sent it to Father. There was a lot more, but it won't come now. When Father read it, tears must have come to his eyes."

She stopped for a moment to cry.

"This might be it. The story's finished. What else to do?"

Disappointed by the abrupt ending, I moved to turn off the tape recorder. But then Aama laughed and continued.

"Father used to say, 'You don't have to face hardship. Your sons will rise up. Live for today, for now. God will rescue you tomorrow.

Don't give your children just a little to eat. Live for today. Tomorrow will go away. Don't feel unhappy.' He said this and then told me a verse.

> What can wealth do?
> Think with your mind.
> You go to heaven praying for Hari.

"'Wealth can do nothing, Daughter,' he said.

"'I am a small person. Everyone wears ornaments. I have no ornaments, Father.' I said this.

"He said, 'Eh, Daughter, you have to be taught. Jewelry is not good. You have to be good. Real gold does not need to be tested. It shines itself. If you are upright, you don't need ornaments. You yourself be upright. Tell the truth. Don't tell lies.' He used to say these things. And I would keep his words in mind.

"See, now I don't have to worry about what to eat. But before, that was a problem. Father used to say: 'Even if it is flat bread made of corn, give it to them cooked, Daughter.' Then I felt satisfied and made another poem.

> Be content, Sister.
> Be content, Brother.
> I feel happy in contentment.
> There are millions to gain in contentment.
> There are few things to gain in being discontent . . .'"

Aama paused to sip tea. She held up the thermos to offer us more. We shook our heads.

"I was married when I was ten. I stayed in my mother's home for one more year. Then I came to husband's house when I was twelve. There was one mother-in-law. There was one buffalo. There was a half-tailed cow. There was a small round house. I went inside that house. It was so small. I had never seen that kind of house among Brahmans. It was more like houses I'd seen among other groups, like Magars. I felt strange.

"I didn't feel like staying home. I felt restless. Where to go? What to do? Going to the spring for water, I used to meet my sisters-in-law.

"I said, 'Eh, I would like to take the cows to graze with you.'

"Then they asked Mother-in-Law to send me out with the cows. But Mother-in-Law said, 'How can she take cows to the jungle? She cannot. Thorns might scratch her. She stays at home.'

"Not able to go with my sisters-in-law, I cried.

"But finally, they took the cows, bullocks, and me too. They took me too! We grazed the cows, sang songs, danced, and played. They made me forget about missing my friends and my maiti. When we came back in the evening, they helped me tie the cows in the shed and brought me back to my house. But I didn't feel like staying home. So, the next day I went with them to the spring to fetch water.

"That way, I spent three twenty-day periods at my ghar for the first time. I could not count twenty-one, twenty-two. So I had to count to twenty and start over. How could I find out how many days I spent in my house? I had an idea. I tied some corn kernels in a handkerchief corner. Every day I took one kernel out and tied it up in another corner until I reached twenty. Then I began with another corner. I tied three bundles of twenty kernels to reach sixty. Nowadays I can count that far, but then it was three twenties.

"On the sixtieth day, who came to fetch me? Father!"

Aama described in detail the happy time she had spent hiking through the foothills with her father to return to her maiti for a long visit. They picked mulberries along the way, eating some and taking the rest as a gift for her maternal relatives.

"These are the things that happened when I was twelve, thirteen years old. Thirteen, fourteen, fifteen, sixteen, seventeen. Still there were no children. Life passed away, working and eating. There was not much land. Sometimes it was dry, and we didn't have enough grain. In the good years, we had fifteen or sixteen measures of rice. Then, I started having children at seventeen, eighteen. First Daughter was born, then six sons. There was hardship. There was no wealth. In this way, over and over again, every two years, I gave birth. Almost every year. The eldest son died at twenty-two years. The one before Pramod died at eleven months. It was hard this way . . ."

Aama talked for several more hours, detailing land sales and purchases and complicated family relationships and conflicts. She paused often to sip tea, cry, or insist: "There's so much more, but it doesn't come. It doesn't come." Then she continued. Anil and I stifled yawns, trying to follow her confusing narrative. I frequently got lost as she jumped from one time and place to another in order to pursue a narrative thread about a relationship, argument, or feeling. I checked the tape recorder often, knowing it was my only chance for teasing some sense out of the story later.

Her stories spiraled around, returning to the pain of leaving her maiti for her ghar at such a young age, the hardship of being a new wife, getting to know a much older man, and the joys and burdens of raising children.

"*Bhayo*, it's finished now," she said. This time, she seemed to mean it. Her white hair, fallen out of its bun, hung in strands around her tired, pale face. Still, her eyes sparkled with exhilaration. After three hours of listening to her stories, I'm sure Anil and I looked more haggard at that point. We returned to Anil's room upstairs. Udaya and Sunil were singing along with Nepali tapes. The rakshi bottle stood empty on the wooden table. Through the window, I made out the voices of Pramila and her friend in the loft over the buffalo shed but no longer heard Amalesh. He must have fallen asleep.

We talked and laughed and then heard footsteps slowly ascending the stairs. Udaya grabbed the rakshi bottle and tucked it behind a cabinet. Aama walked in as it fell to the cement floor and rolled back and forth. She pretended not to notice the clattering or the sake-like aroma that filled the room. Although many Brahmans drink in secret, most Brahman households don't openly tolerate alcohol in the house. Yet Aama and Bua condoned the occasional indulgences of their sons, grandsons, and American daughter-in-law.

Aama sat beside Sunil on one of the beds and held up a notebook. "I had my *jivani* written here," she said.

Anil and I looked at each other with raised eyebrows. Udaya and Sunil giggled.

She explained how she had asked her late brother's grandson, who had been visiting a few weeks earlier, to write down her life story. I silently calculated and realized I had been in Kathmandu then, to see Pramod off. After weeks of waiting and then a long evening of trying to capture Aama's life story on tape, I felt confused. Was the written version the outline or the rough draft for what she had begun telling us that night? Whatever it was, writing had once again entered into the process of her oral storytelling.

She handed the copybook to Sunil, who sat on the cot beside me. "Read my poems and life story," Aama said. Sunil looked tired, bored, and dazed from the whiskey. But he read.

After each song or the conclusion of a passage in the story, Sunil paused, hoping perhaps that he might be relieved of his duties.

"Is it any good or not?" Aama asked us all.

"Yes, yes, very good," we all murmured.

Sunil continued reading. Anil and Udaya snickered occasionally.

"Chup! Keep quiet and listen up," Aama said.

We heard footsteps on the stairway. Pandit Kedarnath appeared in the doorway and looked around the room. Sunil stopped reading. He and Aama moved over and patted an empty space on the bed. Holding his jaw in his hand, Pandit Kedarnath sat down.

"My tooth hurts," he said.

Aama said to Sunil, "Go on, keep reading. Now your grandfather can hear my life story too."

Sunil continued. Pandit Kedarnath held his jaw and listened quietly like the rest. Finally, the written story came to an end.

"We should sleep now," Aama said. At last, she and the others went downstairs. I gave my father-in-law several acetaminophen tablets on his way out.

That night, I didn't sleep much. Excited that we had begun recording Aama's stories, I worried how I would use the material. As with most of my research projects, the abstract ideas had seemed sound when I was writing funding proposals in the States. But in practice, I wondered about the ethics and practicalities. Should I keep Aama's stories as true to her voice as possible and risk losing English-speaking audiences? Or should I rework the stories to illustrate themes I thought important?

Anil had been arguing for the former approach, insisting that North Americans should learn how to appreciate not only the content but also the meandering ways in which people like Aama tell stories. I agreed with the spirit of his argument but also knew that publishers and readers had expectations of how stories should flow and would have little patience for confusing narratives.

I thought back to issues that had troubled me for years. Why was I studying others? So I could gather information to share back home? To further my academic career? To make the diversity of human experience more visible? To counter stereotypes of women in Nepal?

The next day Aama looked exhausted. But after finishing household chores, she hunted for songs that people had written down for her over the years. Each time she brought a fresh pile of papers or copybooks, she looked over our shoulders as we read.

"Does it work or not?" she asked.

Anil read some aloud for her.

"Rewrite them, make them better," she said, and left to find some more.

That night Anil and I continued with our translation work upstairs. Soon Aama joined us to tell more of her jivani.

Aama sat with us many more nights, ticking off the months and years on her fingers. As we transcribed hours of her stories on tape, Anil and I realized that Aama had left out or edited down to the barest bones those we liked best. Before recording her, I'd heard her tell clear and vivid stories of picking mulberries, of clandestine picnics with other women while working in the fields, of trying to stop husbands from beating their wives. When being recorded, she changed her voice and her style. Many stories became lifeless, dull, and incomprehensible.

Aama vacillated between enthusiasm for sharing and worry that people in a developed country like the United States would read her stories and songs as the ramblings of an old, naive, uneducated woman from a backward country. I found myself going back and forth with her.

SCANDAL

O NE MORNING, news of a gathering interrupted my translation work with Anil. I rushed across the pasture and down a
small lane where scores of women and men milled about.

"Which is the young man?" I asked.

The woman next to me pointed toward the tree in the middle of
the fallow fields behind the house.

"The one in the gray sweater and brown scarf," she said.

I couldn't see his face. Other men surrounded him. They pointed
their fingers, shook their heads, and cut their hands through the air
like exclamation points.

Within listening distance of the men, Aama sat with a young
woman wearing a faded red shawl over her bowed head. I remained
at the edge of the fields with the majority of women and girls.

The men walked back toward the house. The women and girls I
stood with giggled and pushed closer, trampling through a field of
peas and recently planted chili peppers. The men scolded, and we
retreated.

Soon Aama and the young woman walked toward the house. I
followed the crowd behind them.

Head covered and bowed slightly, the young woman walked
slowly. In the same modest pose, she stopped next to a haystack. She
had determined eyes and the kind of small, pointed nose favored
among Brahmans. But by the same standards of beauty, her walnut-
colored skin would be considered a shade too dark. I later learned
her name but will call her Leela here. I vaguely recognized her from

mass gatherings of women. Or perhaps she'd been among some gag-
gle of girls who had often stopped by during my pregnancy.

Aama stayed with her and shooed curious girls away. Then
women and men formed into small, mostly sexually segregated
groups and discussed the scandal.

I hadn't seen such excitement in Gunjanagar since women first
made attempts to claim their meeting space. In their efforts to win
land, they had united across caste divisions. But after they got their
land and built their center, they could no longer agree on a direction for the Women's Awareness Organization, or NJS. The divisions became even more apparent after 1990, when the new electoral
process pitted parties against one another in every arena, including
women's organizations.

Party politics tugged at women's loyalties. Like others in Latin
America, Eastern Europe, and other parts of Asia, women and
men in Nepal had sacrificed their land, their careers, and even their
lives to bring democracy to their country. Now that democracy had
come, they could not betray their parties. But neither did women in
Gunjanagar want to betray a nonparty women's organization that
they had helped build through struggle and hard work.

Pramila and Siddhi still taught literacy classes in various hamlets but relied on meeting places closer to students' homes. So the
newly built Women's Awareness Center stood padlocked most of
the time. It had been used a year before for a Women's Poetry Festival organized by members of the Parajuli family—Aama, Pramila,
and Siddhi. It was used annually for the International Women's
Day celebration and occasionally for a meeting. But mostly it stood
silent, empty.

Before he had left to return to Syracuse, Pramod had urged me
to ask Ishwarya—NJS's first and only president—for the key to the
Women's Awareness Center.

"You can gather women and interview them there," he said.

I hesitated. The unused building depressed me. It was a concrete reminder that women's mobilization might, as many men had predicted, sputter out.

"Many women probably won't go there anyway," Aama said. "They think Nari Jagaran is Nepali Congress now. Communist women think they're not welcome there. Sukumbasi women are afraid to go there unless there's a big meeting. And for others, it's too far away. If you want to listen to women's songs and stories, go where they are."

I agreed and followed Aama's advice rather than Pramod's. But I wondered what role I should play in NJS and in women's issues generally. When women had been temporarily united, my role had been easier. Now, with no unity, I had to decide which side to work with as I collected songs and stories and tried to support various efforts.

Crowding the lane between several houses, some NJS leaders asked for Leela. Aama led her into the group. In a soft voice and with her eyes fixed on the ground, Leela told her story.

"I slept with Mohan. We were neighbors. He said he loved me and would marry me. I became pregnant but told no one. Then this morning, I found out they plan to marry him tomorrow to someone else. So, I brought my case before Nari Jagaran."

An older woman in a pink polyester sari with a frayed hem pushed into the crowd. Leela stopped talking and kept her eyes down.

"Come on," the woman said. "Let's go."

Someone whispered to me that the woman was Leela's brother's wife. "Look, the boy already agreed to marry her," she said. "So now you can all go home and leave them alone."

"Well, then," a woman in the crowd said, "bring him out here so he can say it in front of everyone." She was a teacher and one of the founders of NJS. I would later learn she was also Leela's maternal aunt.

Leela's sister-in-law and aunt argued. Aama stood by Leela's side and reassured her. With the crowd swelling by the minute, Aama led Leela and her sister-in-law and aunt toward more privacy. Women and girls surged behind them. Angry relatives of the young man and woman blocked the way.

With all the other gawkers, I stood around and waited for the next dramatic episode. Sadhana arrived with Amalesh in her arms.

"I wanted to be with you, Aama," he said in Nepali, throwing his arms around my neck and crawling into my arms.

I stroked his hair and nuzzled his cheek. "There's a big meeting here. We're going to listen to what people are saying. Can you do that?"

He squeezed me tighter. "Yes, but I want to be with you." He spent so much time visiting neighbors and aunties and uncles and rarely showed any signs of missing his mother. I savored the rare moments when he couldn't seem to live without me.

"That's fine," I said. Reassured, Amalesh loosened his grip and looked around. I tried to peel him off me and put him down, but he hugged me tight again. I tuned back in to the conversation.

"That boy is a good-for-nothing rascal," one young woman told those around us. "And that girl . . . well, she has a bad reputation too."

Others agreed.

"Even though that boy went with that girl, he wouldn't want to marry her," a young man explained to me, speaking in English. "He found out what a bad character she has."

"What do you think about this situation?" others asked, turning to me. "What do you think should be done?"

When some pointed out the girl's "bad character," I fought back anger. But I hesitated sharing my opinion. As a researcher, I knew I should not influence people's ideas by sharing my own. Yet I never liked feigning anthropological neutrality, in which the researcher is supposed to act like a kind of impossibly objective observer. People often asked for my opinions, and I usually gave them, not because it furthered my research but because I believed that people who asked me questions deserved answers.

"I don't know anything about the character of the boy or girl.

Perhaps they both made mistakes. But she will have to suffer for the rest of her life for one mistake while the boy goes free."

"Yes, it's not very fair, I suppose," the young man said, perhaps more out of politeness than conviction.

Others spoke of caste. Leela did not come from Upadhyaya Brahmans like the young man. She was Jaisi Brahman, a lower status that marked her family as already having a history of scandals.

One young woman came over to talk to me.

"Your son has grown so much," she said, and pinched Amalesh's cheek. Amalesh laughed and buried his face in my shoulder.

"Yes, he has."

"He looks so robust. Must be because he's a bikasi. A developed breed," she said. "Our children here are not so good. They're locals. But see what happens when you mix a local and a modern? You get a strong hybrid."

The talk of animal husbandry tugged another birth memory to the surface.

After Amalesh was born, Pramod stepped outside the delivery room for a moment to tell friends and relatives we'd had a boy. He came back in laughing. He told me about an elderly man standing nearby. Pramod didn't know him. But the man expressed shock at seeing Pramod. The man pointed through the small window of the swinging door and said, "The female is a developed breed, I could see that. But the stud? Now I see! He's a local."

Far from erasing inequalities in Nepal, development gave people another way to talk about them. Those on the bottom of the caste and economic hierarchies were backward. Those at the top were more developed, but not as evolved as people in the West. I had tried arguing against such notions, but with little success. Ironically, the people who shared my discomfort with elevating Westerners to such high status were the most conservative Brahmans.

Leela and Mohan appeared from behind a house. The crowd mobbed them. Bodies jostled for the best view. Voices rose and mixed in a deafening cacophony of both anger and amusement. I briefly glimpsed Leela speaking to Mohan. She faced him directly but kept her eyes down and her head covered with the red shawl. I still couldn't see his face well. He turned slightly away and looked toward some distant low point on the horizon. Attempting to follow the conversation, the crowd hushed enough that I could hear Leela's soft voice. I didn't hear any response from Mohan.

Aama stood inside the circle near Leela. One tall, middle-aged man from farther back in the crowd said something to Aama. She responded. Their voices started off too low for me to make out the words, but then rose. I overheard the last part of what he shouted: "Would you want your son to marry such a woman?"

"My son brought an Amrikan," Aama said, and continued in rising staccato phrases. "He asked for my permission. He wanted to marry her. 'Then you get married, if that's your wish,' I said. Parents must accept the son's choice. So, the parents of this boy—they must also accept what their son has done. He made his choice already. They must accept it. That is all."

"It's true . . . Well said . . . Indeed," other women standing in the circle murmured.

Shaking, Aama joined other NJS leaders to nudge the two young people away from the crowd and around the back of an adjacent house. Others barred the crowd from following.

"The boy wants to be left alone with the girl for a while," voices from the crowd said. "They want to speak privately."

The mob broke into smaller hubs of heated conversation. Weaving among them, I paused near some young people I recognized as students at the Institute of Agriculture and Animal Science in Rampur.

"Wasn't the young man's family talking about having a blood test done?"

"Could such a test really determine the father of a child?"

They turned to me for an answer.

"I don't know."

With Amalesh astride my hips, I set out for home.

Over the weeks and months that followed, Leela's case consumed much of our energy. Mohan disappeared, and Leela lived with her brother and his wife. We heard of attempts to blackmail Leela's family into giving money and land to bring Mohan back and ensure her marriage to him. But it was often hard to separate fact from rumor.

Although unrelated by blood or marriage, Aama remained a central mediator throughout the conflict. She believed that Mohan wanted to marry Leela but had been forced into hiding by his relatives. Others, including Siddhi (who often dropped by to visit), suspected that Mohan had chosen to run away. We heard rumors he had gone to India and other rumors that he was hiding in a neighboring village.

We had many late-night conversations in our house about the what-ifs.

What if Mohan did marry another? Could Leela claim common-law marriage with him and file a polygamy complaint?

What if Mohan's family gave her some inheritance? Aama often asked. Then she wouldn't need to be married. Others reminded her of the law, how she could get some of the boy's land only if she'd been married to him for fifteen years or if she was over thirty-five. And then there was what often happened to a woman who tried to claim inheritance: before reaching thirty-five, she might be murdered or framed for a crime and jailed. Human rights activists in Nepal had documented hundreds of cases like that.

What if maternal aunts and uncles sheltered and supported her? They had plenty of land and money, and many of them supported NJS. Why couldn't they build a house for her and her mother? Maternal uncles owed no inheritance to their sisters' children, either sons or daughters. That was probably why relations between maternal uncles and aunts and their nieces and nephews were considered so special and loving: there was never any potential conflict over property or money. Yet in this case, an uncle giving a piece of land to a niece in trouble might set a good example for the community.

What if Ishwarya came forward to share her experiences? After becoming a widow in adolescence, she'd had an illicit affair and become pregnant. She'd had a son and raised him on her own. Through personal determination and the support of men in her politically active family, she had become a respected leader. She'd never remarried but for years had fought legal battles to gain some inheritance for her son. Because of all that, many believed, she should have some sympathy for Leela. But we knew that Ishwarya's relatives, also prominent in NJS and the Nepali Congress Party, had sided with Mohan's family. And Ishwarya had more important political battles ahead.

"What if we make trouble?" Aama fixated for days on a scheme to gather vocal women—mostly Tamang, Damai, and Sarki women from the sukumbasi settlement—to attend a court hearing for Leela.

In a Nepali imitation of spitting, Aama puckered her lips around her tongue tip and exhaled sharply as she pulled her tongue back: "*Tuuu-khaaa!* We'll spit on the men and pressure the court to decide in Leela's favor." She turned to me. "Will you drive the jeep?"

I continued to be surprised at all the ways family and villagers helped me make use of the old Land Rover Pramod and I had bought in Kathmandu that winter. The jeep was heavy and hard to handle and didn't always start as hoped. We had justified the purchase to ourselves by pointing to other research projects and extended stays we planned together in years to come. A jeep, we reasoned, would allow us to travel to distant villages where public transportation was sparse. The jeep could carry at least ten people (plus some animals)—maybe more if we squeezed tight—and had the rigor to ford streams and bounce over potholes. We could ferry family members to weddings and picnics. And I would be able to drive to Rampur or Narayanghat more often on my own to buy vegetables and packaged goods: chowchow, muesli, toothpaste.

I had used it for all of that. I also carried villagers to the hospital in Bharatpur now and then. But I didn't think I had any business driving a group of women to a courtroom to spit on judges.

Anil and I suggested we learn a bit more about the laws before disrupting a court hearing.

"Others know about the law and will go to speak out," Aama said. "The rest of us will go to make trouble."

The what-ifs came and went with no clear answers or actions. What was clear was what my interviews with sukumbasi and my dissertation had shown: a small turn in a woman's life can separate her and her children from any claim to land and have repercussions for generations.

While others in the community focused on the scandal, Siddhi, Pramila, Anil, and I turned our attention to goats. The Local Development Office, headed by a distant relative of ours, was making loans available to women's groups to purchase goats.

I still found it hard to embrace income-generation schemes without a lot of ifs and buts. Yet, I could now see more clearly what women in our village meant when they said they needed income. It was so easy to fall into poverty and so hard to climb out. The market economy had already infiltrated villages like ours; there was no going back, not without some major shift in the global economy, or at least in India and China. And with the market economy defining their daily lives more and more, women needed money.

We saw promise in how the government had set up the goat-rearing scheme. It encouraged both collective and individual gain and gave only modest amounts of money with a low interest rate. The chances of women becoming indebted and dependent on the lending institution were low.

Pramila called NJS members from various villages for a meeting at the Women's Awareness Center. Most said they didn't want to raise goats.

"We don't have any jungle nearby . . ."

"There's nothing to feed them . . ."

"We'd never be able to pay back the loan . . ."

"Then there's the interest . . ."

Finally, a group of women from Vijayanagar, a village adjacent to Gunjanagar, said they were ready to apply. They had just finished a literacy class led by Siddhi and Pramila and had been looking for a chance to work together on a project. They also lived near the Narayani River in an area that retained some jungle along its banks. They could gather fodder there. They were one of the poorest community groups associated with NJS and had a clear need for some income to support their families. And like most residents of Vijayanagar, all the women were communist. They would not be divided by party politics. They had the support and enthusiasm of their husbands, who saw the project as a way to work for the common good.

Many NJS supporters objected to such a choice development project going to a communist area. Leaders haggled over getting the loan for their own areas to serve their own political interests. But none could rouse interest among their constituents. Reluctantly, they agreed to submit an NJS proposal for the loan on behalf of Vijayanagar. The Local Development Office approved the proposal, and women in Vijayanagar organized into credit groups to purchase goats.

Bringing the Bride In

✦

"You used to do something about all the quarrels in the village, no?" Anil said.

"Yes, I would resolve those quarrels," Aama said.

Anil and I were trying to prompt Aama more. I encouraged other family members to sit with us and ask questions too. That approach elicited better stories. It also drew us closer together as a family.

"Tell us. What would you do?"

"The other husbands and wives who couldn't get along with each other used to come to me and say, 'La, this has come to us.' I'd go and resolve things, write it down or get someone to write it down, and keep that piece of paper with me. Then they became a bit scared. But we could do nothing about that man, M—. He married. He himself brought the trouble."

"Did he beat his wife?" asked Anil.

"He used to take her by the hair and throw her around—a very bad habit. He drank whiskey and beat her. He was a very bad man. When he was a boy, he studied with my children. But I would not let my sons beat their wives."

"What other kinds of quarrels did you resolve?" Anil asked.

"I told men, 'If you don't like her, then you have to give her an inheritance. You cook your own food. She will cook her own food. In any case, we will make you give her half.'"

"And what's his name? B—?" I asked. "Didn't he beat his wife?"

"I don't know if he beat her or not. He gave her a lot of trouble.

He scolded her. He never noticed her work. She had many hardships. She wanted to kill herself. Then he went to stay in Pokhara.
After a while he saw how well my son Tirtha got along with his wife
and came to his senses."

"So these days, he doesn't mistreat her?" I asked.

"No, not these days. There are a lot of children around these
days. Youngest Nephew used to beat his wife," Aama continued.
"He tied her up and made her eat grass. His mother cheered him
on. Maybe it was because he thought she didn't work. What a life as
a daughter-in-law! So many wonderful things about mother-in-law
and daughter-in-law, husband and wife."

I smiled at the sarcasm Aama often used in talking about those
relationships.

"But it was not so with me and your grandfather. I did whatever
there was to do. I didn't speak," she laughed. "Father worked outside.
I worked inside. There were no other couples getting on with each
other like we did. We never quarreled at all."

"What about now?" asked Anil.

"These days, we get cross with each other. He wants me to study
the Vedas with him. But I don't agree. 'For fifty years I followed you.
Now you have to follow me,' I say. 'But I know more than you,' he
says. 'But study and experience: both are just as good,' I say. 'I have
experienced many things in seventy years. I have lived in experience,
no?' I say so.

"'This won't do. Come with me,' he says.

"Then I had this dream. A shed for storing grain caught fire.
There were two babies inside. I wondered: should I run away and
save my life or go inside to save the babies? I went inside and tried
to get the babies out even though it was very dangerous. Your grandfather kept saying, 'Run away, save your own life.'"

Aama had been mulling over this dream for months. She told us
many times that it showed the main difference between her and her
"old man." She described herself as an activist. She had to intervene
when she saw pain and suffering in the here and now. Pandit Kedarnath was different, she said. He was not insensitive to suffering,

but believed more in unveiling his atman—his eternal self—and preparing for his ascent to nirvana. The only way to get there was to renounce worldly concerns and his worldly self.

"You didn't quarrel with Grandfather in Kahung?" Anil asked, referring to the family's hill village.

"No, no quarrels at all. He did not have to do anything, did he? I used to wake up before dawn and finish all the chores. He didn't know whether or not some guests were coming, whether or not there were vegetables, when to bring grass, when to take food to the laborers in the fields, when to work inside, when to work outside, when to go to the festival. I took care of all those things. Maybe because of that, we did not quarrel. If I had been like your grandfather, doing anything I pleased, there would have been quarrels all the time.

"But he didn't complain about food. He didn't say, 'You didn't do this or that.' He didn't beat me. I kept some money for myself. He didn't complain about my spending. He didn't complain about anything. But then, I didn't spend a lot of money either.

"Your grandfather worked hard reading his Vedas and doing the work of a pandit. He did puja. People gave him some rice. He wrapped it in a bundle. He brought it and I cooked it for the children to feed them. It has taken a lot of work, no less."

Aama's stories and actions that spring confirmed what I had long suspected. While some might have been tempted to attribute Aama's activism and critical ideas to my influence, I couldn't. She had been fine-tuning her progressive approach for years. I didn't believe I had inspired her. Perhaps my presence—as well as changes in Nepal—simply emboldened her.

Wearing a yellow kurta salwaar, Leela sat by herself on the verandah of the Village Development Committee (VDC) office, formerly the village Panchayat. Names for administrative divisions at all levels had changed after the king dissolved the Panchayat system in 1990.

Leela's pregnancy had begun to show. She looked directly at women and men when they spoke to her. She wore no head covering and had fastened her shiny black hair in a ponytail, a hairstyle popular among young women and girls. I remember details of her appearance because they contrasted so starkly with expectations for a pregnant Brahman woman. She should have been married, and, at least then in rural Chitwan, married Brahman women wore saris, not the kurta salwaar of young girls. And married women attending public events usually braided their hair with red yarn and tassels. They didn't wear unadorned ponytails.

Leela had submitted a letter asking the all-male, multi-caste committee to recognize her union with Mohan as a legal marriage. The fifteen or so elected committee men, plus other men bringing business that day, seated themselves on chairs in a central circle. The women found places on the grass behind them and on the verandah. The meeting began. The men talked about fencing the village common lands and maintaining irrigation canals. The women who had come to listen to the debate on Leela's case sat patiently.

After an hour or so, Pramila approached one of the male officials. "Excuse me, sir. Could we review Leela's case soon? So many women have been waiting. They have a lot of work at home. They can't stay much longer."

The men wrapped up their business, and then leaned back and relaxed their administrative faces into grins as if to say: let the entertainment begin.

A clerk brought out Leela's letter. An official read it aloud to the group.

A few elderly high-caste men argued soberly that the community should work to see the case settled in a proper way. Trying to look serious, other men argued that the committee could do nothing without Mohan or his father present. Bawdy jokes and laughter punctuated the discussion.

In a long speech, one Tamang committee member teased Brahmans about their prudishness. Tamang, Magar, and Gurung leaders howled.

"We Tamangs would never have such a problem. We always let

the boy and girl choose each other. It's easier for everyone that way. What's the problem? A girl and boy go together. So what? It's easy, no? You Brahmans make your own problems."

With some serious comments, much joking, some caste rivalry, and repeated descriptions of the scandal and its aftermath, the discussion stumbled on. Finally, the committee agreed on a day when Mohan's family would perform a common-law marriage (Bitryaune, or Bringing the Bride In).

Later that night, Aama explained the practicality: "If the boy comes, they can be married. If he doesn't come, they can also be married."

"How?" I asked.

"The girl will be allowed inside the house. This is one kind of marriage. The boy does not need to be present. She can formally enter the house and become a daughter-in-law."

I seethed with snarky thoughts on that, but kept them to myself. Instead, I asked, "How can such a marriage be forced with the boy's family so unwilling?"

"Committee members will enforce it," Aama said.

The day for Bringing the Bride In arrived. Women and men gathered again at the VDC office in the early afternoon. After another long discussion about fencing and irrigation, the committee moved on to Leela's case. The discussions and revelry from the previous week repeated.

The laughter stopped when Mohan's father stood and began to speak. He said he was ready to accept whatever decision the committee made. He'd sign a paper to give Bringing the Bride In status to Leela. He would recognize her as a daughter-in-law and not humiliate her. For a moment, it seemed as though the case would resolve.

After he sat down, another man stood and shouted, "How can she be your daughter-in-law? How will you accept her cooking? After all, she is a Jaisi Brahman, and you are Upadhyaya."

Several elderly men stood and made long-winded speeches about why Jaisi Brahmans—who had fallen in status because of ancestral misbehavior—couldn't cook for the purer Upadhyayas and the importance of Brahmans marrying virgin brides.

Some women shouted them down, pointing out that Mohan should have thought of all that before sleeping with Leela in the first place.

Soon the meeting broke into small groups arguing over Leela's fate. I overheard one elderly woman yelling at Aama, "If so many people had not come to the house that first day, then maybe the boy would not have run away. Things might have turned out better, if people hadn't brought politics into it."

"Please, sit down everyone," a village official shouted. "Let's resolve this."

But no one listened. Arguments continued in small groups. Finally, people drifted toward home. No marriage took place, and no one made further plans for resolution.

Multiparty

In the cowshed, the shepherd still lives.
The poor are hungry. "There's development," the
government says.

But there's no development until the stomachs of the poor
are full.
Government! Satisfy the people and develop Nepal.

The government loves to exploit the poor and the wealth
of our land.
What can I say with the poor eating nettles and wild yams?

"Nepal is small, but its exploiters are many," cries the heart
of the poor.
The government felt threatened only when a member spoke
out in the month of Asar.

We will count the gold coins in our hands!
We will call you our government only if the poor get grain
from other lands!

Perhaps there are so many exploiters that the poor aren't
seen as human.
Nepal cannot improve until His Majesty's Government is
shaken.

AAMA SANG her old song slightly off-key with frequent prompt-
ing from Udaya and Anil, who were reading the song off
pages from one of Pramila's old school copybooks. Udaya was going
through stacks of other notebooks and single sheets of paper, some
tattered, and copying all of his mother's songs into one larger, new
book. He had written her name in big letters on the front: Parvati
Parajuli.

"I had not known what politics was," Aama began. "Others might
have known. I didn't know. Although we did not know, we knew
we needed multiparty. Then we went and campaigned for it. Some
campaigned for Panchayat, but I campaigned for multiparty."

Aama was referring to that period in 1980 when King Birendra tried to defuse growing opposition by holding a referendum.
Citizens were allowed to vote on whether to retain the one-party
system or allow multiple parties to compete in future elections. Of
course, the referendum was carefully controlled and meant as a
rubber stamp to continue authoritarian rule. Opposition activists
suspected the process was rigged, but they participated to expose
corruption and build support. Idealists like Aama believed they
might make a difference. Her children were grown and gone by then,
and she wanted to be more involved in politics. She campaigned for
multiparty democracy that year by walking from village to village,
carrying a water pot, a cloth bag, and an umbrella for shade.

Like all her stories, the narrative included a lengthy mapping out
of the places she went, whom she met, how they were related, and
the details of greetings.

She emphasized all she said to convince villagers. "We should
help multiparty to win. We should bring democracy. This Panchayat has given us a lot of hardship. There are many exploiters in the
system. We cannot speak freely. Now we must choose between one-
party and multiparty. It is easy for us now. It will be harder later on.
The king has given us a chance. We should choose multiparty."

She went on to describe how some old Panchas—Panchayat
supporters—opposed her efforts "to twist the people."

"'Aama, you are going to ruin Nepal,' he said. 'Why do you want to bring multiparty? We should keep the Panchayat. Nepal will be done for if multiparty comes.'

"'Eh Babu,' I said. 'Why do you say so? Without multiparty, you see, people can't speak freely. It's too hard, too oppressive. People always threatened. So many people silenced. We should bring multiparty.'

"'No, Aama! The leaders of multiparty are not strong. I have gone up to Kathmandu and met them. They are not going to be able to win. I turned to Panchayat only after I found that it wins.'

"'You say so now,' I said. 'You say we should not bring our freedom. Such intellectuals as you say so. But Indira Gandhi has been running such a big country with freedom. Can't I also be like Indira Gandhi?'

"'Without knowing anything, how can you speak of Indira Gandhi?'

"'Then do whatever you like,' I said, and went on my way."

She described going to another village where some twenty or thirty people had gathered.

"'La! Heh, Babu! Ho!' I shouted. 'If you do not pay attention this time, we will have to shed a lot of blood next time. This is the time for us to think. If Panchayat wins again in this time, then next time many people will be killed.'"

In between travels, she returned home to cook meals for herself and Pandit Kedarnath. She remembered the challenge of that—campaigning, and then having to tend the house with no daughters-in-law to help.

She went out after dark sometimes too, with a lantern. One night, she came across another Pancha. She didn't want to stop and speak to him but remembered her angry thoughts. "'What can you do, you nobody?'"

He chided her as she passed.

"'Don't go around in the night, Aama. Somebody might break your leg.'

"I didn't say it but I thought: 'Who has courage enough to break my leg? Even if somebody breaks it, I will still talk then and there.'"

More calmly, she encouraged him to see this as a time to think things through, to consider the advantages of multiparty to save Nepal from greater conflicts if authoritarian oppression continued.

After the Panchayat won the referendum, some multiparty supporters feared retaliation, so they apologized for their votes and vowed allegiance to the Panchayat again. Aama understood their fear but encouraged them to think ahead.

"'Don't be scared. The chance for multiparty will come again. We should bring it again,' I said. What to do? People did like this. They did not understand things. They sided with whiskey. They sided with chicken. They sided with goat."

She was alluding to the bribery that had occurred when politicians hosted feasts to win votes.

"The Panchas had money. We did not have money. But even without spending a rupee, we got two million votes. The Panchayat, they won only by four hundred thousand, even with rigging. So we knew."

She paused. "How many years have gone by since then?"

"Twelve," Anil said.

"What?"

"Twelve," Anil said, a little louder.

"Twelve years? After twelve years we finally brought multiparty. So many lives lost."

I shivered, remembering those months of terror in 1990. Pramod and I had been safe at Stanford then. What had it been like to be in Chitwan with militia on the rooftops aiming rifles at villagers, ready to shoot to kill if any gathered in groups? I had gotten a bit lost in her story but finally understood the point Aama was trying to make. She had been part of a larger effort to forestall that violence. If only democracy had come sooner.

"Then you were right when you said that so many lives would be lost," Udaya said.

"It's true, isn't it? But when the king gave us the chance to choose between Panchayat and multiparty, we people could not think carefully. People sided with meat. They sided with money. The Panchas even distributed gold."

"But you tried to convince people?" Udaya said.

Aama went on to describe a song she sang at Tij after the referendum. People warned her against it, but she sang it anyway.

"Which song?" Udaya asked.

"That His Majesty's Government . . . No! No! That the prime minister . . . The people could not elect . . . What else . . . ? It doesn't come to mind. I forget."

"Was it the one you just sang?" Udaya asked.

"No. It was another."

"Which one?" I said, flipping through the stacks of paper. "Nepal's intellectuals, the king has corrupted?"

"Yes, I made that song. How does it go?"

I handed the song to Udaya. He read it line for line. Aama repeated it, singing:

> Nepal's intellectuals, the king has corrupted
> and the people's money elsewhere deposited.
>
> To India to do work, the shrewd people go
> and then return as Lahori. Poor souls!
>
> If the king gave work, why would they leave?
> For them, there would have been so much to eat.
>
> If we had democracy, why would the poor wail?
> Who would have taken the way to hell?
>
> We want the government that we've elected.
> This is not the one that we have selected.
>
> The poor, the king does squeeze
> and puts the money in accounts overseas.

Too much oppression the people have borne.
At Tij in the year 2038 [1981], this I have sworn.

After she sang that song, a Pancha told one of her relatives to warn her that if he ever heard about her singing it again, he would inform on her. She would be arrested.

When her relative relayed the message, Aama said: "'I have written only what has happened. Can't I make a song out of it? Where is this law written? Show me! I can look at the law. What's wrong with singing? I will sing whatever I feel in my mind. Let them take me to jail. My duty was to educate my four sons. I have done that. Who could stop me now? Even if I go to jail, the sons will bear the expenses. I will eat. I will stay. Why worry?' I became angry."

She described Pandit Kedarnath as being furious on her behalf too. She wasn't sure how things unfolded from there but suspected he talked to authorities and calmed them down. Word of her transgressions never reached those higher up in the Panchayat.

"They didn't take me to the jail. But if they had sent me, I was ready to go."

Aama laughed and shrugged her shoulders. "So it was then. The teachers arrested, the school closed. Wasn't that bad?" she asked, turning toward me.

"Yes," I said.

"My mind saw that as bad. I made a song because of that. 'What do I have to lose? I have no child to breastfeed,' I said. Even if I had, I would have gone bringing that child with me, no? Then I sang a song like this. I think I remember how it goes."

Aama closed her eyes and sang.

Let's dig a pit and put in it
Mahendra's Pan-cha-yat.
In the city, market, village, and house, let's go planting
The multiparty system brought by striking.

Putting together the government's various wrongs,
I have made this song.

    Udaya, Anil, and I collapsed laughing and couldn't stop. Aama opened her eyes and joined in, wiping away the tears streaming down her cheeks. Maybe it was because we needed relief from Aama's long, meandering story as well as the weeks of drama over Leela's case. Or maybe it went deeper: all those years of authoritarian rule, the hard-won struggle to break through it. People finally felt free to find some humor there.

    For the rest of the evening, Udaya flipped through pages to find Aama's other political songs. A surprising number called for burying Panchayat leaders in pits. In a serious voice with dramatic hand gestures, Udaya sang them one by one. The rest of us held our aching bellies and tried to stop laughing long enough to join in.

ELECTIONS

Ama and I sat on straw mats in the Women's Awareness Center among eleven other women. Anil, the only man, sat beside me. The small cement room with several windows was cooler than outside but would become hotter as the morning wore on. Ishwarya opened the meeting.

"I've heard that some people want to hold an election for president of Nari Jagaran," she said. As always, she wore a white and green sari on her ample frame, her thin white hair pulled back in a bun.

Ishwarya had stepped into the presidency when the organization formed. The bylaws called for elections every year on International Women's Day. Yet elections had never been held and Ishwarya continued as president. Some women had been talking about the need for new leadership.

"Well, that would be fine if I'm the only candidate," Ishwarya continued. "But if anyone runs against me, I'll drop out. I will not even support Nari Jagaran. How can you work against me when I've dedicated so much time and effort to women's upliftment? Why do so many people want to undermine my work? Maybe I'd support an election if I thought someone else could get the work done. But I don't see anyone else who could lead Nari Jagaran. I know there's been some discontent, so I want things to be clear. Let's have a vote of confidence. Everyone tell me whether or not they would support me in an election. If you all agree to support me, then we don't need an election, do we? If you oppose me, then I will quit Nari Jagaran right now."

I'm glad so many communist women are present, I thought. They'd been grumbling to me, Pramila, Aama, and Siddhi for months about Ishwarya's leadership. Now they could tell her what they thought.

Even Aama had been disappointed by Ishwarya's lack of initiative in helping to resolve Leela's case. "She went through the same thing herself when she was young," Aama often said. "Where has she been all this time?"

Five woman, all communists, spoke in turn. And each one affirmed support for Ishwarya.

It was my turn. All women looked to me, waiting to hear what I would say.

I considered my options. I could politely bow out of the confidence vote. I disagreed with the process. But who was I to try to impose my vision of how a local organization should operate? After all, I'd done my own share of behind-the-scenes maneuvering to make sure women in Vijayanagar got their goat-rearing project. The problem was that I couldn't oppose Ishwarya's authoritarianism without invoking my power as an American citizen. I was a white woman from a country with a bloody history of strong-arming other countries into accepting our version of "democracy." And if I did oppose Ishwarya, what consequences might be unleashed for those who, unlike me, had no power to leave and lead other lives?

Yet by passing up my turn to speak, I could be seen as giving silent support to Ishwarya's authoritarianism. How would that make me any better than my own government refusing to see the atrocities committed by so-called allies?

I wished I were somewhere else. I should never have come to this meeting, I told myself, never have gotten this involved. I remembered a lifetime of efforts to both escape and belong, how they had all led me to this moment, where I had to lean away again. There was no good way out. How far would I lean? And where to?

I locked eyes with Aama and recognized the anger in her trembling body. I knew she was waiting to hear what I would say. I couldn't betray her. And I knew I'd rather be heard for my words than my silence.

I considered speaking in English and having Anil translate into Nepali for me. But I wanted to speak for myself. I'd become proficient enough in the elevated Nepali used in politics to give short speeches.

"*Didibahiniharu*! Sisters! Let's not do it this way. This is working against democracy." The movement that had toppled the Panchayat system and brought free elections had glorified democracy. We hardly went a day in Chitwan without hearing talk about it. I hoped an appeal to those values might carry some weight.

I turned to address Ishwarya.

"Although you seem to be giving women a choice, you are not. You're saying: 'You better do it for your own good. But not doing it might hurt you.' That's not democracy. Let's find a better way to do this."

Many women nodded their heads and smiled.

Ishwarya leaned over to the woman sitting next to her. "Foolish girl," she said, pretending to whisper but speaking loudly enough for me to hear. "What does she know?"

The day before she had visited our house and begged for my support in other matters: "You come from America. You're educated. You're Pramod's wife. You must give advice to your sisters here. Tell us what to do." But now my participation defied her leadership, so she foisted another identity on me: Not Nepali. Not Brahman. Hardly even a woman. Just an American. And a "foolish girl." My emotions took me back to those rainy pregnant days over the buffalo shed, when conservative priests had tried to put me in my place. Amid an unfamiliar culture and language, I had felt like such a child that I didn't know how to recognize my allies.

My stomach knotted.

Anil sat beside me. The women asked him to speak next. He said he had come along only to help Aama with reading and writing and me with translation. Women said they wanted his opinion too, so he expanded on my appeal to democratic principles.

All the women smiled and nodded their heads in agreement with Anil as they had with me. Then, continuing around the room, six more women voiced support for Ishwarya.

Aama's turn came. Although I rarely saw it, I knew her look of pent-up anger well. She stood.

"You are all cowards. You say one thing behind her back and another to her face. If no one else will oppose her, I will. I will run in the election. The election will be held."

Ishwarya rose and pointed at Aama.

"I denounce you. I want nothing more to do with you Parajulis. That buhari from America. What does she know? She comes from America. She knows nothing of Nepal and our ways here. I want nothing to do with her either, nothing to do with any Parajulis."

Aama repeated her commitment to run in the election. Then she motioned for me and Anil to follow her as she walked out the door.

The conflict between Ishwarya and the Parajuli family had been brewing for some time. I knew I was marginal to the event and the central issue: the leadership of NJS. I was a tool that could be used in power struggles. And I could just as easily be discarded. It was the web of power I could not escape in Gunjanagar.

Ishwarya wielded local power. She had lost a bid for leadership in district-wide Nepali Congress Party elections the year before. She had been marginalized by the party she had dedicated her life to, so she was trying to build a local constituency of her own. She needed to bring the work of NJS to the attention of regional, national, and even international people of importance. That's where I came in. She hoped to use me to show international support and bring the recognition she desired. By opposing her power play, I was no longer useful.

At the time, I felt powerless. But I wasn't. I could never be powerless in Nepal. That was the problem. I could be belittled in local debates about caste, purity, and culture: not Nepali. Not Brahman.

But I had power that Ishwarya and other local leaders could never hope to have because I was an American. I did not have to be smart, compassionate, dependable, or ethical. I could travel anywhere in the world and claim authority simply because I had a U.S. passport, U.S. dollars, and white skin. I had power handed to me. Why begrudge those fighting for the meager crumbs of power and influence doled out to rural Nepali women in the global economy?

No matter how much people tried to use and discard me in local power struggles, I had a choice that others did not. I could walk away, return to my maiti, find success elsewhere.

Despite my anger, I felt a perverse admiration for Ishwarya's strategy: attempting to use my American privilege as long as it worked to her advantage and denouncing me when it did not. I had grown weary of people in Gunjanagar fawning over me because of my white skin and nationality. As much as I didn't enjoy it, I had often wished for more of India's postcolonial attitude, where people eyed foreigners with more suspicion and calculation and challenged our wide-eyed wonder and simplistic proclamations. With multiparty democracy allowing women and men to emerge from behind decades of smiling façades in Nepal, people like Ishwarya had to experiment, find ways to assert their power against foreigners. It was bound to be rocky. In any case, it was about time someone in Nepal pushed back.

I followed Aama out the door.

On the walk home, I only half-listened to Aama and Anil reviewing the meeting. I pondered what it all meant for my place in the village and family and for my research. That moment of deciding how to respond to the confidence vote crystallized so much. There had been no room for wishy-washy indecision, no time for questions like am I this or am I that? Am I here or am I there? In the heat of the moment, I had found it easy to take sides. How could I have made any other choice?

Natural Births

❖✦❖✦❖✦❖✦❖✦❖   ✦❖❖✦   ✦❖✦❖✦❖✦❖✦❖✦❖

A FTER ISHWARYA denounced us and Aama declared her inten-
tion to stand for election, our family had some heated discussions. Everyone—Siddhi, Pramila, Pandit Kedarnath, Udaya,
Anil—questioned Aama's ability to head an organization. As much
as I admired and respected Aama, I understood what they meant.
In her stories, I heard Aama's longing to be a more extroverted activist, a good orator and a fiery leader like Ishwarya. She took pride
in moments of defiance. But from what I'd seen, her courageous
attempts to organize for some grand action usually sputtered out.
She often fell back to a quieter, behind-the-scenes role where she
was more effective—the kind she'd been playing with Leela and the
goat-rearing project all spring. We all praised her for that. Every
social movement needed people like her.

Siddhi, Pramila, and Anil softened their doubts with a broader
concern: as long as party conflicts ruled, NJS could not be changed
much anyway. Let go of the power struggle in Nari Jagaran, they told
her. Concentrate on the goat-rearing project. That promises success.

As much as I wanted to stand beside Aama in the drama of an
election against Ishwarya, I could see the wisdom of the family's
counsel. So did Aama. She backed down from her hasty decision to
oppose Ishwarya in the election. With that, NJS leadership resolved
easily. No election was held, and Ishwarya continued as president.

I decided to steer clear of NJS—at least for the rest of that
spring—and did not carry on with the research on women activists'
life stories. I had gambled on NJS becoming a creative grassroots

organization, even while suspecting it would devolve into something more mainstream and contentious. At least, the turn of events that spring had confirmed my dissertation findings on class and caste conflicts among women. Out from under the shadow of Pramod's endless optimism, I began to embrace a new persona: a hard-nosed realist with little patience for romanticizing social movements.

NJS leaders continued to grumble about the goat loans going to communists in Vijayanagar, especially since our family had championed that so strongly. But aside from the ongoing literacy classes, the goat-rearing project turned out to be one of the most successful carried out in the name of the organization.

The simplicity of goat rearing made it hard for me to glean any career-making stories for research. The seamless fit with what women already knew how to do, local demand for meat, and the landscape—at least where fodder was abundant—also made goat rearing unremarkable. That's why it worked. I liked the idea of giving my energy over to something quiet, effective, and simple. Aama and I visited the home of each woman involved and found healthy goats and kids. Women had begun selling the offspring, earning income, and paying back their loans. They talked about pooling their money and launching more cooperative projects. Less heartening was Leela's case. She lived with her brother and his wife with no news from Mohan. Uncertainty, as well as her pregnancy, dragged on. Even Aama began to doubt there would be a good solution for Leela.

With fewer meetings and NJS conflicts, I spent more time at home working with Aama on recording her stories and translating her songs and enjoying the pleasures of family.

Every few weeks that spring, Udaya brought home a chicken or two to feed us. He usually cut them up roughly—fat, gristle, and all—for a spicy stew. I can't remember whose idea it was, but at some point he set up a small grill outside and began to cut larger, more recognizable pieces for roasting. I had drifted between vegetarianism and white meat omnivorism for years. The gateway leading back toward a meat-enhanced diet usually involved charred chicken. Soon, I was the one begging for another roast.

One day, Anil and Udaya bicycled around Gunjanagar, offering cash for scrawny birds. They finally found a family willing to part with one. They brought it home and spent several hours slaughtering, gutting, plucking, cutting up roasting pieces, and preparing hot coals.

Udaya, Anil, and I gathered cross-legged around Udaya's small grill on the verandah, turning each piece to perfection. The sizzle and smell made me wild with hunger. Finally, we declared them done. Udaya piled breasts, thighs, and legs on a stainless steel plate. As we each grabbed one, we heard voices on the path. Two men rushed out of the darkness into the courtyard and approached us.

"We need your jeep," one said in Nepali. I recognized him as belonging to a house down the lane beyond the sukumbasi colony but didn't know his family well.

"My wife is giving birth and has to go to the hospital. She has to be cut open. Last time she had a baby, they cut her open. It won't be safe for her this time at home. Can you take her?"

I liked how the jeep gave me yet another simple and effective way to help neighbors. But I felt puzzled by this request. These men were clearly aware of the dangers of vaginal birth for a woman who had once had a cesarean. By local standards, they weren't poor. So why had they waited until the last minute to make hospital arrangements? Still not knowing how to ask such intimate questions in Nepali with men I hardly knew, I suspended my doubts.

Always quick to respond to emergencies, Anil relinquished his chicken and ran into the house to get the jeep keys. Udaya and I looked at the untasted chicken, at the men waiting for us, and then at each other.

We dropped our meat on the stainless steel plate. "Hari-Shiva-Narayan!" Udaya sighed and picked up the dish, put it on a shelf inside the cooking room, and covered it with another plate to protect it from mice and cockroaches.

We made a plan. Anil would fetch the woman in the jeep. Then he'd return and pick me up. Whether traveling by foot, jeep, or bus, I'd grown accustomed to always having a relative along. The companionship wasn't primarily to protect me or my modesty; it was simply how people preferred to travel: not alone. The family made sure I always traveled in the culturally favored way.

Anil drove off with the two men. I dashed upstairs and changed into a kurta salwaar. Then came a moment of maternal panic. Where was my son? I recalled seeing him wave goodbye from the back of a cousin's bicycle earlier in the day and relaxed. His aunt Sakuntala was no doubt stuffing him with fresh milk and sweets at that very moment. I raced downstairs to find Sadhana waiting for me on the verandah.

"That woman, Asha, is such a worrier," she said. "And that husband of hers is even worse. There's nothing wrong with her. She was like this during the last one too."

Like Aama, Sadhana knew a lot about her neighbors. She spent much of her free time listening to their fears and concerns.

"But," I said in Nepali, "if she had her belly cut open once, she really should be in the hospital this time."

"Eh, they didn't cut her belly open. Those men don't know what they're talking about. They just cut a bit down below where the baby comes out." Although young, Sadhana was calm and sensible. She had little patience for decisions made in panic. I trusted her judgment but asked Udaya to translate her explanation into English to make sure I understood. Embarrassed but practical and always helpful, he did his best to explain what his wife said without detailing women's anatomy.

"You mean, she didn't have a cesarean?" I asked. "Just a cut down below?"

"Yes, that's what Sadhana says," he said, averting his eyes from mine.

"We shouldn't take her to the hospital for that," I said in Nepali. "They do that to all women in the hospital. It doesn't mean she has to go this time." A scene from my hospital stay five years earlier flashed into my mind: patients on straw mats along both sides of the hallway, screaming and moaning. "If everything else is all right, it's better for her not to go."

Sadhana nodded and returned to the kitchen.

Udaya brought a bicycle from the shed. I pedaled. He straddled the rack behind and held a flashlight to show the way.

We turned into the courtyard and found Asha waddling forward. I had seen her around the village before. We'd exchanged greetings but never talked much. Her two sisters-in-law held her arms. Usually slight and graceful, she clutched her swollen belly. Several times, she stopped, leaned back into her supporters, and screamed. When the contraction finished, she shuffled forward again, fixing her eyes on the jeep.

I confirmed with Asha's husband that she'd had an episiotomy, not a cesarean. Then I explained to him and others gathered around why she should stay home. Even if I did take her, I said, the pains were coming so fast, she'd probably give birth in the jeep.

I remembered the tempu that had taken me to the hospital, how I'd put off calling for it as long as possible, how people looked at me as though they might never see me again, the pain of bumping over potholes while I had contractions inside, my screams drowned out by the unmuffled engine.

"Narayan! Narayan! Prabhu! Narayan!" Asha leaned into the women holding her. They rubbed her back and stroked her arms. After the contraction subsided, Asha grabbed my arm. "Please take me, sister. Take me to the hospital. I can't bear it. I'm going to die. Please help me. Eh, Narayan! Help me! Here it comes again."

"She worries too much," her oldest sister-in-law said, holding her up. "We can't get her to relax."

"Does everything seem normal?" I asked. "Is the baby in the right position? How much longer do you think it will be?"

"It shouldn't be long now. We just have to get her relaxed. She's such a worrier. It was like this last time too."

"It better be a boy this time for all the trouble she gives," muttered Asha's mother-in-law, standing to one side.

"Please take me! Take me to the hospital, sister. I can't bear it. I want to die." Her classic Brahman beauty distorted by pain, she gasped for breath.

"Didi," I said, stroking her arm. "I'm not going to take you to the hospital. You'll do better here. These sisters can help you here, but they can't help you in the hospital. There you'll be alone. You can't get food or water there, and it's very dirty. I stayed there myself once. It wasn't good."

My mouth said those words, but my mind drifted elsewhere, to a place it had refused to linger during the past six years.

"Having babies is a lot of hardship and suffering," the women had agreed as they waited for my next contraction.

"Remember how my first baby died right after birth?" Sakuntala said. With muscles toned by a lifetime of agricultural work, she held my legs open and pinned my feet to the floor. "I was working all day in the fields and then had this baby. Maybe I was too young and didn't know what to do. Maybe it wasn't meant to live. Anyway it died soon after it came out."

I had hoped to limit the number of people attending my delivery. After long discussions with all members of the family, Pramod and I believed we had reached an agreement: only Pramod, Nurse Bhagvati, and Aama would be with me. All others would remain outside. But when the time came, Sakuntala arrived to tell me disturbing stories and force me into uncomfortable positions. Then came Siddhi, Sharmila, Pramila, Urmila. More distant relatives popped in too. All asked questions that first irritated and then began to scare me: Why is it so slow? What's wrong?

"Please stop!" I said and pushed Sakuntala's hands away. I threw the blanket off and pulled my legs together in glorious relief. *I've been betrayed*, I thought. They led me to believe it would be easy and natural, like ripe mangoes plopping on the ground. Now they talk of agony and dead babies. Again, I felt Sakuntala's strong hands prying my legs apart and replacing the blanket. She continued warming her callused hands over the three-legged iron pot filled with hot coals. She then pressed the heat into my back and belly.

"Go away. Leave me alone," I screamed.

Aama put a woolen hat on my head. I tore it off and threw it as far as I could manage in my exhaustion. Everyone laughed. Trying her best to tend to her American daughter-in-law, Aama fetched the hat and put it back on my head. She then disappeared to prepare yet another strange concoction of food and drink. The more I screamed, the harder she worked to come up with new culinary inventions, hoping to hit on something to please me.

For what seemed like hours, I pushed away hands imposing hats, scarves, blankets, horrible foods, and painful massages. My own body made plenty of heat. I fantasized about rending my clothes and rolling on the cool wooden floor to labor's natural rhythms. That had been my image of a natural birth—one that followed the rules of women's nature and biology, not Brahman culture or Western medical culture. As an anthropologist, I should have known there is no nature separate from culture. As a feminist, I should have been wary of romanticizing women's nature, even in childbirth. Still, clinging to my delusions, I imagined my body freeing itself from the bonds of culture and laboring in primeval glory. But there was no relief from my labor or from Brahman women's management of it until the next morning when I left for the hospital.

Asha and her in-laws asked me to stay during the delivery. I thought of the chicken getting cold back home. Perhaps I felt uncertain enough about my refusal to drive the jeep that I figured I had better compensate with my presence. And maybe I wondered what it would be like to be a different kind of foreigner here: the kind of foreigner who helped midwife actual babies rather than guiding convoluted stories and messy social movements into being. How could I live up to all that people seemed to want from me? Could I learn more tangible ways to help?

I agreed to stay. Anil and Udaya left the jeep and pedaled home. Thinking again of the chicken my family would now enjoy without me, I followed the women and young girls into the house. The mother-in-law closed and bolted the wooden doors behind us. The men waited outside.

The women stoked the fire in the cob stove and heated water. They seated Asha facing the far wall with her back toward the fire. I sat at the bottom of the wooden ladder that led up to the sleeping loft, trying to keep away from the shifting path of the smoke. The eldest sister-in-law held her hands over the fire and then pressed them into Asha's back and belly. Young girls worked together to boil mustard oil in a skillet, adding pungency to the dense wood smoke choking the small room. The younger sister-in-law poured oil onto her hands and rubbed it into Asha's back, belly, legs, arms, and hair.

Earlier in my life, I might have looked at a snapshot of that scene and imagined a charming example of natural childbirth in a women-centered environment. Even during pregnant ruminations in my loft over the buffalo shed, I based my fantasies on such images. Now, I remembered Sanumaya's daughter and other women who had nearly died—or did die—during or after childbirth.

"It's too cold," the eldest sister-in-law said. "We have to warm her body. Then the baby will come out."

"Too slow, too slow," the younger woman said, over and over. "Something must be wrong. Maybe she should go to the hospital."

"Eh, Narayan! Please take me! Take me to the hospital! I'm going to die! Help me, sister," Asha said, rolling her head toward me.

I had looked to others to save me too. But now, I felt paralyzed.

I had leaned back on pillows and spread my legs so Bhagvati could insert two gloved fingers and measure cervical dilation. She poked here, prodded there. I felt another contraction coming on. She withdrew her hand and said something to Pramod in Nepali. A little delirious, I could hardly follow English, let alone Nepali. I asked for a translation. He had to explain several times what made no sense in any language: Bhagvati could not find my cervix.

"What?"

"Her hands are small," Pramod said. "And she says your vagina seems longer than those of Nepali women."

I didn't understand. She had explored up there before and found everything just fine. With skill and compassion, she had delivered hundreds of babies and knew her way around all sorts of vaginas and cervixes. Was my body so different?

Maybe she had begun to question her role. I imagined others in the village seeding her doubts: "What are you thinking? A Nepali village midwife delivering the baby of an American mother?" I'd had moments like that, when I sensed critical eyes, judgment, a pressure to perform, fear of humiliation or dire consequences if I didn't do well. Flustered, I couldn't do the simplest things—turn a knob, remember a word. But how can you lose a cervix?

Maybe that's where my body began to lose confidence in itself and stalled. I never faulted Bhagvati. I chalked it up to another strange cultural clash. On a later visit, she did find my cervix. I remember her assessment: "six centimeters, four more to go." Only four centimeters! I thought at the time. It seemed like such a small distance.

"Just a bit longer," the eldest sister-in-law said, massaging Asha. "Remember how worried you were with the last one? It was like this. But everything came out fine."

"Except she had a girl," the mother-in-law said and dropped a razor blade into the pot of boiling water.

Remembering other young women in the village who had been denied food and medical care after they gave birth to girls, I found myself hoping Asha would give birth to a boy this time. Then I wondered if I should have taken her to the hospital just so better care might be available if she did have a girl.

Hours passed. The women worried aloud, reassured one another and Asha, and then worried some more. Asha's screams and pleas for help turned to low moans. The older women urged the younger ones to massage Asha and keep her hot. Asha twisted and strained during each contraction, testing the strength of all the women who held her body back from the fire.

I felt overwhelmed trying to observe and note all the details and file them in a mental category: Traditional Childbirth Practices Among Nepali Brahmans. I knew I would do what I usually did: write down what I remembered the next day. But I sat there for hours and had sufficient time to take notes in real time. I could have asked for paper and pen. But I couldn't bring myself to do it. I refused to play anthropologist that night the same way I had closed myself off five years earlier to insights that had come to me as nagging: wrap a cloth around your belly, don't look at an eclipse, put a cap on your baby's head. No matter how much I wanted to learn about Hindu ideology and gender, I couldn't bear to hear anyone describe women's bodies as dirty, filthy, sinful. I had absorbed so much through skin and muscle and blood that I feared letting too much into my brain at a time. So, I sat and watched. And rather than making mental notes on what I saw, I continued to let observations filter memories.

"The contractions are coming too fast," I yelled, looking at the tube in my arm. "I'm going to die." I recalled a passage in one of my pregnancy books. It advised careful monitoring for women using Pitocin to accelerate labor. An excessive amount could harm the baby or mother.

A capped and aproned nurse came into the room. She twisted the toggle switch regulating the drip. In the certainty of delirium, I knew that people rolled switches like that, back and forth, when they weren't sure of the proper direction for increasing or decreasing something. I imagined the chemicals flowing through my arteries and veins, leading to a contraction that would never let go. The only relief would be a big bang, exploding my body into a million pieces.

Satisfied with her placement of the switch, the nurse left the room. I remembered the precautions I had read and screamed again. Pramod massaged my back through every contraction and spoke comforting words. I kept screaming. In between contractions, I had moments of lucidity, but they brought guilt. I considered all the sick women and men laid out on straw mats in the hospital hallway. What right did I have to claim the attention of doctors and nurses in this understaffed and underfunded hospital in one of the poorest countries in the world? I longed for compassionate care and comfort for everyone, not just myself, but during each contraction, I cared for nothing but relieving my own pain.

After an hour or so, the doctor came in, scowling.

"What are you screaming for?" she said in fluent English.

"It's coming too fast," I said. "The drip. I can't bear the pain. Please take me off the drip."

"You must bear this pain." She fondled her stethoscope like a Shaivite fingering his *rudraksha* rosary. "All women must bear this pain."

I howled through another contraction. The doctor put the cold stethoscope on my belly and pressed down. Hard. I stifled a scream.

"What are all these men doing here?" she asked, looking at Pramod and two of our nephews. They had returned from buying sheets for the cot and were waiting to see what other errands needed to be run.

"They're family," said Pramod. "They've come to help out."

"Didn't any women come?" asked the doctor.

"No, they couldn't come," said Pramod. "It's too far. They have so much work, you know?"

The doctor rolled her eyes. I was afraid she would chase all the men, including Pramod, away. But perhaps she gave up on customary hospital practices.

I lay exhausted, waiting for another wave of pain. I didn't care what either women or men saw of me at that point. And I found more comfort in the familiar faces of Pramod and our nephews than in the doctor's glare.

"Please take me off the drip," I said. "It's too much. It's dangerous."

"You want to have this baby or not?" She said something to the nurse, who adjusted the switch. The Pitocin dripped faster. Both doctor and nurse left.

Asha grunted and clenched her teeth. I heard a cry from between her legs.

"Here it is," the eldest sister-in-law said. She lifted the blanket covering Asha's legs and scooped up the baby.

"It's a girl," the mother-in-law said. "Too bad. We don't need another girl from this one. Still, she's white and beautiful."

None of the women smiled. Asha bowed her head.

The mother-in-law, who had been giving directions throughout the labor but not touching Asha much, took the razor blade and a piece of string out of the boiling water. She tied off the umbilical cord and sliced it away. With a remnant from an old red sari, she wiped blood and mucous from the infant.

"You're a pretty little thing, aren't you? Too bad you're a girl. We needed a boy."

Asha sat alone while the others busied themselves with the baby. One of the girls warmed the milk left over from the evening meal for her.

In the hospital delivery room, I screamed through one final push and then felt a slithering down, followed by a loud wail.

I was shaking so hard I could see nothing more than a blurry shape in the nurse's arms. Pramod continued stroking my hair and gripping my hand.

"Don't you want to know whether it's a boy or a girl?" the nurse asked Pramod.

"Well . . . okay," he said, as though it didn't matter. He'd been telling me all along he'd be fine either way. But until that brief hesitation, I hadn't believed him.

"A boy," said the nurse. She handed the newborn to Pramod. He wrapped the wailing baby in a piece of flannel cloth and walked him over to me.

"Do you want to hold him?"

"I . . . c . . . can't . . . n . . . now," I said through chattering teeth. I wanted to hold that baby more than I've ever wanted to hold anything but couldn't control the spasms. I feared I might drop him. "I'll . . . w . . . watch."

Making sure I could see, Pramod washed our son—still screaming—in a tub of warm water. In doing that, I knew Pramod added one more stain of ritual pollution to himself. Exhausted and shaking, I ballooned with so much love for him and our son, I thought that might be the final spasm that would explode me.

Pramod swaddled our baby in a blanket and offered him to me again. I took him for a moment but couldn't hang on. I gave the bundle back to Pramod. I would have to deliver the afterbirth and rest for a while before I could hold my son and nurse him.

Supported by her sisters-in-law, Asha stood up.

"The afterbirth should come soon. Why is it taking so long? What's wrong?" asked one. They massaged her belly and warmed her up again. Soon the bloody mass slid out onto the straw mat. The mother-in-law wrapped it in some dirty cloth and set it aside.

Asha drank milk and removed clothes soaked in sweat, blood, and mucous. She asked for the soiled petticoat, sari, and blouse she had worn for working in the fields the previous day. She would not be allowed to bathe or wear clean clothes for the next eleven days. I was tempted to intervene, to encourage some cleanliness to prevent the kinds of infections I had seen among other women. But I kept quiet. I had been invited to take her to the hospital and then to sit nearby to provide reassurance. Nothing more.

More women and girls jammed into the room to view Asha's baby. Shaken by all I'd seen and remembered, I stood to make room.

I had long known that the "natural" childbirth I had once naively hoped for, and still sometimes regretted not having, was a figment of my own cultural imagination. I knew that even as I sat pregnant in my loft over the buffalo shed spinning fantasies. But seeing another woman give birth pushed the realization out of me in a new way, as though some bit of afterbirth lodged inside me for years had finally broken loose. Asha's delivery took place in a more rustic setting and had been less medicalized than mine, but it still had as much to do with culture as nature. The older women had managed the process in culturally accepted ways, just as the mother-in-law would continue to control Asha's life. Asha would, most likely, soon become pregnant again to try to have a boy.

I would always define myself as a woman who survived a traumatic birth in Nepal. But what had been so traumatic? There had been the physical pain, of course, but although worse than any I'd ever known, it was nothing new or unusual for women. Afterward, I probably suffered some postpartum depression. Again, nothing unusual there or in the fact that I never bothered to seek diagnosis or treatment. Part of my depression oozed, I knew, from a cognitive crack—that distance between the birth I wanted and the birth I gave. But that's also true for millions of women. How many ever get the birth experience they hope for? How many more don't dare hope for more than a live birth? How many suffer much worse than unfulfilled dreams: damaged wombs, damaged babies, postpartum abuse?

And, of course, there were plenty of Buddhist neighbors who claimed—and might have tried to tell me—that all expectation causes suffering.

I had returned to Nepal with a research grant to ask women to parse through memories of their lives. Yet, I had to sit by and watch a woman survive childbirth before I could face my own jagged memories. I would need time to replay in detail the scenes of the morning we came back from the hospital to my first sutkeri shunning. But the worst was over. And now, maybe, I could begin to forgive myself and others.

I wove through the crowd toward the door. The younger women moved aside for me. Some of the older ones rushed toward me.

Perhaps I should have done more, I thought. But beyond being a sympathetic observer and a standby taxi driver in case of emergency, what else could I have contributed?

The older women surrounded me and took turns squeezing my hands.

"Thank you so much. You've been so helpful."

"We're so glad you didn't take her to the hospital. That's no place to have babies."

"Yes! Home is best."

"Besides, it would have cost us money," the mother-in-law said, taking her turn at holding my hand for a moment. "There's no reason to spend money on this one. You saved us money."

"These know-nothing men!" one of the eldest in the group said. "They worry too much. They wanted to go to the hospital because they don't know about these things. We old women know what to do. We have given birth to so many babies."

Over the heads of the women, I looked back at Asha, sitting by the fire and sipping some milk. She looked up at me.

"Yes, thank you. What would I have done in the hospital? Maybe I would have died. Thank you for not taking me."

Stunned at being so warmly thanked for doing so little, I said my namastes, walked outside, and sat in the jeep, grateful for a moment alone in the dark.

Was there really nothing more for me to do? It felt so anticlimactic. When I first found out that Asha had never had a caesarean, my decision to convince the family not to take her to the hospital came fast, without reflection. But now, I began to imagine how much more useful I would have felt if I had driven Asha to the hospital. I could be returning now in this very jeep with a sense of pride and accomplishment. I'd already be spinning the story, how I pulled myself away from roast chicken and a pleasant evening at home to drive a woman to the hospital. It was an emergency, I'd say, a true emergency. I steered that jeep through ruts and around potholes as fast as I could, I'd tell people, but not so fast that I hit a bus or caused pain for my patient in labor. That took some skill. And en route, I had to be ready to stop at any moment and help deliver a baby. In any case, I may have saved a life—no, two lives.

As I imagined that scenario, I knew I probably would have done nothing more than drop the family off at the hospital and then return home. That's what I usually did. But I could see myself doing even more. I'd bustle into the hospital, demand a private room, pay for it, hover over nurses and doctors, insist they treat Asha well.

The jeep windows were all open. No one was about. The women and girls had stayed inside with Asha. The men had all gone to bed. I heard dogs bark in the distance.

I was alone, but I wasn't. I don't remember where Aama was that night. Sick in bed with a cold? Off visiting a relative? In any case, I heard her voice the way I would often hear it years later. It was as though she squatted grasshopper-like beside me on the jeep seat, as she did on a table by the stove to pop corn or stir lentils. In my imagined conversation with her, she echoed what Asha's in-laws had told me: urging Asha to deliver at home was the right advice. Asha had no need for chemical or surgical intervention or the extra expense and trauma of a hospital stay. There were hard things for Nepali women beyond that, but neither a jeep ride, nor a hospital, nor an Amrikan could easily fix them. Hadn't I seen how hard it was for Nari Jagaran to help Leela?

I started the jeep and drove along the lane Pramod and I had walked on my first arrival in Gunjanagar seven years earlier. Off to the right streamed all I had tried to make sense of: the village administrative buildings and the new Women's Awareness Center, then the crowded huts of the sukumbasi settlement, and finally, the remaining pasture. By trying to measure my accountability to profession, Nepal, and family through all that, I had set up impossible ideals for myself. And others too. But I had grown weary of that part of me. For so long, I had wanted to be someone else—a dynamic grassroots organizer, a charismatic mover and shaker ... more like, well, Pramod. And in trying to be more like him, I gave up the power of becoming myself.

The air through the open windows was cool, but pleasantly so. In a few more weeks, I knew, even the nights would become unbearably hot. I drove home slowly to enjoy the temperature and unclog my smoke-filled lungs with deep breaths of barnyard air.

I downshifted for the left turn into our courtyard. Here was where I had stood when Pramod called out to his brother in the dark, and I wondered if we'd arrived at the right place. Beyond, I could make out three trees silhouetted on the chautari Aama had made. Those trees had grown tall and sturdy. I could imagine Amalesh and Sebika hiding there now—my little monkey children, eyes glowing in the dark, giggling, making me look for them as they climbed higher and played hide-and-seek behind ficus leaves.

In the courtyard, I turned off the engine and stepped out.

My ghar. I wasn't sure I'd ever want to settle here permanently. But the scar tissue I had shed scraped out a new sense of possibility: raw and uncertain, but open.

I never had learned much about the gods and goddesses Pandit Kedarnath made offerings to every day in the holy basil shrine still choked by weeds at the edge of the courtyard. What I had come to understand was that each had at least one twin avatar. Bloodthirsty Kali—drunk from slitting throats and dancing among her corpses—morphs into Kali Ma, Mother of the Universe, and nurses Shiva back to life. Vishnu asleep yawns into Vishnu awake. In a fit of unfounded jealousy over his wife's suspected infidelity, Shiva cuts off his own son's head. Soon after, he molds clay into an elephant head, puts it atop his son's body, and breathes life into Ganesh, the party god. With time pushing us forward, we mortals must choose a path through all that destruction and creation.

I stepped onto the verandah and remembered the chicken. I figured it had been eaten and didn't bother peeking into the kitchen for leftovers. It didn't matter. Tomorrow, I'd wake to hot chia and popped corn, stories and laughter. Maybe, Aama and I would talk over plans to walk to Vijayanagar to check in with our goat-rearing friends. Meanwhile, Sebika would crawl into my lap for a brief cuddle. At some point, Amalesh would ride into the courtyard on the back of a cousin's bicycle, hop off, and call for Sebika to climb trees, look for bugs, or pick mulberries. But first, Aama would coax them into the kitchen. They'd sit on the bench, swing their legs, and wait. Aama would stoke the fire, set water on to boil, and reheat the pot of buffalo milk. Before Amalesh and Sebika launched into their first fight of the day, Aama would skim firm threads of sweet cream from the warming milk and drop some into each grandchild's cupped hand.

I tiptoed up the stairs. I had learned the height of each rise and the depth of each tread so well I didn't need a flashlight. I also knew where to place each foot to avoid creaks and groans in the old boards. I rarely thought anymore of the night I'd tumbled down and sprawled on the landing. And when I did, I laughed.

Glossary

With a few exceptions, I define most Nepali words within the story or make them clear through context. Here I list words that are not defined or that appear again far enough beyond their original definition that a reader might appreciate a reference.

aama: Mother.

babu: Little boy, son.

bhai: Younger brother.

bhanja: Sister's son.

bhanji: Sister's daughter.

bhat: Cooked rice.

bigha: Unit of land measurement equivalent to about 1.6 acres or 0.67 hectare.

bua: Father.

buhari: Daughter-in-law.

chautari: A resting place formed by shade trees planted in a raised earthen platform.

chora: Son.

chori: Daughter.

chup: Hush; be quiet.

dai: Older brother.

dal: Cooked lentils.

dal bhat: Lentils and rice. Can also refer to any regular meal (e.g., breakfast, dinner) as in, "Have you had your dal-bhat yet?"

Dalit: Literally, "the Oppressed." What those once known as "untouchables" increasingly call themselves.

daura suruwal: Tight-fitting tunic and drawstring pants made for men.

dhaka topi: A unique Nepali man's cap sewn from colorful hand-woven cloth.

dharma: In common usage in rural Nepal, it can mean duty, moral law, code of conduct, custom, or religion.

dhoti: A long, rectangular piece of unstitched cloth worn by men in South Asia. It is usually wrapped around the legs and hips to form loose pajamas and then knotted at the waist.

didi: Older sister.

dukkha: Hardship, troubles, suffering.

ghar: Husband's home.

hazuraama: Grandmother.

hazurba: Grandfather.

hukumbasi: Landowners; literally, those who live in a place from where they can eat and give orders.

Jaisi Brahman: Lower-status Brahman.

jivani: Life story.

khukuri: A Nepali knife with an inward-curving edge, used as both a tool and a weapon.

kurta salwaar: Long tunic and drawstring pants worn throughout South Asia. Also known as salwaar kameez.

Lahori: A Nepali who has worked abroad. Literally, those who have returned from Lahore. The term comes from British imperial times when Nepalis who joined Gurkha regiments were often garrisoned in Lahore (in what is now Pakistan).

lungi: Sarong. Can refer to the plain, striped, or plaid ones often worn by men or the flowery ones worn by women.

maiju: Maternal aunt.

saili: Wife of the third son.

maiti: Maternal home, natal home.

momo: Dumplings, usually stuffed, made with spicy meat and steamed. A Tibetan specialty now popular throughout Nepal.

Pahadi: hill dweller or hill-born. Can refer to people in any caste who trace ancestry to hill areas of Nepal, no matter where they currently live.

Pani Nachalne: Those From Whom Water Cannot Be Taken, or "untouchables." Many now prefer the term Dalit (literally, "the Oppressed").

rakshi: Home-brewed liquor, usually made from rice or millet.

ratauli: A women-only Hindu dance celebration that takes place at the groom's house, while the formal wedding ritual takes place at the bride's home.

rudraksha: Seeds from several species of trees in the genus *Elaeocarpus* that are commonly made into beads and strung on rosaries used for repetitive prayer throughout Nepal and India. Literally, "Rudra's (Shiva's) eyes."

sal: *Shorea robusta.* A tall, straight tree native to southern Nepal and North India. Highly valued as hardwood timber.

saniaama: Little mother/aunt.

sasu: Mother-in-law.

sasura: Father-in-law.

sel roti: Deep-fried bread made from sweetened rice flour. Much like a donut but lighter and thinner.

Shaivite: Devotee of Shiva.

shakti: Female energy.

sukumbasi: Landless. Literally, "those who live in a dried-up, insufficient place."

sutkeri: A woman who has just delivered a baby.

tarai (terai): The narrow strip of lowlands between the Himalayan foothills and the Gangetic plains of North India.

tempu: Motor rickshaw, three-wheeled scooter taxi.

thuliaama: Elder mother/aunt.

Tij: A festival that falls in August and September during which women purify themselves and also show off their seductive and rebellious side through dancing and singing.

tika: A smudge of rice mixed with water (and sometimes yogurt) and coloring (usually red in Nepal, although certain occasions and individuals call for other colors) placed on the forehead as a blessing or protection.

Upadhyaya Brahman: High-status Brahman.

zamindar: hereditary estate owner, landlord.

ABOUT THE AUTHOR

ORN IN Seattle, Elizabeth Enslin earned her Ph.D. in anthropology from Stanford University. She is the receipient of an Individual Artist Fellowship Award from the Oregon Arts Commission and was awarded an Honorable Mention for the Pushcart Prize. Her academic essays have been published in *Cultural Anthropology* and *Himalayan Research Bulletin*, and her creative nonfiction and poetry appear in *The Gettysburg Review, Crab Orchard Review, High Desert Journal, Raven Chronicles, Opium Magazine* and *In Posse Review*. She lives in a straw bale house in northeastern Oregon.

© Jerry Gaffke

ACKNOWLEDGMENTS

WHEN I lived in Nepal, many laughed off a "dhanyabad," or "thank you," in the same way they'd push away money offered for what was given freely, as a gift. "Thanks is already understood in our culture," people would say. "No need to go on about it."

Still, I often found it hard to overcome my American impulse to gush out a dhanyabad whenever handed a cup of tea, a bowl of popcorn, or a tangerine. And now, faced with the task of singling out a few people and institutions for acknowledgement here, I see myself as a bumbling foreigner again, wanting to shout thanks in every direction but unable to explain the deeper gratitude embedded in every layer of how this story came to be.

Let me start with dhanyabads to those who might be the first to refuse them: the extended Parajuli and Bhattarai families, especially the households headed by Pandit Kedarnath and Aama, Siddhi and Sakuntala, Udaya and Sadhana, Tirtha and Sarada, Madhumaya and Tara. I'm especially grateful to elders who bent customs to accommodate me and to the younger generation––Sharmila, Urmila, Suman, Sujan, Anubha, Anjita, Keshav, Yadav, Sunil, Binita, Dipesh, Sebika, and Subash––for easing my way into an unfamiliar culture and language with such warmth, humor, and patience.

Among the younger generation, I owe special thanks to Pramila Ghimire and Anil Bhattarai, who became both fierce supporters and tough critics of my work and showed me inspiring examples of what can be accomplished in Nepal by creative, thoughtful leaders. Many thanks also to Anil for helping translate Aama's stories and songs from Nepali to English. I'm also grateful to Anjan Parajuli, Archana Parajuli and Sanjog Rupakheti for frequent momo parties in Portland, Oregon and their encouragement for pushing this story forward.

I am indebted to the residents of the sukumbasi settlement in Gunjanagar and the participants in Nari Jagaran Samiti in western Chitwan who allowed me to interview them, observe and participate in their meetings, and record their stories and songs. Thanks also to Bhagvati, my midwife, for how well she guided me through all my fears and worries during pregnancy. I still wish she could have been the one to deliver my son. I'm also grateful to many friends and neighbors in Gunjanagar who shared laughs, plant starts, food, whiskey, chia, and so much more over the years—especially Sanumaya Ghimire, Vishnu Vilas, Annapurna and Indira, Padma Raj and family, Thulodai and Kansididi Tamang, Buddiama Mahato, Thulodai Mahato, Sukmaya Mahato, Meena Mahato, and Mohan Gurung and his family.

As a first-time author, I had much to learn about the team effort that goes into producing a book. Thanks to She Writes, especially Brooke Warner and Kamy Wicoff, for sponsoring the book proposal contest that won me a publishing contract. And thanks to Seal Press for believing in this story and guiding me through the publication process. If I were a better poet, I'd write odes to two brilliant women: Executive Editor Laura Mazer, who led me through difficult decisions and unfamiliar procedures with wisdom and compassion, and Anne Horowitz, developmental editor extraordinaire, who understood what I wanted to express and helped me write it more clearly and convincingly. Thanks also to Beth Partin for sharp copyediting, Gopa for a beautiful book design, and Jesse Wentworth for a smart publicity campaign. I'm also grateful to The Community of Writers at Squaw Valley and the Bread Loaf Writers' Conference for generous scholarships to attend summer nonfiction workshops and the faculty and participants there who helped strengthen various sections of this book with thoughtful feedback.

In sorting out the directions of this story, I found great support and encouragement through a 2009 Individual Artist Fellowship from the Oregon Arts Commission. Thanks also to Portland friends, especially Maya Muir, Rick Comandich, and Amy Ambrosio, who nurtured my writing aspirations over the years and critiqued some early, rough drafts of what would go into this book.

Writing this story has rekindled my appreciation for anthropology. I'm especially indebted to those who gave me strong roots in the field many years ago: Sonja O. Solland, Bud Winans, Donald Donham, Jane Collier, Sylvia Yanagisako, Akhil Gupta, Gerald Berreman. I'm also grateful to foundations that funded the research and analysis threading through the story: The Social Science Research Council, Advanced Area Studies Grant; The Rockfeller Humanities Residency Fellowship, Women's Studies Program, University of Iowa; Wenner-Gren Foundation for Anthropological Research; The Institute for International Studies, Stanford University.

Many thanks to literary journals that published various pieces of this book in earlier forms: *The Gettysburg Review*, *Crab Orchard Review*, *Raven Chronicles*, *The Truth About The Fact*.

In my new home in Wallowa County, Oregon, I'm grateful for all that Fishtrap does to inspire and support literary arts and writers in our remote region (and throughout the American West) and for the many ways they have helped me launch this book. Special thanks to sister board member Elizabeth Oliver, who has championed my writing since we first met and also given me a comfortable place to crash whenever I need to spend a night in town.

Among family, I thank my mother, Judy Downs, for sparking my curiosity about other cultures and my stepfather, Oran Downs, for playing the practical, paternal role my birth father refused. Thanks also to Johanna Hoaglund for being a second mother to me and to Erika and Janna for letting me be their big sister. I can't imagine any of my achievements without picturing all of them standing with me, cheering me on.

My marriage to Pramod Parajuli set the stage for this story. I will always be grateful for his unwavering support for my research, teaching, and writing, and for all that we continue to share as parents, thinkers, and activists.

Abundant thanks to Jerry Gaffke for his patient and practical ways of loving me, for understanding my obsessive need to work through this story, and for giving me the gift of time to write.

Finally, I come to the two greatest teachers in my life—Parvati Parajuli, my Aama, and Amalesh Parajuli, my son. Fumbling for words to thank them returns me to where I started. I can thank my son for letting me share stories about his birth and childhood, but how can I use the same word to marvel at his very being and all that I learned from him and family in Nepal by becoming a mother? Deep, unspeakable gratitude is already there, embedded in every touch, every laugh, every moment of compassion, hospitality and kinship rippling across many lives. Maybe that's what Parvati tried so hard to teach me. I'm forever humbled and honored that she entrusted me with her stories and songs and waited patiently for me to find some way to share them.

Selected Titles from Seal Press

Fast Times in Palestine: A Love Affair with a Homeless Homeland, by Pamela Olson. $16.00, 978-1-58005-482-9. A powerful, deeply moving account of the time Pamela Olson spent in Palestine—both the daily events that are universal to us all (house parties, concerts, barbecues, and weddings) as well as the violence, trauma, and political tensions that are particular to the country.

Beyond Good Intentions: A Journey into the Realities of International Aid, by Tori Hogan. $17.00, 978-1-58005-434-8. Tori Hogan takes on the controversial task of revealing the downside of international aid, through the lens of her personal experiences abroad.

Wanderlust: A Love Affair with Five Continents, by Elisabeth Eaves. $16.95, 978-1-58005-311-2. A love letter from the author to the places she's visited—and to the spirit of travel itself—that documents her insatiable hunger for the rush of the unfamiliar and the experience of encountering new people and cultures.

A Thousand Sisters: My Journey into the Worst Place on Earth to Be a Woman, by Lisa Shannon, foreword by Zainab Salbi. $16.95, 978-1-58005-359-4. Through her inspiring story of turning what started as a solo 30-mile run to raise money for Congolese women into a national organization, Run for Congo Women, Lisa Shannon sounds a deeply moving call to action for each person to find in them the thing that brings meaning to a wounded world.

The Other Side of Paradise: Life in the New Cuba, by Julia Cooke. $17.00, 978-1-58005-531-4. A young American journalist shares her experience of living in Havana and offers an evocative and revealing look at Cuba's youth culture.

Find Seal Press Online
www.SealPress.com
www.Facebook.com/SealPress
Twitter: @SealPress